AGEING, INSIGHT

Meaning and practice across the lifecourse

Ricca Edmondson

First published in Great Britain in 2015 by

Policy Press
University of Bristol
1-9 Old Park Hill
Bristol
BS2 8BB
UK
t: +44 (0)117 954 5940
pp-info@bristol.ac.uk
www.policypress.co.uk

North America office:
Policy Press
c/o The University of Chicago Press
1427 East 60th Street
Chicago, IL 60637, USA
t: +1 773 702 7700
f: +1 773-702-9756
sales@press.uchicago.edu
www.press.uchicago.edu

© Policy Press 2015

British Library Cataloguing in Publication Data
A catalogue record for this book is available from the British Library

Library of Congress Cataloging-in-Publication Data
A catalog record for this book has been requested

ISBN 978-1-84742-559-1 paperback
ISBN 978-1-84742-593-5 hardcover

Cover design by Policy Press
Front cover image kindly supplied by Billy Alexander
Printed and bound in Great Britain by TJ International, Padstow
Policy Press uses environmentally responsible print partners

MIX
Paper from
responsible sources
FSC® C013056

Contents

List of figures

Acknowledgements

I am anxious to thank, for their inspiration and very often for their kindness, H.R. Moody, with especial gratitude for all he has done to support the development of this book, and Thomas Cole, Ron Manheimer, Jay Gubrium, John Vincent, Eileen Fairhurst, Hans-Joachim von Kondratowitz, Lars Andersson, Chris Phillipson, Bill Bytheway, Stephen Katz, Chris Gilleard and Paul Higgs, as well as many colleagues in or near Utrecht, including Jan Baars, Peter Derkx, Joep Dohmen and Hanne Leceulle; those who attend symposia of the Galway Wisdom Project, including Jane Pearce, Michel Ferrari, Monika Ardelt, Trevor Curnow, Eva and Rüdiger Kunow; the members of the Ex-OP Group in Germany and Austria, including Richard Kliem OP, Wolfgang and Florentine Schmidl and Karlheinz Hülser; the members of the international Aristotelian discussion group, including Marja-Liisa Kakkuri-Knuuttila and Robert Bolton.

For sundry forms of help in understanding meaning I thank Gundel Schümer, Almut and Klaus-Werner Schulz, Martha and Karl Ulrich Mayer, Terry Eagleton, Willa Murphy, Anthony Heath, Kate Kenny, Howard Bowman, Carmel Gallagher, Ernest Hess-Lüttich, Dieter Genske, Karsten Harries, Elizabeth Langhorne, Cecily Kelleher, Joe Dunne, Lily Hong Chen, Sigrid and Peter Weiler, Siniša Malešević, Pat Armstrong and Christel Bürck; also friends and colleagues on the Ageing committees of the International Sociological Association and the European Sociological Association, especially Sara Arber and Harald Künemund; and those connected with the *European Journal of Cultural and Political Sociology*, including Charles Turner, Zeynep Talay, Eeva Luhtakallio, Pertti Alasuutari, Robert Fine and Siobhan Kattago; as well as friends and colleagues in the School of Political Science and Sociology in the National University of Ireland, Galway, including Chris Curtin, Anne Byrne, Mark Haugaard, Kevin Ryan, Vesna Malešević, Kay Donohue and Henrike Rau; in the Department of Philosophy, including Felix Ó Murchadha, Heike Felzmann and Richard Hull; and at the Irish Centre for Social Gerontology, including Tom Scharf and Eamon O'Shea.

For their illumination and insights I should like to thank Imam Khalid Sallabi, Fr John Keane, Rabbi Lionel Blue, Pfr. Frank Hörtreiter, Hannerl and Wastl Schwaiger and many of my students, not least Elaine McCaffrey and Anna King; as well as friends and neighbours in or near Connemara, including Rachel Latey and Tony Carroll, Niall Ó Murchadha, Bartly Griffin, Mary Troy and Charlie Lennon.

I should like to express warm thanks and sincerest gratitude to Judith Phillips, the editor of this series, and at Policy Press, Emily Watt and especially Isobel Bainton.

For their always stimulating conversation and many other forms of help and inspiration I should like to thank Markus Woerner (also a member of many of the groups mentioned here), Tom and Abby Woerner-Powell and Christopher Woerner.

A further note concerns references, which are used in texts for various reasons, sometimes treated as proofs of the assertions to which they are attached. That is not the aim here. Rather, they are intended to show that reasoning is carried out within a vast network of people and to begin to give credit where credit is due. It became increasingly clear to me while writing the book that without conversation in groups with different theoretical and experiential backgrounds it would be impossible to synthesise the aspects necessary for approaching the complexities of talking about meaning and ageing. Heartfelt thanks to the many people who have talked to me in such insightful ways.

Foreword

Harry R. Moody

The book you are about to read responds to the most important question you could ever ask: What is the meaning of my life? Ricca Edmondson has put together a vast array of resources to help us all respond to this question. She has guided us through the territory, for which we owe her gratitude. Wendell Berry said we live the life we are given, not the life we have planned. In his felicitous phrase, we encounter the question of this book: How do we find meaning in the 'life we are given', that is, the actual life we have lived, whether from individual intention or though structures imposed by the world around us? How do we connect the life we are given with 'the life we have planned' – that is, with our hopes, ideas, interpretations, and the deep structures of society around us? This question becomes ever-more insistent as we grow older. I write these words a few days before my 70th birthday. I, and we, have less time ahead of us, more time behind us. The plans we had for our future are now replaced by memories of what has happened. With the coming of age, the question of 'the meaning of life' is no longer philosophical or hypothetical.

Ricca Edmondson is concerned with illuminating the details of lives-as-given during the last phase of life. Others in gerontology have also been interested in this project, and Edmondson has read and assimilated what they have to say. She is not content with how mainstream gerontology deals with these questions. Formulations like 'successful ageing' or 'life satisfaction' evidently will not do the job. Edmondson's approach is an inductive one, recovering the messiness and complexity of lives-lived, reluctant to reduce that complexity to any simple categories. Her approach is a phenomenological one, a hermeneutical one, or choose from among many other terms. The formulations are not important, and each has different methodological claims, such as qualitative research, oral history, ethnography, autobiography and so on. Edmondson draws on all these discursive resources. All are helpful, all are found wanting because we cannot reduce 'the life we are given' to methodologies.

And we stumble, again and again, across dualities: structure and agency, modernity and tradition, youth and age. How do these dualities play out in the last stage of life? For example, what happens when individuals move from the (celebrated) 'Third Age' into the (denigrated)

'Fourth Age'? What of the duality between the 'well-derly' and the 'ill-derly', or between those with limited life expectancy (such as centenarians) and those who are terminally ill? Is ageing a 'disease' as some ambitious biogerontologists would argue? Perhaps the dis-ease in question is not in the elders but in the observers, among those of us who are suffering from 'hardening of the categories'. Edmondson has given us a glimpse of the territory far more nuanced than what we get from the dominant discourse.

Edmondson understands all too well that our language, our categories, our public discourse, have impoverished our understanding of the last stage of life. For instance, we too easily accept the prevailing liberal presumption that 'meaning' is private. The greatest of our liberal philosophers, John Rawls, codified this duality by insisting that public ethics should only address the Right, but not the Good. The rest, the realm of meaning, is banished from the daylight world of rationality into some other dark place of privatism. Alasdair MacIntyre, among others, understood that making this public–private duality into a wall of separation has been a fatal forgetting of our history. The result, all too familiar, is that 'values' become private, as Charles Taylor has shown in his magisterial analysis of our historical condition. Yet language itself, as Wittgentsein understood, is inherently shared, therefore public. There are no private values, any more than there are private languages. But once banished to the night-world of privatism, meaning becomes invisible in the dark.

Ricca Edmondson's project, and it is a magnificent one, is to recover the discursive resources we desperately need for genuine human flourishing over the entire course of life. This project is far more than an endorsement of 'happiness' because Aristotle's idea of eudaimonia is better translated as 'human flourishing' and not what marketers or psychologists deem to be happiness.

The condition in which we find ourselves today, early in the 21st century, requires an analysis which is both historical and cultural, and this is what Edmondson offers us: a snapshot of lives in the West of Ireland, the UK, Germany, and the US. Western, all of them, and therefore perhaps not as global as we would want. But a global history of the search for meaning in later life remains for others to do. We begin where we are, where we can see both differences and similarities, as in cultural worlds close enough to our own. An inductive or phenomenological approach is difficult enough without trying to encompass peoples of the Amazon or the Kalahari desert. Too vast a landscape would cause us to lose track of the details, which are critical. Moreover, as we have seen in versions of popular anthropology, too much attention to diversity provides another drumbeat for relativism, another excuse for repressing the search for meaning and banishing it into privatism.

'I don''t feel old' is the spoken version of this privatism. 'You're only as old as you think' is another such phrase. Both responses reflect the epidemic of ageism that is the dominant ideology of our time. We think of ageism as 'discrimination against older people'. True enough, but irrelevant. The actual discrimination is older-people-against-themselves. Ageing is the great repressed element of our contemporary life and so its meaning eludes us. Ironically, ageism is most evident in societies which, in demographic terms, are vanguards of 'population ageing', especially Japan and Europe, of course. But now, with falling fertility rates, the trend of population ageing is global. Ageing is all around us, but it is 'hidden in plain sight' because we will not look at it, will not listen to the voices of elders. Ricca Edmondson wants to look and listen, and she invites us to do so as well.

The triumph of relativism comes as joy for those who promise one-to-one marketing: 'Have it Your Way' was the advertising slogan of Burger King. Neoliberal primacy of choice has made this slogan into the watchword of an entire historical epoch, which is our own. Proponents of autonomy in bioethics rush to agree. So it is that we die alone and we die by individual choice, even if our lives and our choices are deprived of meaning. Here is the final irony of ageing: in the Fourth Age, we are more and more deprived of meaningful choices, by healthcare system, by dependence on others, by the body itself. No wonder Sophocles said, call no one happy until they are dead.

It was Sophocles, at age 90, who wrote 'Oedipus at Colonnus', the culmination to the Oedipus story, where we, like the aged Oedipus, might finally grasp the riddle of the Sphinx: What creature is it that walks on four legs in the morning, two legs at noon, and three legs at twilight? The human being, of course. But we, like Oedipus, cannot grasp the true riddle of our existence, the meaning of our lives, until we have lived, not the life we have planned, but the life we have been given. To see that meaning in its fullness is what Ricca Edmondson invites us to do in this book.

Harry R. Moody
March 2015

Series editor's foreword

Judith Phillips

Wisdom, the meaning *of* and *in* life, lived experience, identity and the lifecourse concepts highlighted by Ricca Edmondson in this book describe the very essence of the 'Ageing and the Lifecourse' series. The book provides a critical approach to how gerontology uses these concepts and incorporates debates, for example around the meaning of life, into its dominant discourses which, as Harry Moody describes above, can 'impoverish our understanding' of later life. The study of ageing and the lifecourse is increasingly an interdisciplinary area of study. Consequently students, academics, professionals and policy makers interested in understanding later life need to look at *Ageing, Insight and Wisdom: Meaning and Practice across the Lifecourse* to challenge the dominant and often negative views of ageing and to open up new ways of thinking about the contribution of later life. The book will be invaluable to all gerontologists, particularly cultural gerontologists, sociologists, philosophers, practitioners and policy makers in the area of ageing and later life. It certainly achieves its aim in opening up the debates surrounding lifecourse meanings and values.

Introduction: the roles of meaning in (later) life

It might seem difficult to deny that meaning in life is important, in later life not least – and perhaps most. But it is surprisingly seldom discussed directly. While meaning does feature in important ways in work on ageing and older people, in everyday life it is more often implicitly than explicitly treated as significant. Much of what older people have to offer is tacitly suppressed by exclusionary practices that frame meaning for older people, and the meaning of older people to their societies, as trivial. This book begins, first by exploring positive approaches that gerontologists take in relation to older people and meaning, particularly in cultural and humanistic fields, then by dealing with some of the ways in which attention to meaning is made difficult in everyday life. Ignoring the importance of meaning in relation to ageing is in many ways the most exclusionary habit of all; if the ways that older people see things and what they have to say do not matter, then little else in connection with them does either and they, with all that later life has to offer, cannot effectively be defended. In effect this is a practice with substantial political implications; implying that the world of work is all that should matter in human lives, it devalues the lifecourse for everyone.

This book therefore analyses in detail some of the key ways in which meaning is treated in gerontology, tracing a range of approaches to talking about meaning that highlight its significance and that of older people's insights and behaviour. This underscores varieties of meaning from commitments to connectedness of different kinds, through meaning related specifically to time and generational meaning, to ethical meaning and grappling with the human condition. Characteristically, these are partly implicit, but not the less key to their holders' lives for that, an importance too often played down or ignored. Most of these are more difficult to perceive if the field confines itself to individual-scale data, so we examine methodological approaches to meaning that aim to respond to the partly social nature of its production and practice. Searching for further discursive resources for resisting the denigration of older age, we recall that older people in the past might be thought of in terms of their potential for wisdom. We enquire what this could realistically entail, how it could be explored further, and what it might contribute. A wisdom–related discourse suitable for use in gerontology would be one that stressed the social transactions of both daily and public life, and the capacity of small-scale behaviour to contribute to humane deliberation; not one that seeks out sages, remote from bewilderment or confusion, but one that responds constructively to the turmoil of everyday lives. Openness to wisdom of this kind could concentrate attentiveness to what older people do and say, emphasising that the meanings they have to offer are potentially illuminating not for them alone, but for everyone.

It should not be so easy to overlook these issues. Some years ago a radio team was exploring conditions for older people in the West of Ireland; the interviewer spoke to a smallholder in his eighties who lived in a cottage on a tiny track halfway up a fell-side, with no water, electricity or access to public transport. All this the team accurately reported, but they cut out his declaration at the end: 'I'm happy as the day is long!' What he could have told us about the source or manner of his contentment, what made his life so meaningful to him, we shall never know.

But the importance of meaning in later life is part of the study of older people and intergenerational relations, even though it is frequently overlaid by other enquiries, or incompletely conveyed. Vital though it is to be able to keep dry, fed and warm, these are not the only aspects of life that matter to people; the meaningful ways in which they take care of themselves and each other are part of the process of survival itself. Early writers in gerontology, the American scholars Arensberg and Kimball in Ireland in the 1930s, later Sheldon, Townsend, or Young and Wilmott in the UK, communicate a compelling sense of the variety of interests, preoccupations and enjoyments they see as mattering to older people. This sense continues through the history of the discipline, though often it is not formally expressed. As the first chapter of this book underlines, gerontologists' investigations of signification and meaning take many forms, with which their literature deals in a variety of ways.

Meaning may be expressed in terms of what people overtly say about how they regard their own lives. One woman in her late sixties, talking to the author, was explicit about her insight into her own life: 'I've decided my life is about encouraging other people. That's what I'm going to be doing now, I'm going to concentrate on things that let me do that.' Meaning and insight may also be conveyed through the ways people engage in activities that are ordinary in themselves – spending time working outside on the land or playing cards at weekends. Another woman of similar age spends much of her time not only working to build up her own garden, but tending flowerbeds on each side of the lane along which neighbours pass each day. This activity also communicates meaning in a way that is important to the person herself and to those around her.

The first of these women is giving her view about the meaning *of* her own life as she currently sees it; the second is conveying meaning *in* life, engaging in an activity she finds significant. Other people find it significant too, though this is not the main reason why she does it. While the first is, for the moment, looking at her own life from the outside, considering its purpose, the other is living it from within; she is not advancing a theory about what her life is for, though perhaps she is expressing one. There is a distinction between taking a view on what is necessary for 'a meaningful life', and finding certain aspects of life meaningful; both are important to the ways people experience their lifecourses. Nor is either of the women in the examples making up her mind in temporal or social isolation. The first is drawing on a lifetime of work as a therapist and of interest in religion and politics; she is searching for what makes her own life meaningful, rather than reflecting on the meaning of life as such. The second lives in a farming community in which working the land is considered intrinsically worthwhile, something a person naturally ought to do. The process of making a garden is meaningful to her, and to the other people who use the lane: it is read by her neighbours as expressing care for the land and, in a sense, for those who inhabit it.

Both these people, each in their late sixties, are drawing on cultural habits and traditions in order to enact meaningfulness both for themselves and for others. They are doing so in worlds whose particular forms of sociality enable them to do it. The first could not encourage other people if no one needed encouragement or accepted that she could give it; the second would find it hard to keep tending the land if this activity were routinely denigrated. This applies to the phenomenon of meaning in later life as such. To the extent that we live in social worlds where, as Thomas Cole or H.R. Moody argue, we are discouraged from finding meaning in later life at all, it becomes harder for older individuals to find meaning in their own lives. Charles Taylor's work on recognition draws on Hegel to explore the mutual relations between the perceived and the perceiver: if no one believes that what you are doing, or what you are, is significant, it is difficult to believe it yourself. 'The politics of recognition' emphasises that the self-belief of entire categories of people may be undermined in this way: in societies where most worthwhile activities can be performed only by the young, or by those in paid work, older people's access to related sources of meaning is heavily obstructed.

There is a distinction between 'finding meaning in later life' in the sense of seeking views or behaviour that one considers important enough to justify positions about the meaning 'of' life, or at any rate of one's own life, and in the sense of practising activities that give one satisfaction. But these overlap, not least because the ways people live their lives express their opinions about it. One lady in the Midlands of the UK, a friend of this author for decades, made a practice, in her case a considered practice, of emphasising the small gestures of everyday: inviting guests to feel comfortable and relaxed, to sit in armchairs airing unconventional opinions as they wished, to savour the experience of drinking cups of tea, admiring the sunshine, eating simple food such as baked beans on toast. She savoured the pleasure of passing encounters in shops, where people might give up their places in a queue for someone who was in a hurry, or remember to ask about each other's grandchildren. This was a personal style she insisted on protecting until her death at the age of ninety. She, and it, were valued deeply by those around her. Yet while she was quite prepared to talk about what she valued in life, chiefly kindness, and a type of unintrusive appreciation of other people's viewpoints, she was not comfortable with offering meta-language for what the meaning 'of' life might be. She expressed great pleasure when her daughter's ex-husband insisted on her presence at his marriage to a new partner. This might have been in part because, despite the break-up of the first marriage, she could see values of consideration and loyalty prevailing, in which the children could feel secure, even though she did not theorise about it in this way.

An American of a similar age, also known to the author for many years, lives his life according to a rather different tenor: critical of governments and organisations, familiar with the ways in which plans are sent awry through vanity and haste, hesitant to claim competence for himself, quick to appreciate other people's viewpoints, preferring witty self-deprecation to other forms of communication. Both these people could be made angry by pomposity or arrogance. Neither claims to be discussing, or enacting through their style of being, the meaning of human lifecourses in general; but both have the facility of communicating value, showing through their styles of living what they consider significant and what we might, too.

To express views on the meaning 'of' life as such appears more demanding. Krause (2009: 101) contends that 'a sense of meaning is the ultimate goal in life and represents the highest state of human development'; he echoes the view that this amounts to 'the cognizance of order, coherence, and purpose in one's existence', with fulfilment to be reached in pursuing and attaining 'worthwhile goals' (Reker, 2000: 41). The two individuals just described seem to convey a more modest attitude to insight and meaning: both enact what is important to them in their own lives, without laying claim to conspicuous order or coherence. Dalby (2006: 5) reviews writers who 'emphasize a search for meaning or "meaning-making" as a central aspect of spirituality', seen as a 'life-long quest'. Here, insight or meaning may be taken to relate to a consistent set of dispositions one is able to attain. Thus MacKinlay (2001) interviews people in a nursing home in their seventies whom she describes as searching for answers to questions 'of ultimate meaning' through activities ranging from prayer and meditation to exploring music or art. She sees them as trying to become self-sufficient, wise, related (to a God or to other people) and hopeful; this contrasts with feeling vulnerable, detached from meaning, isolated or fearful. These are not the respondents' own terms; they are categories MacKinlay offers the reader, in order to communicate the force of what she takes her respondents to be doing. The concerns they express may have been lifelong, but for her they gain urgency in efforts to transcend the constraints of older age and the losses it may bring.

Studying life-course meaning: an interdisciplinary project

While there are strong bases for the study of life-course insights and meaning in sociological and psychological contributions to gerontology, the multidisciplinary nature of the field adds both conceptualisations and methods to its arsenal. Political contributions concern both the politics of recognition and the effects of differential distributions of power and resources stressed by critical gerontology; they interrogate how discursive practices shape and are shaped by the ways people perceive the world (Freeden, 2003; Malešević, 2002). Philosophical accounts of meaning and thought are also relevant to insight and life-course meaning in major respects. First there is the contribution of Wittgenstein and other 20th-century writers to understanding the ways in which human language is shared rather than private, a topic earlier broached in enquiries by Aristotle and other classical theorists into the practices underlying social and political communication and behaviour. Second, methods in the behavioural sciences are always underpinned by implicit or explicit models of the human being: images of and assumptions about what people are and how they can be understood.

It follows from the first point that these models cannot reasonably be entirely individualistic nor embody rigid distinctions between cognition and emotion (Edmondson and Hülser, 2012). Positions in philosophical anthropology are implied by methods in other ways too. Work on older people standardly maintains that they ought to be treated seriously and their views attended to. This may seem to suggest, for example, consulting older citizens about their preferences for cityscape design or types of housing with different degrees of nearness to family or friends. Yet as soon as we consider *why* these questions are being asked, it becomes clear that they presuppose profounder issues – not only about how people wish, or might be hoped or expected to wish, to spend their lives, but also about how we envisage what a person is: whether individuals are basically separate or basically intertwined, for example, whether they conduct their lives on the basis of conscious decisions or whether the concept of decision making itself needs revision in order to make sense of life-course practices.

Third, exploring insight and meaning cannot be divorced from issues connected with ethics, the question of what human flourishing can mean, or enquiries into arts of living. Many of these topics have been explored with more engagement in the past than they are now. From the beginnings of recorded history, concerns about lifetime insight have produced a variety of creative responses; historical perspectives are crucial in understanding how ageing has been linked with meaning in different social and political predicaments. Fourth, debates in aesthetics enquire how, and for what purpose, meaning is communicated through artistic products: whether the arts expressly teach about meaning and the way it is worked out through human lifetimes, for instance, or whether their main purpose is distraction or pleasure. These discussions help, at the same time, to show what it is about meaning that can be conveyed by cultural practices in general.

Both literary texts and their critical analysis can give detailed expression to people's senses of life in ways that the social sciences usually do not, for example focusing on the components of moral experiences: how they impact on those who undergo them and what we can learn from reading about them. Thus Theodor Fontane explores how it can come about that parents can fail to show adequate affection and understanding for their children, and what consequences can flow from this failure. In contrast to taken-for-granted assumptions about how older generations should behave, he scrutinises 'inverted parent roles: cold, dominant mothers and warm-hearted, weak fathers, both too egoistic to acknowledge their daughters' individuality' (Hoffmann, 2013: 40). Aristotle would say that literature like this is significant because it shows what *can* happen, casting light on possibilities and dangers inherent in human lives. Erikson or Moody might conclude that Fontane's characters illustrate what occurs when people evade confronting key developmental tasks in their own lifetimes, and how this impacts on the lifetimes of others. When gerontological work shares in techniques used in literary texts, it can enhance reflection on such topics; students of ageing such as MacKinlay use theological categories with the same aim. The writing in the Eriksons' empirical work together with Kivnick (1986), however, conveys their subjects' feelings for life directly, engaging readers' imaginations so that they can infer what is important to the older people they describe. As people often are, the people in these texts may sometimes have been reluctant to put such attitudes into words; often, it is the Eriksons' style of writing that conveys them.

Cultural gerontology tries to respond to issues such as these, drawing on hermeneutical or ethnographic methods to understand the worlds of meaning within which people move, and also to communicate them: seeking to achieve an impact that extends readers' horizons of understanding. Understanding these accounts relies on the fact that cultural habits and traditions do not belong solely to individuals, who both draw on and change them when they act and think (Holstein and Gubrium, 2000; Kattago, 2015). This applies to readers too. Authors supply fragments of data in texts, for instance brief extracts of talk taken from interviews, but these are normally read in terms of some imputed cultural background or setting – whether readers are conscious of this or not. When readers encounter quotations from older people in gerontological writing, they inevitably read them in terms of cultural assumptions that augment their interpretation. Deliberately or otherwise, authors direct them to do this as constructively as possible, as well as to care about what they read (Edmondson, 1984). Thomas Cole's account of a recent interview (2014) appeals consciously to literary as well as historical methods in an effort to convey more faithfully what he has learned from his respondent. He refers to the breeze blowing over his interlocutor's garden or his own insecurity about what the conversation ought to be about or what he ought to say, in effect showing how he and the other speaker build the meaning of their talk together.

'Culture', here, may refer to the norms and practices that structure any human activity, from the culture of everyday life to the culture of science; or it may refer to cultural products, from Shakespeare's plays to bowling. Some cultural analyses explore meaning using the tools of ethnography; others use instruments taken from the arts and their analysis. Cole, in the example just mentioned, uses both, and does so in order to study life-course meaning specifically, trying to understand the ways in which interpreting the meaning-practices of everyday helps us to comprehend life-course meaning better. This illustrates something of the constant interplay between versions of the 'meaning' of life to which different sorts of *content* are ascribed – as we explore in subsequent chapters – and the major ways in which human beings *convey* meaning to each other. This is shown heuristically in Figure 1.

Figure 1: Life-course meaning and its communication

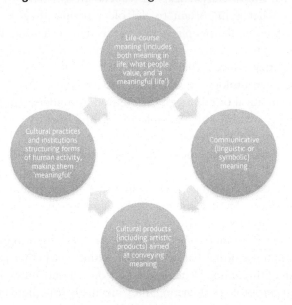

These types of meaning are normally in play together, even when meaning is denied. Thus, when I went to take my 85-year-old mother, who had previously lived with us, to a nursing home after six weeks in hospital, she and I wanted to wash her now bedraggled hair to prepare for entering her new social setting. The ward nurse ruled this out: 'It doesn't matter.' Perhaps unintentionally, she indicated that this older woman's appearance was of no significance within anyone else's account of what is meaningful in life. This implied absence of meaningful content at the same time cut out any possibility of using the normal means for conveying it. It thus conveyed too that my mother's appearance failed to achieve any kind of symbolic communication; was not to be counted a cultural product (like the creative hairstyle a young person might have assumed, designed to convey a message about who the wearer was); and no longer formed part of any significant social practice. It is characteristic of humanistic and cultural gerontology in particular to respond in detail to the ways in which using communicative methods in particular ways, or being prevented from using them, is not clearly separable from content.

Meaning in lived contexts

Because the topic of meaning is approached so differently across the field, this book begins by recalling the political context into which the discipline of gerontology itself was born, and which heavily influenced how meaning became customarily treated in the subject. After the experience of the Second World War and all that led up to it, debate on ethics and politics had come to seem untrustworthy; 'science' was imagined to be a more neutral and more reliable path to human progress. Quantification, studiedly neutral language and articles following 'scientific' formats seemed to promise the most reliable conventions for gerontology, as in the other human sciences, as well as the most prestigious. At the same time, in the course of subsequent decades the language of ethics itself became transformed – some would say, undermined. Ethical statements began to be treated as expressing subjective emotional preference rather than conveying serious conviction (MacIntyre, 1981). The status of ethical debate was further dislodged by post-modernist endorsements of relativism, the still-popular view that any position can be understood in relation to its context, but that no one context can be held to be better or more convincing than any other, so that no ethical position can, either. This sounds convincing only if we see ethical positions as more like instant promulgations than they are like negotiations; as Parekh (2000), for instance, shows, workable ethical agreements can surprisingly often be negotiated over time even between people with radically different backgrounds.

Ensuing neoliberal stress on the language of 'choice', and the view popular among economists that human aims and values cannot be discussed reasonably, could only compound these effects. It is still widely held to be positive *that* individuals can choose how they shape their lives, but that *what* they choose is of no public interest. This position effectively supports a stylistic preference for neutrality and calculation in gerontology, seeming to undermine the need for any other approach. These (cultural) developments, taken together, have an ironical result: they interpret a concern with culture and meaning itself as a subaltern discourse, a minority taste. However significant the meanings of their lives may be to human beings as they age, within gerontology they have come to play a more modest role.

There are certainly other discourses that struggle, more or less effectively, to survive in this climate. Hans Joas (2013) explores the 'sacralization of the person' inherent in the idea of human rights, for example. (This significant historical development is sometimes obscured by the impression of objectivity and quantifiability on occasion attributed to it.) In the realm of gerontology, the preference for eschewing debates about values is enough to make it hard to discuss lifetime meaning at all. H.R. Moody comments,

> Ironically, quiet desperation is what shows up in dominant images of 'positive aging' all around us today. Later life in the early 21st century seems increasingly shaped by shallow ideals like 'Successful Aging' or 'activity theory': in short, by desperation masking itself as wishful thinking (2002: 715).

Peter Derkx (2013a) stresses that relatively little research has been carried out on the question of what it might mean to lead a meaningful life. As a result, it is not obvious what means to use to counteract the influence of these 'shallow ideals'. Derkx's own work explores possible contents of life-course meaning, such as a meaningful life described in terms of dignity and autonomy; he expands on work by writers such as Baumeister (1991) to argue that self-fulfilment or flourishing require not only competence and control, but also senses of coherence and connectedness, besides the opportunity for wonder and curiosity. This is not to suggest that everyone agrees about what meaningful lives should look like; artists and writers such as Hugo Hamilton (see below) precisely seek not to be in control. Bikhu Parekh (2000) stresses strong cultural influences on what is considered most meaningful in life; in non-Western societies, many communal virtues count as more significant than a sense of autonomy. Derkx, therefore, seeks to weigh such claims for the potential reasonableness that can be ascribed to them.

In efforts to avoid imposing a single vision, ethicists increasingly often return to the Aristotelian notion of 'flourishing' as what fundamentally makes sense of human lives. Nussbaum (2006) offers a list of ten key capacities intended to form a threshold that must be reached for human beings to be said to flourish, including the ability to live to old age. But, unlike 19th-century philosophers such as Bradley, Bosanquet or Green, who were prepared to talk at length about the possible contents of human beings' lives and the concrete choices they might face, many contemporary philosophers take trouble to avoid undue prescriptiveness. Commentators argue, too, about applying these debates to lifecourses: what it means to say that someone has, or has had, a happy life, and whether this is a judgement that needs to refer to the person's whole life or just to some, perhaps culminating, part of it (McKerlie, 1989; Temkin, 1993). Can someone be said to have led a happy life if its last 20 years were isolated and abandoned? Or, as long as their latter years were not blighted in this way, has the person had a 'successful' life? We might recall the reactions of one of Gubrium's interlocutors in a nursing home: 'It's come to this' (Gubrium and Holstein, 2009: 75).

Given that most people hope eventually to enjoy old age, it is of pressing interest how older people, both for themselves and in conjunction with other generations, create meaning in their lives – even though finding out more about it is not always straightforward. Some scholars apply a 'meaning in life' scale that asks respondents to 'take a moment' to think about what makes their existences 'feel important and significant' (Steger et al, 2006) before responding to statements such as 'I have discovered a satisfying life purpose.' But most of the evidence discussed in this book takes a more tentative approach. Scales like this one may be most useful in circumstances where people have already had the opportunity to reflect on meaning and insight in their lives, and are replying in terms of an on-going conversation. But we take seriously the warnings by Holstein and Minkler (2003) against imposing a 'univocal' language on gerontological discourse (see also Edmondson, 1984). Thus the concept of 'successful' ageing may occlude value-judgements rather than explicitly debating them (Holstein and Minkler, 2003). It seems crucial not just to ask people if they think their lives hold meaning and significance but to examine their indirect modes of communication too: what they do and how they do it. This is, not least, because there are strong cultural influences on the readiness with which respondents do, or do not, feel at ease verbalising their inner thoughts and feelings (Edmondson, 2000b; Pincharoen and Congdon, 2003). Too much research in the behavioural sciences is implicitly predicated on the counterfactual expectations that respondents will be willing and able to verbalise their profoundest views and attitudes; and that social phenomena can automatically be accessed via data that is overwhelmingly derived from individuals.

In addition to investigating aspects of meaning that can be addressed overtly, gerontological approaches thus need also to be hospitable to the creativity entailed by more flexible methods: exploiting an ethnographic grasp of cultural meaning (Geertz, 1973), using a phenomenological methodology (Biggs and Powell, 2001), or taking relatively pragmatic approaches to social construction (Alasuutari,

1995, 2009). Simon Duncan (2011) takes people's moral commitments to their lives' meanings seriously, using the many-sided theoretical assumptions in 'bricolage' to investigate what light their everyday practices cast on the meanings they attribute to what they are doing; Fairhurst (1990) underlines the fact that methods must respond to the pressures of the moment in the field, including moral and emotional ones. Everett Hughes argued in 1971 that it behoves us to be 'suspicious of any method said to be the one and only'; but all should involve 'the intensive, penetrating look with an imagination as lively and as sociological as it can be made' (Hughes, 1971: xviii–xix; cf Denzin, 2001).

As Peirce or Gadamer stress, we inhabit worlds of meaning that were already constituted before we were born, and that shape the possibilities we can conceive. The institutions we inhabit convey meaning (including institutionalised aspects of the lifecourse itself, as Kohli (1986) contends). Communicative meaning is by no means exhausted by the sentences uttered or practices engaged in by individuals; these draw on, and in their turn modify, backgrounds of shared understandings. While much scientific language needs to minimise, or regulate, its relationships to immediate context (even if it cannot dispense with relationships to theory), social language cannot be understood in the same way. This applies even to the simplest instances, as when we contrast clock time, with its computational connotations that do not change according to place, with the temporal meaning contained in, say, a Libyan imam's explanation of the time for afternoon prayer. He said: 'It's time when the sun's rays on the walls of the houses begin to turn orange.' He was demonstrating a grasp of inhabited time (Rau and Edmondson, 2013), one that is not expected to incorporate the relative certainty of mechanical chronology, which has now come to be independent of everyday views or opinions. The imam is content to rest his view of time on estimations made by himself or other people, based on judgements others have been witnessed making in the past, looking out at landscapes where walls are painted white and the movement of the sun remains a significant aspect of the daytime; this view of time is social too. While social constructions like this are in principle familiar in the social sciences, methodologically there remain difficulties in coping with the sociality of thought and language. These will persist as long as social-scientific data is still collected and interpreted predominantly on an individual basis – a method that tends to under-estimate the force of meaning that is indirectly expressed.

Many of the examples in this book are therefore intended to explore ideas about life-course meaning, illustrating how we might respond to their different expressions, particularly in the context of partly-occluded discourses. They have an abductive effect too (Peirce, 1958: 121ff): if meaning can be conveyed in the ways we suggest in these cases, this at least strengthens the argument for expecting it to happen more widely. Many of the examples of discourse used here are taken from research carried out since 1993 in the West of Ireland, the United Kingdom and Germany, occasionally the US. They comprise conversations about meaning set within contexts that often contrast with each other, though they can show surprising similarities too. It is customary, and valuable, to supply at least some of the ethnographic background for such excerpts, though this entails some dangers: it can seduce readers by offering a narrative that appeals to their sense of what is plausible in a way that may in fact be spurious. Communicative uses of silence, for example, are familiar to people living in rural societies from the West of Ireland to the Tirol to the north of Finland, in all of which places it might often be considered sensible to refrain from explicit judgement, letting events develop, for a variety of reasons that contribute to local views of what a person is and what to expect from human beings. Readers from more urban settings might be more convinced by motivational accounts of silence, for instance references to reluctance to offend. Such readers may find motivational interpretations convincing because they share a philosophical anthropology in which individual motives are thought crucial to explaining behaviour, but the inhabitants of the original setting may not do so. For space reasons there are limits on the extent to which we can interrogate all the contexts referred to here, but the point of referring to them is to help indicate that lifetimes can be experienced *differently* in different places.

Societies such as that in the West of Ireland are significant in themselves, but they also intimate something of social interaction in semi-traditional settings close to how the majority of people have lived in the past. The question of what social interaction *used* to be like has been a preoccupation in gerontology since the advent of modernisation theory, with its claim that the technical progress associated with urban living tends to make older generations seem superfluous (Cowgill, 1974). People from the West of Ireland would recognise much in the tale of the elderly man who appeared at a house in northern Finland when its owners returned from their weekly work in the town, taking for granted his right to use his neighbours' sauna. They might understand the viewpoint of an older man in northern Austria who described his wife's work before their marriage, when she was employed as a chambermaid in the same hotel for 16 years. He said proudly: 'That tells you something!' He meant it showed her capacity for commitment to a task, an enterprise, a place and the people in it. In London, the same observation might be heard as casting deep aspersions on the lack of personal ambition with which his wife had chosen to shape her lifecourse. While this contrast illustrates the importance of interpreting what people say with reference to the background of practices that make their meanings more intelligible, this is not a simple urban–rural distinction (Edmondson and Scharf, 2015), or one that illustrates only emotional as opposed to instrumental relationships (Sánchez Rodrigez et al, 2014). In (often working-class) urban settings, inhabitants may also be expected to show a commitment to place, for instance the 'Kiez' in Berlin or 'quartier' in Paris. In all these arenas, lifetimes and their meanings tend to be treated in a fashion heavily contextualised by places themselves and the (sometimes) solidary networks within them (Rowles and Bernard, 2013).

Clifford Geertz (1973) emphasises that human beings live 'suspended' in 'webs' of meaning: human life is possible because almost everything in the world has a meaning to someone: something is a pot to cook rice in, or a terracotta pot bought abroad, or the pot one's grandmother cooked in. The meanings ascribed to objects or practices may or may not be expressed in words, by their users or anyone else, and may or may not be conscious; individuals as well as cultures have different degrees of sensitivity and attachment to the cultural messages that make up their lived environments. Cultural gerontology in particular explores and makes explicit these messages (Edmondson, 2013b). To show 'the meaning' of living in a certain social setting it is not enough to piece together how people need to behave for their conduct to make sense to each other, difficult though it is to do that; ways of behaving express opinions that should be taken seriously too. Practices that clearly express views of the lifecourse range from hanging parents' wedding photographs on the wall to standing up for older people on the bus; *how* these practices are carried out is as significant as the fact that they are carried out. On a visit to the UK in August 2013 to escort a friend in his mid-eighties, an Irish countryman, to visit his equally elderly sister, the author discovered that people in every part of London were delighted to give up their seats, eager to use their phones to find better routes to our destination, glad to book taxis; the pleased alacrity with which these transactions were forthcoming suggested a need to help on the parts of these individuals that was as great as our need to receive it. What they would have *said* about this is a different matter.

Developing the argument

Chapter One of this book highlights the urgency with which gerontologists have underlined the need to discuss older people in connection with life-course meaning. To neglect this aspect of lives bitterly misrepresents them: making meaning is a socially and existentially significant activity. To ignore this does not absolutely entail regarding older age as simply a time in which people should either work or else pay their own bills in some quiet corner; but it opens the way to a view of life defined exclusively along such pared-down parameters. By default, it advances the ideology of work as the be-all and end-all of life. The chapter therefore explores a range of different approaches by gerontologists to what meaning and insight in later life do involve. To do this, they may draw on discourses of religion and spirituality, of developmental or positive psychology, or of social and political crisis. Gerontologists, like other people in everyday life, do not as a rule embark unannounced on overt discussions of meaning in the midst of debates about food or medication; they require a context in which to do so, and these three foci of interest all offer discursive conventions in which the significance of meaning has an intelligible place. (For this reason, spaces for 'any other comments' at the ends of questionnaires can have limited usefulness: they expect respondents to communicate without being able to know what their readers will understand or value.) At the same time, such gerontologists are vividly aware of the significance of everyday behaviour. The work of Erikson or Frankl makes clear that the ways in which people carry out their everyday lives contribute profoundly to the meaning of living for themselves and those around them. Like writers in classical times – Aristotle, Cicero, or the Stoics – they are conscious how morality, and the meaning of the lifecourse, are constituted in large part by the practices of everyday life.

Since the work of the Chicago School specifically appreciated the nature and implications of everyday interactions, the ways people lived, it is not surprising that writers influenced by it continued to explore the embedded nature of meaning in daily life, as the work of Glen Elder on the Depression shows. Elder's approach to meaning specifically highlights the ways it is constructed in interaction and how it is experienced. Thompson and his colleagues too, in I Don't Feel Old (1990), deal with the 'search for meaning' and the 'vital resilience' needed to find it (1990: 245) – in a style that effectively conveys what is like. For them, individuals make constant efforts to retain their sense of immersion in everyday experience as well as to keep in touch with the symbolic patterns of their lives that they have built up over a lifetime. These accounts of meaning do not preclude awareness of political and economic pressures on individuals as they strive to make their lives make sense. Like Elder, Thompson et al believe that an egalitarian public policy is indispensable in supporting these efforts, though it cannot replace them. Social support for meaningful lives can also ensue from shared social norms. Mehta, dealing with Singapore, or Gallagher in Ireland, show how religious and other conventions can make it easier for older individuals to see their lives as making sense. In the UK, by contrast, Lie et al (2009) see older volunteers as struggling to assert a commitment to meaningful citizenship in the face of a banal official language that tends to delete its expression.

The work by Lie et al describes meaning as it is embedded in and arises from everyday actions; their respondents carry out activities and talk about them, but Lie et al themselves take on the task of explicating what it is that these actions and conversations more fundamentally express. Not everyone thinks about their activities in terms of how they contribute to the theory of citizenship; this does not mean that such a contribution does not exist. Other writers interrogate meaning as its practitioners' views on it are expressed more explicitly. Tornstam, in Scandinavia, offers evidence for arguing, like Dillon, that people can evolve a special commitment to the Golden Rule in later life. For them, later life as such has a meaning, in addition to what their own experiences mean to them. Cole or Moody, however, expose features of contemporary society, politics and culture that militate heavily against attributing meaningfulness to older age. They include the influence of ideologies of science and the philosophical anthropologies attaching to particular historical periods and political/economic forms of organisation, together with the ideas about justice, including justice between generations, that these purvey. Their work shows that several factors need to converge in a self-aware gerontology, not least practices of resistance that are needed to confront the impacts of ideologies and stereotypes.

There are, then, compelling reasons for expecting older age to be meaningful and often enjoyable, bringing insight to older people and to others, even from a state of comparative vulnerability; yet common discourses and major social practices in connection with ageing standardly thwart this expectation. Chapter Two explores claims by Christina Victor and many others about the prevalence of stereotypes that denigrate older people or – just as effectively – fade out their activities and contributions from public attention. For scholars such as Hepworth and Featherstone, systematic social attitudes block out the significance of older people's contributions to society; this chapter draws on insights from philosophy and other disciplines to investigate underlying conditions for these attitudes. Even in the practical theology of the churches, Coleman shows, inattention to older people's spiritual needs illustrates a dearth of socially-meaningful public languages that accord significant status and interest to older people. In the context of the overwhelming age-consciousness and the relentless chronologisation of everyday life described, for example, by Bytheway (2011), this leaves no room for the compelling interest of what older people do, feel and think. This chapter argues that multidisciplinary methods are needed in order to critique the construction of lived meaning as of merely secondary importance, with the effects it has on how we can understand ageing itself.

Gerontologists such as Outi Jolanki and James Nichol chart the struggle for language that older people face. Not least, 'active' approaches to ageing can have the effect of occluding older people's linguistic freedom to discuss spirituality, ethics or wisdom. The languages of active ageing tend to function on an individualistic basis that underplays the sociality of meaningful communication. The chapter therefore interrogates the construction of public discussion of life-course meaning, ethics and wisdom. Contemporary 'social imaginaries' appear dominated by ideologies featuring forms of relativism, on the one hand, or neoliberalism, on the other; both make it impossible to perceive the lifecourse as offering insights of permanent value. Thomas Cole sees the advent of capitalism as key to this change; there is support for this view in Adam Smith's contention that 'commercial society', whatever its other advantages, has an intrinsic tendency to undermine judgement about values. Simone de Beauvoir and writers from Robert Butler to Gilleard and Higgs also claim that attitudes to ageing and older people derive from endemic practices underlying much broader social structures. Under these circumstances it is not surprising that some older people find the idea of ageing repulsive, even though gerontologists such as Krekula find more positive evidence of resistance to such a reaction.

In order to explore these cultural preconditions of lifetime-related discourse, the chapter draws on philosophical explications of the way debate is undermined when even those who want to support ethical stances treat them as merely a matter of preference or choice – a move that leaves social and political choices to be dominated by technical experts. Though Simon Blackburn insists that people still desire ethical narratives to their lives, MacIntyre (1981) has exposed the domination of 'emotivism' in contemporary cultures, which effectively undermines the import of such narratives by suggesting they are mere matters of preference. This saps the significance of discursive resources available for conceptualising the lifecourse, which become envisaged simply as a sequence of one choice after another. Old-fashioned metaphors attempting to express what might heuristically be termed 'cosmic, social and individual dimensions of meaning' come to lack authority (Cole, 1992: xxix). These problems are compounded by the further assault on life-course meaning that emanates from hyper-rational conceptualisations of thought itself, presenting cognition as divorced in principle from feeling and action (Edmondson and Hülser, 2012). This has the effect of denying authority and interest to interpersonal forms of reasoning about the social and political world, in particular destabilising the conception of wise thought (Edmondson, 2005, 2012, 2013). The term 'wisdom' continues to be used and referred to in everyday talk, and the idea of wisdom plays a significant part in social life, but it tends now to occupy an 'interstitial' role rather than being overtly explored and acknowledged. As a concept, its key advantages include its capacity to absorb and analyse diverse aspects of the human condition: ethical discourse, the sociality of thought and the absence of certainty in private and public life, as well as the varieties of significance attributable to experience. Enquiring how to re-establish the status of the language of wisdom, the chapter turns briefly to its potential for evolving effective ways of communicating about social and political needs.

Chapter Three reiterates that, despite their subaltern official status in contemporary discourse, life-course meaning and insight remain stubbornly of key significance – both to people as they live their lives and to the ways these lives are written about. The chapter therefore sets out to excavate the literature on the content ascribed to meaning and insight in older people's lifetimes. It builds on the ways in which such concepts are used both in texts and in everyday practice, in order to delineate major sets of key approaches to them. Within each of these major sets, there is a range of possible variants, and the lines between them may be blurred. Nonetheless we can suggest a three-fold division, each of which covers three types of meaning. The first group stresses references to different forms of connectedness between individuals and some wider set of circumstances. These include 'vital engagement' or appreciating the point of certain activities, a position whose theoretical significance was underlined by Boethius in the 6th century. Again and again it appears – even if this is not expressed directly – that having values that go beyond oneself is a key aspect of attributing meaning to life. Viktor Frankl argues that valuing something or someone for its own sake can make the difference to survival itself in life-threatening circumstances. Secondly, this group includes 'spiritual' meaning, in the sense of transcendence, or a feeling of connectedness with some wider aspect of existence; this includes but is not limited to religious spirituality. Thirdly, the group includes commitment to ethical meaning. The term 'ethical' can be understood broadly, as Nussbaum (1990: 231–2) does in her commendation of Wayne Booth's position in *The Company We Keep: The Ethics of Fiction* (1988):

> It covers everything that pertains to asking and answering the question, 'How should one live?' Enjoyment, distraction, even contemplation of form, are all aspects of the ethical as Booth understands it – so long as they are seen as forming part of a human life, and are assessed accordingly.

Ethical questions, therefore, are not to be understood solely in terms of obligation. The quotation from Nussbaum continues,

> The question he asks is nothing so narrow as, 'What does it show me about my duty?' It is, rather, 'What relationship does my engagement with it have to my general aim to live well?' – and to live, we should add, as a member of a society, since Booth insists that human beings are social and political beings.

This asserts an explicit connection between ethics and living a flourishing lifetime; the details of older people's ethical views and behaviour, and how they develop them over their lives, ought surely to be of absorbing interest.

The second group of meanings focuses more explicitly on the lifecourse in a sense that takes special account of the role of time. It contains, firstly, references to personal development and what are sometimes referred to as 'tasks of life' – a term associated with facing challenges in relation to one's community, work or relationships: how to learn to be courageous, for example, or how to be honest. Secondly, there is the pride or lack of it that people may take in their own lifecourses; and thirdly, the concept of generational meaning, which encompasses a consciousness that individuals can be understood in terms of their place in the flow of generations, and the attitude known as generativity.

The third group of meanings concentrates more specifically on meaning in the sense of insight. The first refers to the way in which older people's very existence can be a source of insight for others; for example, older people may be regarded as part of the symbolic order of the world, making possible a broader or deeper understanding of what life entails. Second, life-course meaning may be taken to refer to familiarity with the human condition, in the sense in which, with experience, people may come to be more realistic in their expectations of others' or their own behaviour, more familiar with the types of snag likely to arise in human enterprises or the degree of success to be expected from them. Third, there is meaning or insight in the sense of wisdom, some versions of which are explored in more detail in the subsequent chapter.

These are interpretations of insight and what older people can offer that have their own implications for gerontological methods: methodological and theoretical questions are deeply intertwined. This is, not least, because different forms of life-course meaning are conveyed by cultural symbols and practices that display their own dynamic over time – affecting and being affected by each other – and operating among larger or smaller groups of people. This demands attention to questions concerning how they can be explored. Characteristically, they are not expressed in terms of linguistic utterances alone. This is because, firstly, different societies and (sub-)cultures have their own impacts on the ways cultural symbolism is used, or on the practices used to convey meanings that are understood to be significant. Secondly, in addition to these phenomena, it is precisely in the case of life-course insight and meaning that individuals often choose to express themselves allusively and contextually, through actions and in their styles of being as much as through explicit sentences.

The chapter therefore explores some features of the sociality of meaning and the way that ethical views, views about being a person, are derived from and influence social ones. It also examines some methodological implications of the fact that texts are social objects: trying to transport meaning from its original social setting to that of readers presents its own challenges. We then review three key areas in which meaning and sociality converge: time, narrative and practice. Attention to time and temporality needs to be a much greater feature of gerontological method, particularly since its subject matter specifically concerns living in and over time (Biggs, 2007; Biggs and Lowenstein, 2011; Baars, 2012). Narrative is important not only because it incorporates time and process, but also because of how much it can convey about both sociality and practice or style of life. The concept of practice is significant not least because it tries to show how different aspects of life blend together, with communicative effects –

undermining the assumption that only utterances and acts constitute evidence of what people and groups believe and feel.

Chapter Four expands on the notion of wisdom, which already has a presence in the literature relevant to the lifecourse and ageing. It includes, for instance, Frankl's association between love and the meaning of life, or Erikson's final stage of life-course development, in which a feeling of identification with future generations may be attained that can overcome fear of one's own mortality. Writers including Schachter-Shalomi and Miller (1995), Moody (2002) or MacKinlay (2005) see wisdom as a key goal of later life. While Gabriel Marcel (1954) underlined the precariousness of this concept in the contemporary world, the idea of wisdom was reintroduced and explored in the last two decades of the 20th century by 'positive' psychologists such as Clayton and Birren (1980), Holliday and Chandler (1986), Sternberg (1990 onwards), or in the work of Baltes, Staudinger and the Berlin group. The chapter explores some of these ideas, and later elaborations by writers such as Ardelt, relating them to ideas stemming from the ancient world.

Thus the chapter connects fruitful conceptions of wisdom with contemporary questions relevant to ageing, such as the capacity for development, change and responsibility for other individuals and generations; 'active listening' and social critique; counter-cultural action, tolerance and concern for justice. It also explores the type of deliberation Aristotle associated with wisdom. He sees it as the characteristic mark of human beings to use logos, human reasoning, to share values and reach decisions about what is right in both strategic and ethical senses. For him, this is the highest type of discourse in which we can engage in our lives in the community.

Some accounts of wisdom tend to be perfectionist, in the sense of expecting an unusual height of achievement, in either interpersonal or intrapersonal senses, while others are more hospitable to human imperfections, also in either interpersonal or intrapersonal senses (Edmondson, 2013). Wisdom may be envisaged as exemplary knowledge achieved on one's own, or, as in the reading of Aristotle suggested by Woerner (1990), it may be portrayed as engaged in by people who are by no means perfect, but able to work together to achieve more insight than they could on their own. Psychologists often aim to interrogate 'wisdom-related' behaviour – behaviour that does not meet perfectionist standards of wisdom but is connected to it. We explore views among positive psychologists, aiming to elicit their positions on cultural and social knowledge, as well as on connections between developing wisdom and the lifecourse. At the same time, we suggest that a psychological interest in personal development can be paralleled by a more transactional approach in gerontology that responds to 'wisdom' in terms of more transient, but still illuminating, contributions to confronting everyday challenges.

The next section explores exchanges on these topics from the history of art or the study of literature. Von Hülsen-Esch argues that successive historical periods have impacted on the ways wisdom was portrayed: she recounts how, during the Middle Ages, the attribution of wisdom to older women gradually became impossible, as their representation became overlaid with contrary meanings associated with feebleness and decay. Aleida Assmann also examines historical tropes communicating different images of wisdom, from the esoteric, magical insights of Prospero to the good counsel and justice attributed to Solomon. We suggest that Montaigne, with his radical hospitality to the ways other cultures conceptualise the world, can throw light on what Staudinger means by 'openness to experience'. Nagy's work (1985) on 'the wisdom of the outlaw' develops connections between capacities for wisdom and social positioning, contending that there are insights that require the perceiver to stand entirely outside the comforts of society. Kunow too (2009) underlines the freedom that may be achieved by standing at an angle to convention – often achieved specifically with age, as in the case of Blaikie's (2002) 'cultures of resistance'.

These are not exclusively recondite themes, as this chapter shows, but have considerable appeal in popular media. They may be explored, for instance, in films approaching questions such as how developing a confidence provoked by challenges in later life can be linked to greater tolerance; how to set priorities between money and power, on the one hand, and human commitments, on the other; how to resist conventions about self-presentation or the concept of 'the loser'; how to approach profound loss. These films identify significant questions, many underlined by writers like Cole, Moody or Tornstam, featuring how much can be learned and achieved in (later) life, what can be changed or aimed for, how and whom to trust and how to become trustworthy oneself.

The remaining part of this chapter gives examples from the author's research that contrast meanings attributed by eloquent individuals to their whole approaches to living with more indirect contributions that need to be understood with the help of long immersion in their social settings. In many cases, to perceive what is taking place below the surfaces of apparently superficial interchanges can become intelligible only on the basis of familiarity with local practices. The approach to discourses involving wisdom that is offered here specifically makes room for the sociality of human discourse, making it possible to explicate attributions of wisdom in the context of everyday transactions rather than on the model of the distant and perfect Stoic sage.

This book tries to make some implicit conceptions more explicit, so that issues related to values and the human condition can be recognised more clearly. This is not to claim that such issues mean the same from every point of view, even in their original settings. They differ in degrees of significance for different individuals; discussing them is affected by cultural convention and by political and economic power. In particular, there are socio-political factors that enable or inhibit emphases on meaning; the contemporary post-modern world deforms the expression of meaning in particular ways that need to be confronted. The overarching tendency in a consumerist culture is to evade or deny the thought that life is always untidy and challenging: it is normal for things to go wrong in ways that need deeper responses than purchasing-power can supply. Perhaps a widespread fear of ageing arises because being old makes it definitely clear that there are some problems that cannot simply be spirited away.

Under circumstances of exacerbated social and economic competition, ageist dismissals of older people's views may contribute to powerful cultural scripts used by both individuals and organisations. This, for Powell and Biggs (2003), lies behind the fact that vulnerable older people tend to be relegated to insignificance while 'successful' ageing is celebrated. The 'generational contract' is not extinct: members of different generations do show concern for each other and support public policies advantageous to other age groups (Scharf et al, 2013: 3; Kohli, 2007). Nonetheless, Bauman or Beck are not alone in identifying economic trends increasingly requiring individuals to sink or swim alone. Bringing a different twist to the question, Gilleard and Higgs (2013) treat generational divides, specifically divisions spurred by the cultural and economic changes in the 1960s, as themselves evolving over time; they outline ideas with the potential to liberate both older and younger generations in future. But both 'social capital' theorists such as Uslaner (2002) and critical gerontologists would predict that social and economic rifts threaten such possibilities. The economic marginalisation of precarious younger generations, or long-hours work cultures that devalue caring activities, are features of (post-)modernity that fundamentally threaten both the experience of younger people and the standing of older people's accounts of themselves and their lives. While intergenerational relations are both normal and fundamental to human interaction, this does not make them impervious to distortion.

Key disputes therefore revolve around the generational allocation of resources, particularly economic and political resources, underlined in critical gerontology (Phillipson, 1998). Generational theorists may draw on work such as Mannheim's (1923/1952) or Bourdieu's (1993), to suggest that there are common habits, rituals, memories and practices that can make one generation's experience relatively distinct from another's, potentially exacerbating these issues; though, as Brückner and Mayer (2005) point out, there is no substitute for empirical enquiry into how different these experiences actually are. Edmunds and Turner (2002) argue that developing a consciousness of sharing significant predicaments, not least common experience of economic disadvantage, can make 'passive' generations of this sort 'active' in pursuing their interests; what creates a generation in this sense is not just chronology, nor just culture, but shared economic and political tensions and problems (Turner, 1998). Thus, with John Vincent (2005), we should expect that intergenerational relationships will not normally be entirely stable, but will fluctuate through time. They cannot be taken for granted, and a concern for older people should entail similar attention to the young.

At all stages, bestowing meaning on one's life is so central to existence as a person that devastation results when someone is no longer treated as a meaning-making being. Older people in care homes who are kept in bed for 12 hours out of 24 are being treated as if this subjection had no meaning for them, in a way that undermines their status and experience altogether. Meaning is a social matter, but also a political one; it affects political life and the preconditions for it are created politically. As Michael Lerner (1996) among others insists, questions of meaning do not simply emanate from politics and economics in an automatic way, but they cannot be seen as separate: they cannot all be solved without attention to sociopolitical processes. It is perverse to delimit cultural questions from political, social and economic ones, as if cultural developments were generated in a sphere of their own, separate from the rest of society. Bringing together questions of meaning with those of politics does not diminish their importance, but heightens it.

Given the wealth of insight that exists on the centrality of meaning, therefore, why is it not more widely accentuated in gerontology? Moody and Cole (1986: 247) sum up this concern:

> Many writers who have thought about meaning and aging
> have sensed something missing in literature on old age. It is
> as if we have enquired about almost every imaginable aspect
> of late life – sex, politics, religion – but somehow missed

what is all-important, perhaps the very thing we wanted to understand in the first place.

This book aims to broaden debate so that issues surrounding life-course meanings – what people think is the meaning of life and what they value in life – can be given a more overt status in gerontological discourse. In this context, contributions by older people to the meaningfulness of human lifetimes can be seen not only as sources of challenge, but also as sources of creativity and hope.

ONE

Lifecourses, insight and meaning

This book explores an approach to ageing in terms of a central concern to human beings as they live through their lifetimes: how they create meaning and insight in their lives, and what meaning both they, and ageing itself, have to others. The importance of meaning in ageing has long been a concern in the study of older people and intergenerational relations. Even if this concern is often expressed obliquely, it is stressed explicitly in such works as *I Don't Feel Old*, by Thompson et al (1990); Chris Phillipson (1998) terms it central to critical gerontology; the idea of meaning is central to the work of gerontologists including Dannefer (with Kelly-Moore, 2009: 405), Cole, Ray and Kastenbaum (2010) or Chris Gilleard and Paul Higgs (2013). Pat Thane's work on ageing (2005) highlights the various meanings ascribed to later life for those who experience it, as well as for people who do not yet see themselves as old; psychologists such as Peter Coleman (2011) regard the transmission of meaning and value as central both to older people themselves and to what others expect from older age. This book explores this debate, trying to become clearer about what creating and perceiving 'meaning' in later life really imply. It interrogates the ways in which issues surrounding meaning impact not only on how we look at ageing and conceptualise older people, but also on intergenerational relations.

The study of ageing by gerontologists, people concentrating specifically on that topic, is, Andrew Achenbaum reminds us (1995), relatively new: it has developed since the end of the Second World War. This timing has not been without its consequences for the study of meaning. As Achenbaum also points out, the early days of gerontology occurred at a time of disillusionment with political debate and political idealism; science, in comparison, seemed to offer a more reliable path to progress in tackling major problems faced by humanity. But 'science' is always envisaged in terms of the culture of the time, its application envisaged within a social and political context that affects how it is understood. The right-wing movements of the 1930s had imagined science to reveal laws of genetics that could transform the health and purity of the human race; in the post-war period, new views of science were constructed, with their own effects on how older people were seen. The 'biomedicalisation' of ageing took itself to be value free, but by concentrating on *problems to be solved* it rewrote the meaning of ageing in terms of pathological conditions that ought to be cured scientifically (Estes and Binney, 1989). The appeal of this perspective can be felt today, not only in popular culture but also in, for example, Aubrey de Grey's 'anti-ageing mission', a crusade to harness medical techniques to counteract cell damage in the human organism (Grey, 2007: xii, 4ff). Yet gerontologists in the human and social sciences are well aware of the sociopolitical and behavioural factors that shape ageing (House, 2001) and that make ageing in comfort depend closely on being situated advantageously in a social structure (Donkin et al, 2002). For them, the biomedical approach can too easily function as an excuse for ignoring social choices and political responsibilities that ought to be faced.

But this can work the other way around too. In his article 'The medicalisation of old age: Should be encouraged' (2002), Shah Ebrahim recalls the history in London of under-treating older people in workhouse wards, when they could in fact have been assisted and discharged (cf Warren, 1943). He contends that 'The warehousing of frail elderly people in nursing homes is a result of medical disinterest and of political ideology, and has led to a social model of care in which medicine is denied a role' (Ebrahim, 2002: 861). Arguing against the 'fair innings' argument as a social reason for failing to make medicines and other forms of treatment available to older people, he contends that medicine should put itself more explicitly at their service. Ebrahim sees political prejudice as at work here again: excuses are being sought for abandoning interest in older people as soon as they become in any way fragile or vulnerable. In other words, the *meaning* of ageing and being old remains at the centre of apparently technical arguments about what medicines work, and to whom they should be prescribed.

It is clear even from this brief overview that the study of ageing and older people needs to be understood in a multidisciplinary way; few of the associated issues can be explored effectively within the confines of a single subject. It is not only the more medical and practical aspects of ageing that need to belong to gerontology, along with sociology, psychology and other behavioural and literary studies, but its philosophical and social-theoretical aspects too. At the point where all these approaches overlap is the question of meaning, the issue of how older age is interpreted by older people and by others, a topic more often pivotal to public debate and private feeling than may at first be apparent.

Some contrasts between public meanings and lived reality are made clear in an influential text in the history of exploring older age, *I Don't*

Feel Old, by Thompson, Itzin and Abendstern (1990). The authors sympathise with the reluctance of the older people they interview to be '*identified* as old' (Thompson et al, 1990: 122). These individuals are all quite realistic about issues such as looking older, or physical decline, but, given prevalent 'negative attitudes or prejudice' in connection with ageing, 'dissociation of oneself from the category of old age might be a very reasonable position to adopt' (1990: 122.). The authors write,

> The fascinating and revealing testimonies of our sample seem to demand a reassessment of our concepts and preconceptions about old age and ageing. Few if any of our interviewees actually fit the stereotypes of old people as being passive, inactive, helpless, dependent, rigid in their thoughts or behaviour, old-fashioned, or unproductive. Instead their lives are characterized by variety, vitality, diversity, activity, energy, interest: by 'youthfulness' in attitude, outlook, and activity (including paid employment) regardless of their age. The people themselves are each unique and uniquely different from each other, and from just about every stereotyped image of old people that exists.
>
> The reality of older people's lives is therefore clearly very different from most people's preconceptions: indeed, different from the preconceptions of the older people themselves (1990: 121).

Thompson et al do not spell out exactly what they mean by insisting on the meaningfulness of their subjects' lives. But the paragraph quoted here is characteristic of these authors' work in conveying an account of meaning that might be summed up in terms of *pointfulness*. The stereotypes of ageing and the old that they mention have one feature in common: passivity, sameness, rigidity: lack of dynamic direction. The older people they actually *meet* are brimming over with dynamic direction, even if they interpret meaningfulness in varying ways. This zest for life may partly depend on their personalities and their physical health; it also depends on the existence of at least local shared practices and discourses that allow them to express the values they attribute to engaging with other people, telling stories, working the allotment or whatever it might be.

Recovering meaning as central to ageing would involve reinvigorating the public standing of these discourses, showing what it is that older people do that is genuinely important. It could also help to counteract tendencies within gerontology that have ageist implications, even though their intentions are quite the opposite. Concentrating on defending older people and highlighting problems they face – from care needs to disputes over socioeconomic resources – can have unintended effects if it takes centre stage. In effect it situates older age and older people within a territory marked by disadvantage. Pressing as such problems are, to allow them to define older age itself is to miscast the process of ageing for human beings, significantly skewing our relationships to older people, to ourselves as we age and to policy on ageing.

The authors whose views are explored in this chapter implicitly or explicitly treat developing meaning as a characteristic human activity, and seek in different ways to re-establish ageing as a central part of this project. Such work is fundamental to reinstating older people as playing crucial roles in our understanding of our own lifetimes, so it is vital to pay special attention to the ways in which these writers understand and communicate the projects concerned. Phillipson's adoption of this concern identifies it as crucial to critical gerontology, but what exactly it involves is approached variously by a wide spectrum of authors. There are a variety of different approaches in the literature to what sense-making and meaning-making are thought to entail.

The question whether older people are significantly involved in exploring 'meaning of life' questions is in part a political one. If they are engaged in enterprises recognised as central to the human project, they can be seen as making a special contribution to social life – which deserves recognition and support. Moulaert and Biggs (2013) argue that strong efforts are being made to discourage us from supposing that this is the case. Surveying a sequence of international documents on ageing policy, they identify a period around the turn of the 21st century in which United Nations documents could still refer to the leading potential of 'the skills, experience and wisdom of older persons' (United Nations, 2002: art. 10). Since that time, Moulaert and Biggs argue, such holistic language has retreated sharply in favour of 'a new orthodoxy of ageing subjectivity' (2013: 23) that emphasises work and self-sufficiency in later life. It concentrates on getting older people to view their past lives in terms of risks taken and choices made, for which they must now bear responsibility. In this view, central to the meaningfulness of lives is the category of *work*, in which active, responsible ageing is equated with work itself (see Biggs, 2004).

Moulaert and Biggs plead for a renewed focus on 'existential life tasks'. This recalls Adler's or Moody's term, 'the tasks of life', whereby people work out the significance of their lives to themselves through a series of linked processes. Adler envisaged individuals as facing challenges as they go through life in terms of key areas: 'problems of behavior toward others; problems of occupation; and problems of love' (Adler, 1935: 5; significantly, modern references to these tasks usually place problems of work or occupation first in the list). These 'problems' span a gamut from morality and philosophy through a variety of forms of knowledge of the world; the question is how to talk about them.

In gerontology as in everyday life, discussion of life-course meaning is seldom embarked upon from nowhere, but usually makes sense through being located in a discourse hospitable to it. Gerontologists may broach this topic in connection with religion and/or spirituality, or with developmental or positive psychology – in some cases, both; or they broach it in connection with crisis or challenge, as in Glen Elder's work on the Great Depression. Questions concerning *cultural* meaning may be connected to any of these. Thus, researchers such as Michele Dillon explore whether concern with spirituality in a religious sense (however interpreted), or with non-materialistic Golden Rule thinking, tends to develop throughout individuals' lifecourses. Her subjects explicitly draw on the cultures they have grown up in or have encountered at subsequent stages of their lives – even if it is to challenge or question them. Kalyani Mehta investigates societies with strong religious and cultural expectations of age-appropriate behaviour for older people, exploring respects in which their circumstances and predicaments, or their social and cultural surroundings, encourage or oblige them to take special approaches to spiritual or ethical conduct. Texts in developmental or positive psychology need not suggest that older people necessarily concentrate on meaning-making *more* than at earlier life stages, but for a variety of reasons insist that their meaning-work is of special interest or importance; examples are Jung's or Erik Erikson's exhibition of the richness of later-life insights in offering contributions *to* their cultures. Exploring some of these approaches to what creating 'meaning' involves, we can enquire how they are related to the discursive contexts in which we find them, and what they offer to the understanding of how human lifetimes are built.

Meaning in gerontology

Chris Phillipson's description of critical gerontology sees its origins in concern with structural constraints and inequalities, especially those involving class, gender and ethnicity, and in eagerness to empower older people who are suffering different types of exclusion. But central in his account too is a 'humanistic' concern about 'the absence of meaning in the lives of older people' and 'the sense of doubt and uncertainty' generated by such an absence (1998: 14). What is it that he thinks is lacking, and in what context does this lack make itself felt? Is it something intrapersonal, does it arise from something absent from interpersonal relationships, is it some form of philosophical crisis, or does it derive from specific society-wide attitudes and opinions? In fact Phillipson's argument does not incorporate sharp distinctions between family or friends and wider social predicaments. It stresses 'the idea of ageing as a socially constructed event', one encompassing different levels of politico-economic impacts on the circumstances of ageing, individuals' active roles in constructing the 'world' in which they live, the 'interplay between the self and society' that this involves and the stories people tell about it (1998: 14, 24). The 'absence of meaning' he points to is thus neither purely subjective nor derived purely from social points of view or circumstances; the two are intertwined. This argument makes room for complementarity between approaches focusing on a sociopolitical 'crisis of meaning' in relation to older people and ageing (as described by writers such as Cole or Moody) and more biographical approaches to the experience of ageing such as that taken by Ruth and Kenyon or in Gubrium's ethnographic work (Phillipson, 1998: 21ff, 23ff). Like these others, Phillipson refrains from imposing simplistic distinctions between different features of people's lives, allowing room for blending ethical with personal and practical concerns.

For Cole or Moody, modern emphases on purportedly 'scientific' effectiveness and an economistic understanding of rationality have leached the profundity from later life, sharply curtailing individuals' capacities to ascribe positive meaning to it, as well as – and through the process of – degrading the status of ageing as such. For both, analysing the impacts of social expectations is linked with a concern for individuals' ability to resist them. Each tries to show how views of ageing change with successive social and historical developments, and to use these analyses to persuade us to see our own views of ageing as historically conditioned too – thus as vulnerable to critique. Pat Thane also takes a long historical perspective in highlighting changes in the meanings ascribed to later life, both by those who experience it and by others: 'The meaning of old age is not fixed and it has different meanings in different contexts' (2000: 5). Like Cole and Moody, she refrains from offering naïve summaries; it is difficult to determine if there is a trajectory showing that 'respect' for older people has waned or waxed through history. This is an issue that has been debated for over two millennia, made more complex by the fact that 'throughout history real life was as richly diverse in old age as in literature and the visual arts' (Thane, 2005: 28).

The ways older people (like younger people) are regarded are overlaid with views and expectations that stretch far beyond themselves as individuals or even older people as a group. One of the oldest written texts in existence, *The Maxims of Ptah-Hotep*, composed in about 2200 BC, is preoccupied with the question how far it is possible for life experience to be communicated by older to younger people; the Hebrew Bible (or the Old Testament) is replete with references to relationships between youth and old age. Resisting prejudice against the vulnerability of ageing has perennially demanded personal effort; Botelho (2000: 113) quotes Maimonedes in the 12th century as defining an old woman as 'One who is called old and does not protest.' When individuals have resisted negativity and stereotyping, they have performed an important service, since views of ageing have always been linked, implicitly or explicitly, with views about what it is to be a human person as such.

It is the effects of contemporary attitudes to this problematic that writers like Moody and Cole critique: they deplore the results of undermining all connections between understanding ageing and reflecting on the human condition. This chapter tries to restore some of these connections by exploring work on older people that does stress the role of ageing and later life in constructing significant types of meaning. Does this entail the development by (at least some) older people of ethical/spiritual insight and wisdom, or are more everyday types of conduct involved, for example maintaining cultural practices that conduce to other people's well-being? In rural Ireland, for example, practices supporting community life include visiting neighbours in hospital – on the basis that they are neighbours, not that they are necessarily intimate friends. It is recognised that older people whose children no longer need constant attention may have more time for such contributions, and at the same time that older people may acquire more awareness of the need for them. Understanding the significance of rootedness in a locality is expected to grow with age – 'You don't know who you are till you know where you've come from; but you don't know that until you're fifty!' This is a culture that is reticent as far as meta-reflection is concerned; commitment to meaningful practices is a way of expressing insight without analysing it explicitly.

In contrast, work on ageing and meaning that is based on interviews or surveys necessarily addresses the verbal expression of interest in meaning; this includes texts by Dillon, Tornstam, Manheimer or – somewhat sceptically as far as theories of lifetime development are concerned – Coleman. Stephen Katz (2009: 12) underlines the urgency of listening to the exact words respondents choose; words carry complex cultural messages over and above their literal imports. Hence it is important to attend to undertones in the ways in which *gerontologists* express themselves too. Their own textual practices may heavily modify their explicit positions (Edmondson, 1984, 2007). Their quotations from people they interview also elaborate their positions; not because writers simply use others' terms to express their own opinions (though they often do), but because in taking over respondents' speech they often choose accounts they feel are especially eloquent, in ways the conventions of academic language may not permit.

Michele Dillon's work specifically deals with religious and spiritual aspects of the search for meaning. She seeks to expand on Wuthnow's (1998) distinction, which is not necessarily mutually exclusive (Wink, 2003: 104), between people who are oriented to religious organisations and communities and their practices, and those who stress personal growth, self-fulfilment and the deepening of a sense of identity, along whatever paths they find appropriate. She sceptically addresses connections between religion, ageing and crisis, and associations within the gerontological literature between later life and social isolation, or later life and the need to resist threats to one's sense of integrity (Dillon, 2009: 52f; see also Dillon and Wink, 2007). In contrast to these misgivings, she argues, Laslett (1991) was right to suggest that many older people, at any rate at the end of the 20th century, were 'in a unique position to enjoy the freedoms that come with the post-retirement years' (Dillon, 2009: 53). She and Paul Wink have taken up and continued a longitudinal study into the lives of two groups of individuals born in California between 1920 and 1929, interviewing 184 of those still surviving, then aged between 69 and 77. A quarter of these were still working for pay at the time of interview, as were their spouses, and Dillon describes most of them as 'economically well off' (2009: 54). Seventy per cent remained married, and of those 88% described their marriages as exceptionally happy, or at least good.

Despite reservations about Eriksonian anticipations of difficulties and challenges in ageing, Dillon refers to both Erikson (1963) and Bellah et al (1991) as stressing 'the importance of purposefulness in everyday life, of living attentively in the present in order to maintain a personally meaningful and socially integrated life' (Dillon, 2009: 54–5). For her, meaningfulness can be an on-going feature of a successful or enjoyable later life, rather than, necessarily, a response to crisis. A number of the respondents she deals with, notably the 'spiritual seekers', do have problems for which they use religious or spiritual exploration to confront, but by no means all of them do. 'David Allen', a respondent aged 76 when last interviewed, 'is an excellent illustration of what might be considered "purposeful" ageing', remaining as 'articulate, insightful, optimistic, and energetic' as he had always been (Dillon, 2009: 56). Though 'among the least religious' of the respondents, he acknowledges the lasting impact of the religious principles of his youth (2009: 57). David Allen has run a mountain resort business as well as being a history teacher, proud of the impacts on them for which his pupils continue to thank him; he has continued to work in property restoration and management, as well as being active in local community politics and environmental organisations. He enjoys good health, playing golf and travelling often to Europe with his family. His life has not been entirely trouble free; he had serious difficulties with relationships with his children on the occasion of his divorce from their mother, and has mourned a son who has died of AIDS. He has risen to meet these challenges, but by and large does not feel it reasonable to "'think religiously'" (Dillon, 2009: 57). David Allen is clearly a favourite respondent: from the author's account of what he says and does we can envisage him almost physically as he engages vigorously in the open-air pursuits of which he is so fond.

While David Allen certainly seems to lead a life that is purposeful and meaningful on a day-to-day basis, another of Dillon's case studies, 'Kate Ward', has been actively preoccupied with spiritual development all her life, at the same time as being 'highly committed, though selectively so, to organised religion' (2009: 63). She speaks of having faith "'in a universal spirit that's connected to human spirit'" (2009: 62), deeply concerned with preserving the integrity of her own search: "'I would do almost anything to allow myself options to grow and to develop ...'" (2009: 61). She is not alone among Dillon's respondents in that her most intense experience of spiritual growth came from her forties onwards (2009: 61); but, unlike David Allen, she discusses the process of spiritual seeking itself, rather than experiencing meaningfulness chiefly through other activities. Yet Dillon herself debates if we should expect older people specifically to try to enhance their 'spiritual' interests throughout their lives. While Tornstam offers evidence that they may, others demur, for instance Atchley's (1999) longitudinal work depicting some (by no means all!) ageing Americans as placing more importance on material considerations as they grew older, feeling less rather than more connection between themselves and other generations. Dillon emphasises, first, the *plurality* of paths one may take as one's lifecourse develops, even though there seems to be lifetime continuity in individuals' attitudes to religion. Second, she stresses that, independently of denomination, level of religiousness, gender or class, 'substantially more participants affirmed a Golden Rule philosophy during late adulthood (63%, 1997–2000) compared to when they were interviewed in early adulthood (29%, 1958)' (Dillon, 2009: 64). This does not seem readily accounted for in terms of historical change, since it was perfectly possible to talk in these terms during the participants' youths. For Dillon, this lends some support to Fowler or Tornstam, 'who argue that a more universalising world view is distinctive of late adulthood' (2009: 65). One 77-year-old respondent tells her,

> 'Well, I think that it really is true that you do have to love your neighbour. I do believe that God really did create us all equal, although we haven't figured out that quite yet.... I think that people have got to quit worrying about sexual preference. I believe that God made us the way we are ... I believe that you have to accept people, truly accept them. And as I said I don't think you have to like everybody. I don't think that's possible. But I do think you have to love everyone. And that includes the criminals and everybody. And no matter how hard that is ...' (2009: 65).

Similarly, 'one highly successful, professional man' also expresses views that correspond with Tornstam's accent on people's capacity to feel their place in the larger universe. In contrast to his own views earlier in his life, this respondent speaks of

> 'A feeling of humbleness and being properly insignificant as a person. Because when you're young you're pretty much self-centred.... And the whole world revolves around what you do. And as you get older you realise that you're not very much. You're just another little spark in the universe' (Dillon, 2009: 66).

A third respondent connects 'the web of life on earth we live in' with doing your best for others, without being sanctimonious: enjoying and valuing nature, and obeying the Golden Rule as Buddhism, Christianity and other religions express it (Dillon, 2009: 67).

There are strong confluences between what is said by some of Dillon's respondents and by some of Coleman's, discussed below. Neither of these authors wholeheartedly embraces a developmental psychologist's expectation that the lifecourse can be defined in terms of successive stages; but they are impressed by respondents' evolving perceptions that their connections with other people and other parts of the universe have deepened, and their views of their own importance diminished. For this reason, we shall examine views of meaning-creation that are more explicitly developmental, notably Erikson's, before examining a further variety of approaches to later-life insight in the gerontological literature: perspectives on the sorts of insight that lifetimes might accrue.

Lifetime and insight in gerontological research

It is a perennial question what, if anything, can be gained or lost in terms of insight in the course of a lifetime; the vizier Ptah-Hotep was not alone in feeling a drive to communicate what he felt he had struggled to learn from hard-won experience. Erik Erikson and Viktor Frankl argue that a lifetime involves effort that can certainly produce significant insight and perhaps ought to do so; Glen Elder's *Children of the Great Depression* or *I Don't Feel Old* by Thompson et al underline the variety of perspectives with which people look back at their lives. 'Life stage' theories like Erikson's stress growing attention to personal and ethical insight amounting to wisdom; Frankl's famous text on incarceration in a concentration camp argues that the role of meaning is so central to individuals' lives that it can make or break their very capacity to survive. But its role is not significant only for distinct individuals. Kalyani Mehta (2009) explores cultures in which ageing is associated with the need to provide a moral compass for others as well as for older persons themselves; part of the satisfaction involved in being older lies precisely in providing this compass. The cultures where she works explicitly stress age-related forms of attention to moral conduct or wisdom; but this attention can be effective even if it is not overtly thematised. Carmel Gallagher (2008) offers an account of more implicit ways in which older people's understanding of life factors into everyday social activities in communities in Ireland.

It is an ancient notion that human lifetimes might be hoped in some sense to have cumulative value. Old age has always been acknowledged to be vulnerable in different ways and to different degrees, involving change in various forms; Aristotle shows that the Athenians feared becoming ground down and bitter in older age through repeated exposure to frustration, disappointment and loss. (Aristotle says little about what he himself thinks about ageing; in these remarks in the *Rhetoric*, he is reporting on how one can argue about ageing and be generally understood, on the basis of common opinions; this is not dissimilar to an early version of social construction.) Yet, since the time of Homer, an alternative trope has persisted: the wise older person (usually, though not exclusively, the wise older man), using what he has learned from experience in order to give the benefit of his advice and example to his acquaintances and to society. Cicero, writing in the 1st century BC, deals in *De Senectute* (*On Old Age*) with the efforts one might make to preserve as much as possible of one's memory and strength, to retain and develop one's friendships and to continue to contribute to one's immediate and wider surroundings. Acknowledging that practical as well as philosophical preconditions are needed for success, he argues that there are pleasures to be gained from older age, given effort as well as good fortune. But in the developmental psychology of the 20th century, the notion that human beings continue to develop throughout their lives, even after attaining adulthood, remained notoriously under-explored. In itself, the idea of life as composed of successive stages is relatively common. Thomas Cole comments that 'stages', like the image of life as a journey, are 'archetypal images' representing fundamental Western 'intuitions of the wholeness or unity of life' (1992: xxx; see Grenier (2012: 192) for additional problematisation of the concept of 'transitions' between successive times of life). But most 20th-century psychologists concentrated almost exclusively on childhood stages; it is an achievement of Paul Baltes, Robert Sternberg and others writing within the ambit of 'positive psychology' to draw attention to this lacuna at the end of the century, carrying on the work of earlier writers such as Erik Erikson and Viktor Frankl.

Erik Erikson's work made such an impact in the immediate wake of the Second World War because it tried to resist taken-for-granted psychological practice and to portray human beings with the potential to develop throughout their lifetimes. The stages Erikson saw individuals as traversing were all heavily imbued with questions of meaning. The identity of his own biological father was unknown to him; Erikson's own surname was self-given, and the lifetime project of achieving insight into meaning was one he took very seriously. For Erikson, infancy involves the challenge between basic trust and basic mistrust, followed after a year or so by conflict between autonomy and shame. The next stage involves initiative versus guilt, and then – until about age 11 – industry versus inferiority; in adolescence, identity is set against role confusion. Erikson sees young adults in their early twenties as struggling between intimacy and isolation as they confront issues in forming marital partnerships and other friendships; but then one entire stage is envisaged as stretching between 25 and 64. This stage is characterised in terms of struggle between 'generativity' with regard to matters such as pursuing a career or raising children, or else stagnation. The eighth stage is posited as beginning around age 65, where the choice is between ego integrity versus despair. Ego integrity is a stage, if it is reached, at which one can realise the continuity in one's own personality and one's meaning for others. (A ninth, more reclusive, very late stage was subsequently added, in 'The Life Cycle Completed', written with Joan Erikson (1987).) Thus Erikson's view of the lifecourse is highly moral. The names of all the stages he envisages are heavily weighted in ethical implications, as are the 'virtues' or potentials they ideally lead to; for him, moral development is built in to human life in a fundamental fashion, part of daily psychosocial struggle. Correspondingly, if we want to describe the point of this daily struggle, it is to moral terms that we must look.

Erikson envisages the different stages as posing characteristic problems, such that the way a person deals with them affects his or her capacity to approach challenges featured in the next stage. Positive or negative aspects of encounters at particular stages are therefore cumulative – even though an earlier 'maladaption' can in principle be made up for later on (Erikson et al 1986: 41). But this is a version of developmental theory that makes room for cultural influences too. Erikson expected social and cultural surroundings to have impacts, for better or worse, on individuals' capacities to encounter tasks at different stages. Like the Athenians, Erikson recognises the real danger of late-life 'despair', especially to those who have coped less well with preceding stages; this is characterised by hopelessness, the feeling that one has achieved nothing, perhaps triggered by the loss of a profession or partner. But he stresses that in principle people have the potential to continue to develop right until the very ends of their lives. Since, for him, the ideal trend of this development is to open up wider and wider concerns, later stages have the potential to be strongly significant, ideally leading even to 'wisdom'.

While secondary accounts of Erikson's views on the development of meaning through a lifetime can render them somewhat schematic, his book *Vital Involvement in Old Age* (1986), written with Joan Erikson and Helen Kivnik, gives a much livelier impression of what he is trying to convey. It deals with 29 of the same set of subjects, born in California in 1928–29, with whom Michele Dillon deals (see above). For the Eriksons, the hope is that people in older age can achieve the strength given by integrity, 'wisdom' in the sense of 'detached concern with life itself, in the face of death itself' (1986: 37). This concern 'maintains and learns to convey the integrity of experience, in spite of the decline of bodily and mental functions' (1986: 37–8), the outcome of 'a kind of creative balancing' between trust, which is 'mandatory' for living well, and 'a "sensible" mistrust – also necessary for existence' (1986: 38). These are mostly not cognitive, conscious, intentional processes, but characterise *the way an individual deals with life* (cf. 1986: 39). In other words, people can be engaged in heavily moral enterprises without necessarily framing them in this way to themselves, without necessarily wishing or even being able to describe themselves and their actions in such terms. Wisdom, if a person achieves it, is, on Erikson's account, not just an extension of the care and creativity he or she may have shown at earlier stages of life; a genuinely new achievement, it 'probably is truly involved disinvolvement' (1986: 51). Ideally, a life cycle 'weaves back on itself in its entirety, ultimately integrating maturing forms of hope, will, purpose, competence, fidelity, love and care, into a comprehensive sense of wisdom' (1986: 55–5). Individuals normally experience an existential dread of no longer being alive; confronting this in the genuine realism of later life involves, Erikson hopes, placing themselves 'in perspective among those generations now living' and accepting a place 'in an infinite historical progression' (1986: 56).

This text is especially important because it does not deal only with the authors' explicit theory, which often takes on a very different hue as successive secondary commentators reinterpret it; it shows how the authors respond to real-life individuals on a personal level in the light of their theoretical approach. Their style in this book foreshadows Peter Coleman's (2011: 35ff) or Thomas Cole's strictures about the need to approach questions of meaning with caution, empathy and warmth. Just as they expect to understand their subjects on the basis of sympathy with the ways they do things, the theoretical stance of the Eriksons' book is partly conveyed by its style. The notions of ego-integrity and wisdom, which might otherwise seem abstract or obscure, take on friendlier aspects as we see the text reflecting how the authors and their respondents behave in everyday conversation. The Eriksons give the example, for instance, of a woman who is trying 'to be old with a sense of humor':

> Her comments do not indicate that the grandchildren think
> of her as old. Rather, they seem to reflect her view of herself
> as she relates to them – always interested, concerned, and
> eager to be supportive (1986: 57).

The older people they describe in this chapter tend to be busy and involved:

Another woman tells an anecdote about her mother, illustrating both her own philosophy of old age and the source of that philosophy: 'My mother was eighty years old and plants an apple tree and says, "In five years we'll have apples"' (1986: 58).

This speaker has recently enrolled in a course to learn sign language, and when she is fluent she intends 'to go to the museum and persuade them to provide tours in sign, for deaf art lovers' (1986: 58). The authors write of changes their respondents notice in themselves and each other:

> For many, these changes include a kind of increased concern for and tolerance of the world and its multifarious inhabitants. These people describe both themselves and their aged contemporaries as more tolerant, more patient, more open-minded, more understanding, more compassionate, and less critical than they were in their younger years. In a variety of ways, many agree that 'patience is one thing you know better when you're old than when you were young.' 'Old people are slower to anger … with people who don't understand their point of view. They are able to take the vicissitudes of life in a calmer manner.' 'Nothing shocks me any more.' 'Now I can see both sides' (1986: 60).

These interviewees 'seem to be open to considerations they used to view as incompatible', with 'a new concern for issues they previously all but ignored' (1986: 60) – though they do not attribute such developments to all older people, and are prepared to be self-critical about any failure of tolerance in themselves (1986: 61). Yet, nonetheless, respondents seem to feel that 'feelings of pessimism, discouragement, and simple exhaustion must be all but excluded from conversation, lest they jeopardize fragile tendencies toward energetic optimism' (1986: 63; cf Jolanki, 2009, who explores the obligation to present themselves as energetic and healthy that older people may feel). Not all are able to contemplate death with equanimity; some are openly afraid. They are afraid, too, of catastrophes they fear for their families and the world – ecological disaster or nuclear holocaust, as well as moral and social failings they perceive in American society (1986: 67). Religion may sometimes be a comfort, but highly significant is 'the acknowledging and accepting of past choices'. This does not imply a facile 'lifelong contentment', since many of the respondents have known 'profound unhappiness and restlessness', attributed to 'misguided decisions' earlier in their lives (1986: 70).

> All are struggling somehow to accept the notion that, whether or not they could have behaved differently in the past, they cannot *now* alter decisions made or courses of action taken *then* (1986: 71).

There is no point in denying pain, even disaster, emanating from past conduct; but

> As the elder seeks to consolidate a sense of lifelong wisdom and perspective, he or she endeavors, ideally, not to exclude legitimate feelings of cynicism and hopelessness, but to admit them in dynamic balance with feelings of human wholeness (1986: 72).

Not everyone, the authors say, is equally successful in doing this; but all are 'struggling to bring lifelong dystonic tendencies into balance with acknowledged psychosocial strengths' (1986: 72). They are 'all involved in the process of trying', and it is 'this effort that is the basis for growth at all stages of the life cycle' (1986: 73). In addition, this effort is not simply self-concerned. It has effects on the respondents' families: Erikson believes that healthy children will fear life less if the adults surrounding them achieve sufficient integrity not to fear death – but also beyond, in 'beliefs that reflect an enduring, underlying concern for community, for country, and for all of humankind' (1986: 100). The people the Eriksons talk to are socially, ethically and politically concerned (1986: 100ff), retaining 'the opportunity to demonstrate real caring in the present' (1986: 104). The examples here do not accentuate introspection in the way some accounts of Erikson's theory might expect; Michele Dillon (2009) casts doubt on the ubiquity of the 'life review' among her respondents, but the everyday details displayed in the Eriksons' text show us something of how meaning can be created without explicit reflection on the process of doing so. The richness and colour of their examples offers insights into how older people can contribute to society as a whole: their *way* of being people has an impact on the world they inhabit.

Erikson and his colleagues thus lay some stress on conveying what they mean by 'meaning' through examples of people leading lives they think of as meaningful, whether helping neighbours or taking pleasure in looking forward to reading novels. At one stage they use

an example from Bergman's film *Wild Strawberries* to give a further
ostensive definition. This emphasis on style of approaching life is not
without precedent; Moody (1986: 19) suggests that the ego-integrity
the Eriksons describe is at root a re-statement of Stoic principles. Even
though the Eriksons' work focuses much more on the enjoyment of
living in practice than in summary, it is certainly a central Stoic tenet
that ethical commitment is shown less through theoretical debate than
through the way someone lives. Erikson himself had experienced the
rise of Nazism in Germany, where ethical and philosophical choices
were not abstract matters, but were made real through the impact of
crucial life choices.

This point is made with lasting force by Viktor Frankl in *Man's
Search for Meaning*, published in German in 1946, in English in 1959;
the current, revised edition dates from 1964. Subtitled *An Introduction
to Logotherapy*, this work starts by dealing with its author's experiences
in a succession of concentration camps, in which almost the entirety
of his family perished. Here

> only those prisoners could keep alive who, after years of
> trekking from camp to camp, had lost all scruples in their
> fight for existence; they were prepared to use every means,
> honest and otherwise, even brutal force, theft, and betrayal
> of their friends, in order to save themselves (Frankl, 1964: 3).

How could the author, as an ordinary prisoner, survive in such
circumstances? By implication, how can his readers survive the lesser
travails of their own everyday lives? Very many did not survive the
camps, including especially 'the best' (1964: 4), and Frankl describes
in immediate analytical detail the emotional, intellectual and physical
torments the inmates endured. Yet the term 'logotherapy' indicates
that the answer is to be found, if at all, in the search for meaning.
After extensive detail designed to make the reader realise the depths
of privation to which the prisoners were reduced, Frankl describes
an event during a march to a work site when the man next to him
whispered, "'If our wives could see us now!'" He hoped they were
better off in their own camps (in fact they were not), and both prisoners
began to think of their loved ones (1964: 36). Frankl says,

> my mind clung to my wife's image, imagining it with
> uncanny acuteness. I heard her answering me, saw her
> smile, her frank and encouraging look. Real or not, her

look was then more luminous than the sun which was
beginning to rise.

A thought transfixed me: for the first time in my life I saw
the truth as it is set into song by so many poets, proclaimed
as the final wisdom by so many thinkers. The truth – that
love is the ultimate and the highest goal to which man can
aspire (1964: 36).

This Frankl terms 'the greatest secret' that can ever be imparted: '*The
salvation of man is through love and in love*' (1964: 36, italics in original).
Even in 'utter desolation', when nothing may be open to a person
except to endure all suffering 'in the right way – an honorable way'
(1964: 36), it may be possible for that person to 'achieve fulfilment'
(1964: 37). He describes the deepening of some prisoners' inner lives
and their profound responses to 'the beauty of art and nature' (1964:
38). Despite the consciousness of imminent death, they might feel
triumphantly that life possessed 'an ultimate purpose' (1964: 39). Thus
'it is possible to practice the art of living even in a concentration camp,
even though suffering is omnipresent' (1964: 43).

For Frankl, despite the fact that inmates constantly succumbed to
temptations to behave utterly selfishly, if a person 'finally suffered a
loss of values' and thus lost self-respect,

he lost the feeling of being an individual, a being with a
mind, with inner freedom and personal value. He thought
of himself then as only a part of an enormous mass of
people; his existence descended to the level of animal life
(1964: 49).

Yet, for Frankl, there is an alternative: people are not solely products
of biological, psychological and social influences, but do possess
'choice of action' (1964: 65). Despite the constant apathy induced by
hunger, exhaustion and fear, 'there were always choices to make, and
some of them at least were heroic' (1964: 65). Even when confronted
with suffering, without which no life is complete, one can attempt
to react with as much courage, dignity and unselfishness as one can
muster (1964: 67). Such 'spiritual accomplishments' must be treated
seriously (1964: 69).

These are lessons Frankl applies to everyday life, believing with
Goethe that if you expect the best from someone 'you will make him
become what he in principle is capable of becoming' (Frankl, 1972).
For Frankl, Goethe's adage is simply realistic. For him, there is such

a thing as 'a *will to meaning*' (1964: 99, italics in original; cf p 105) that looks to a person's future and gives sense to his or her life. 'Man's search for meaning is a primary force in his life,' a search that is 'unique and specific' to each individual (1964: 99; cf p 111). Notwithstanding 'pseudovalues' of various kinds, there is such a thing as an 'authentic and genuine' desire for values that can be defended as profoundly as possible, 'detected' rather than invented in an existential sense (1964: 100f). People who are unemployed can run the danger of seeing their lives as meaningless (1964: 70); this happens, for Frankl, when they lose confidence in themselves and become isolated from social support, rather than because working is the only thing they should be doing. He is gravely concerned about the 'existential vacuum' he perceives in the 20th century (1964: 108ff): a 'form of nihilism' (1964: 13) that gives little credence to the seriousness of 'spiritual' needs.

This work by Erikson and Frankl takes seriously the later years of life, presenting this time as important and responding with warmth, interest and respect to individuals they encounter. The same applies to Glen Elder's 1974 *Children of the Great Depression*, though it challenges the usefulness of expecting life to unfold in identifiable stages. It too takes human development seriously, both in youth and throughout the lifecourse, and in particular it highlights the interactions between individual effort and social-historical change. For Elder, his findings present an irrefutable argument in favour of supportive social policy. His particular respondents prospered in life more than they might have been expected to do, given their original circumstances, and more than other waves of respondents did, *as long as* they were able to benefit from opportunities such as access to higher education, like that offered by the GI Bill, or stable marriages. Famously, he inferred from his analyses five principles for life-course investigation: that development is lifelong; that individuals' lifecourses are historically shaped by the specific events they experience; that 'timing' is significant – the impact of an event or transition in someone's life is affected by *when* it happens; that lives are interlinked, within networks of shared relationships; and that individuals construct their own lifecourses through choices and actions within the possibilities and constraints that confront them. These 'principles' are not intended to be abstract, but to be read through the inflections of empirical detail that show in detail how they take effect.

Elder's work begins from a large philosophical question about the effects that history can have on the lifecourse. As his former director, John Clausen, puts it, Elder's combination of historical, sociological, psychological and longitudinal individual analyses starts from radical reflections:

Depressions, wars, and periods of extreme social ferment often produce major reorientations of society. That the life course of individuals may also be reshaped by such periods of crisis is apparent from personal experience and from biographical studies. Some lives are cut short or stunted, while others find purpose and opportunity to achieve beyond all prior imaginings (1974/99: xvii).

Elder begins his book with a quotation from Dickens' *A Tale of Two Cities*:

'It was the best of times, it was the worst of times, it was the age of wisdom, it was the epoch of incredulity, it was the season of Light, it was the season of Darkness, it was the spring of hope, it was the winter of despair' (1974/99: 3).

This is not accidental: Elder explicitly wants to discourage us from seeing even the Depression in over-simplified terms. He has a historian's sense of the interwoven complexity of the strands of experience lived through in any period, and the different ways in which events impact on and are responded to by those caught up in them. The experience of living through the Depression was not the same for everyone:

Severe physical want and poverty were concentrated among the urban and rural lower classes, in particular, while status or reputation loss and related anxieties were especially common in the middle classes (1974/99: 3).

Individuals remembered the Depression very differently – not just because their experiences actually were different, but also because 'The past is often reconstructed to fit the present' (1974/99: 4); hence the significance of the archival material from which Elder himself worked, which has contemporary impressions to offer. Like that analysed by Erikson and Dillon, this was data collected at Berkeley, California, but Elder's 'Oakland' cohort was begun two years later, in 1931–32, examining 167 children born in 1920–21; it studied them intensively until 1939, then added five subsequent waves of exploration until the early 1980s. Though it was only one of the cohorts that passed through the Depression, the 1916–25 cohort 'has historical significance as a major source of World War II veterans, the postwar "baby boom," and the presumed generational gap'; these people's early years were marked by scarcity and those of their children by affluence (1974/99: 5). Elder's work differs from Erikson's in that it does not envisage individuals as facing successive waves of psychosocial tasks, but it does see them as giving meaning to their lives in different ways: both in seeking ways of responding to situational challenges and in trying to interpret or make sense of the circumstances around them.

Here Glen Elder's approach follows a tradition influenced by the Chicago School (Elder, 2005); for instance, in stressing the interdependence of all areas of life – as when family relationships and cultures are affected by socioeconomic change but in turn adapt to produce new forms of reaction to those same socioeconomic circumstances (1974/99: 114ff). It also addresses failings he perceived in the sociological approaches common in his youth (some still visible today): they 'tended to slight the role of father, the development of parents as well as children, the reciprocal nature of social interaction (that children influence parents and vice versa), and the educative dimensions of family influences' (Elder, 2005). In his later work he was interested in the conditions under which fruitful intergenerational bonds can be formed, for instance between teachers and students. Thus 'resilience and vulnerability' continued to interest him as, in a variety of cultural settings, he sought 'pathways out of disadvantage and risk' (Elder, 2005). This goes right back to the interests of W.I. Thomas in the early years of the 20th century (Elder, 1974/99: 7): how do individual people respond, as time goes on, to the events in the social structures in which they find themselves? These responses involve continuous adjustments in *meaning*. For example,

> Crisis situations are a fruitful point at which to study change since they challenge customary interpretations of reality and undermine established routines. The disruption of habitual ways of life produce[s] new stimuli which elicit attention and arouse consciousness of self and others. Control over events becomes problematic when old ways are found lacking as means for dealing with social demands and satisfying basic needs or standards. Situations enter the crisis stage when they are interpreted or defined as such by a group or individual, and thus constitute a problem which calls for novel solutions and lines of adaptation. For the child in a family which has suddenly lost income and status, adaptation may involve redefinition of self and others, the restructuring or clarifications of goals, and the assumption of a new status or role (1974/99: 10).

Interpretations are challenged, routines and habitual practices disrupted, attention is given in new ways, consciousness of self and others changes; people feel less in control because old approaches seem inadequate; but the crisis makes its impact through being 'interpreted or defined as such', and it is this process of social perception that creates a problem calling for new solutions. Individuals' whole views of themselves and others may be redefined in consequence, as may their goals and their understandings of what they should be doing.

> We have assumed that children from deprived and non-deprived families experienced themselves as a social object through their interpretation of the responses, which others directed toward them. These interpretations frequently differ from the actual views of others, as we have seen in this chapter, and do not correspond in a simple one-to-one relation with established views of self, especially in situations of drastic change. Any change of this sort tends to alter the framework of meanings in which the self is anchored, creating a disparity between an acquired image of self, constructed from stable relations in the pre-crisis period, and interpretations of social judgments or evaluations in the new situation (1974/99: 145).

Elder credits W.I. Thomas with having seen that 'Life organization is … constructed and reconstructed in the course of self-reflection' in such crises; individuals differ in capacities such as the ability to tolerate ambiguity, or to take empathetic or objective views of their surroundings (1974/99: 11), but their impacts on each other are also decisive. In *Children of the Great Depression*, meaning is central – less in the sense of ethical meaning specifically than in the sense of what experiences are *like*, and how it is that they come to be experienced as they do within the overall, complex structural influences at hand. 'The meaning of economic deprivation and unemployment depends in part on the relative importance and consequence of prestige loss and financial strain' (1974/99: 62). Within families, the power of one parent or another 'for children is largely a function of how they perceive it' (1974/99: 87); interrogating the confluence of sociopolitical and cultural elements in a given case shows how meaning is created in interaction among individuals, within their overall, and changing, circumstances. Elder's approach takes social construction extremely seriously, in other words: accentuating *both* how it arises in interaction among numbers of people *and* how it is experienced.

The work by Thompson et al mentioned earlier, *I Don't Feel Old* (1990), like Elder's, begins by referring to profound questions about history, humanity and change. Thompson and his colleagues stress the impacts of social changes on the process of bestowing meaning on ageing and coming to terms with death. The virtual eradication of childhood mortality means that in countries like the UK it is now 'only the old who have to deal with the universality of death':

> Once loudly and publicly proclaimed, death has become private, secret, almost shameful: so much so that nobody of any age wants to talk about it. That makes facing one's own death, and the crushing pain of bereavement through the death of others, even more bewildering. The very changes which have lengthened life have made the coming of death feel stranger and harsher from its new unfamiliarity (1990: 22).

Yet, though this book demonstrates in many ways how its subjects make their lives meaningful, the authors seldom discuss this issue directly. This book, whose subtitle is *Understanding the Experience of Later Life*, conveys meaning and subjectivity by communicating diversity and vividness of impression, its pages packed with vignettes about everyday life – food eaten, daily activities engaged in – and, significantly, quotations from individuals that allow readers to picture what their lives must be like.

> A London chemist, a sturdy, blue-eyed man with a long white beard, would take his grandson for walks. Once, going through a churchyard, 'he held my hand ... He said, "Don't fear," he said, "the dead don't hurt you, it's the living that hurt." I've remembered that all my life' (1990: 73).

Thus, rather than hearing people's *opinions* about the meaning of life, we hear details of what they *do*. One woman describes how her husband, though he had lost his job, 'wasn't any bother,' 'because you see he did the garden. Oh, he loved gardening' (1990: 160). It is what he did rather than his internal life that she feels able to mention.

In a sense, this book conveys its message by mimicking the diverse helter-skelter of its subjects' lives. Its authors are conscious that 'To a greater or lesser extent' all the stories they record convey a 'search for meaning' and the 'vital resilience' needed to find it – and which not everyone may possess (1990: 245). Thompson et al identify a number of contemporary approaches to 'particular sources of meaning':

including 'house and home', 'daily routines', memory and the act of remembering, and 'a sense of personal continuity over the whole life span', in which individuals symbolically connect meaningful past with current experiences. Efforts to maintain these connections are potent in counteracting loss: 'loss of paid work, loss of full physical energy, loss of loved companions' (1990: 245). For Thompson et al it is, therefore, immersion in everyday experience as well as a sense of personal patterning over a lifetime that go to make up meaning, and these senses must be striven for continuously in the face of vulnerability or pain.

They are clear that public policy needs to support equality in respect of the material basis people need if they are to make the effort to resist the impact of heavy losses and 'to make the choices which construct individual meaning'; but at the same time they emphasise the decisiveness of 'the culture of particular families' in supporting individuals (1990: 246). They see the areas of work, leisure, grandparenting and intimate relationships as highly significant; here too active engagement is required. People need to make individual decisions to win their grandchildren's affection, to rebuild difficult relationships or to compensate for those that have been lost entirely. Far from being static and unchanging, later life is therefore 'a time of constant reconstruction'; the 'myths' that 'help to make sense of life' and of the lifecourse are misleading about or even 'degrading' of ageing and must be resisted (1990: 250). Thompson et al conclude,

> Later life from the inside – like life at any age – is a story with its dark side, its pain and suffering. But the message which comes most strongly from these accounts is of resilience in the face of the twists of fate; of adaptability; and in some of these lives, of a powerfully continuing ability to seize or create chances for fulfilment, whether in work, leisure, or love (1990: 252).

Many other writers approach the ways in which older individuals' consciousness of life-course meaning contributes to their families and communities; they both use and develop the cultural resources those settings provide. Mehta (2009) deals with older people in Singapore whose different cultural and religious backgrounds frame 'ageing' in such a way that they can see themselves as helpful, setting examples to others. For her, 'the search for meaning and purpose in life is far from a speciality of the young' (2009: 37), but it is satisfied in different ways by recourse to different cultural resources. She interviews older

Chinese, Malay and Indian individuals who all live in Singapore, seeking to understand how they 'seek, and indeed create, meaning in their lives and those of others' (2009: 37). While Chinese respondents emphasise remaining useful to family and society until the end, they are conscious of the need to behave ethically, humanely and with propriety – resisting temptations to avarice, for example (2009: 39). Malay respondents, in contrast, feel obliged to become more religious because of the closeness of death, and to earn the respect of younger people by providing them with good examples to follow (2009: 40f). Indian study participants also emphasise the need for spiritual and religious pursuits, in the context of expecting reincarnation. All Mehta's respondents see older age as meaningful; they do not feel marginalised, but connected to an 'active web of ethnic community bonds' (2009: 44), happy to socialise with members of other generations in these contexts.

Gallagher (2008), in contrast, describes small-scale interactions among older people that contribute to community in Ireland, giving life meaning by making it liveable. Apparently small gestures, such as greeting people in the street or watering their plants while they are away, are keenly appreciated and, for Gallagher, have a significance that runs deeper than surface appearances suggest. Gubrium, in *Living and Dying at Murray Manor*, emphasises the continuous everyday processes that go into creating and maintaining meanings in the 'places' people inhabit; 'unwitting routines' invest places with meanings, maintained 'as practical solutions to getting on with the affairs of living together' (1975/1997: 1, 40). The different 'worlds' to which places are attached bring with them criteria expressing values and expectations about what works, what is important, what should be taken seriously, and what can safely be ignored.

Lie et al (2009), writing about voluntary work in the UK, also infer to a set of meanings that are rather indirectly expressed by their respondents. They explore the extent to which voluntary organisations depend on the contributions of older people. For Lie et al these individuals' behaviour as well as their comments in interviews express their commitment to participation as citizens in the common good. This commitment is of great benefit both to those they assist and to themselves, but it would be a mistake to see it as carried out *in order to* reap such rewards. Instead it may convey an implicit conceptualisation of citizenship that is superior to that used by government agencies. The authors hold that 'The meanings that people attach to their volunteering offer a richer way of accounting for their activities compared to "motivations"' (2009: 702). They argue that their respondents' comments in in-depth interviews express, in effect, a philosophical view, what the authors term a 'republican' position: 'a strong commitment to society and fellow citizens among older people that counterbalances individualistic and instrumental reasons for volunteering promoted by the state and market' (2009: 702). Everyday conversation and actions can obliquely express social, ethical and political commitment to insights gained in later life.

Exploring approaches to meaning

The work we have begun to investigate here in different but complementary ways treats meanings and insights achieved by older people as embedded in the lived experience of everyday life. This third section deals with writers who would not disagree that this is so, but who even more explicitly focus attention on methods of eliciting meaning in a gerontological context. They include Lars Tornstam in his work on gerotranscendence, H.R. Moody on ethics and wisdom, or Ron Manheimer in his humanist approach to meaning in later life. Like Thomas Cole, with whom we begin, they all argue that creating meaning is a central project in ageing, and that people in later life have significant views to offer on human conduct. We shall examine what sorts of claim these writers are making and the sorts of evidence they advance for them.

Thomas Cole's *The Journey of Life: A Cultural History of Aging in America* (1992) tackles the question of meaning directly. A 'notoriously vague concept', it is, he says, usually employed in two main ways, which have become disconnected in the contemporary world.

> The *scientific* questions about meaning are part of the human attempt to develop logical, reliable, interpretable, and systematically predictive theories. The *existential* questions about meaning are part of our human quest for a vision within which one's experience makes sense. The concept of meaning, then, contains a crucial ambiguity … The generative power of meaning as a concept derives from this seminal ambiguity, which allows one to connect the world of public understandings with the inner struggle for wholeness (1992: xviii).

Significantly, he argues, the first of these approaches has come to dominate public life and thought. The dominant mode of visualising ageing has succumbed to 'secular, scientific and individualistic tendencies' that have 'eroded ancient and medieval understandings of aging as a mysterious part of the eternal order of things': old age has now been redefined as a scientific problem (1992: xx). Older people – Cole exemplifies his own grandmother – have succumbed to 'historically conditioned feelings of failure' they now associate with their failing bodies (1992: xxiv). While 'All cultures maintain ideals of aging and old age', therefore (1992: xxv), 'the rise of liberal individualism and of a moral code relying on physical self-control' undermines the capacity 'to accept the ambiguity, contingency, intractability and unmanageability of human life' (1992: xxvi). Cole does not, of course, challenge the usefulness of scientific evidence, but he seeks to restore some of their status to religious and spiritual discourses, and to the richness of metaphorical language that attempts to come closer to ideals of transcendence and morality.

For Cole, as for writers such as Vincent (1995), Katz (1996) or Bytheway (2011), the meanings we attach to later life are heavily influenced by the cultural discourses that predominate in the worlds we inhabit. We are now living out a 'chronologically defined, bureaucratized course of life' – whose origins Cole locates in 'the search for religious and social order in early modern Northern Europe' (1992: 4). We cannot understand ageing, or our own views and expectations in connection with it, without recognising that our 'growing interest in individual lifetime' needs to be understood 'in conjunction with the "spirit of capitalism" described by Max Weber and the "civilizing process" described by Norbert Elias' (1992: xxix). As the aftermath of strict Calvinism waned (1992: 161), the revolutionary generation passed away, and American society became more industrialised in the early 19th century, old age itself became infused 'with increasingly sentimental images of lost patriarchal authority' (1992: 74). The story of Rip Van Winkle illustrates this process. Rip falls asleep before the American Revolution and wakes to witness 'the continuing rationalization of individual behaviour in a market society', 'unattuned' to the self-interest now expected of farmers, still preferring the 'communal rhythms' of his countryside childhood. He prefers to 'starve on a penny than work for a pound'; but

> Rip's fate foreshadows the obsolescence of the old man in a secular society where women become rulers of the home, productivity becomes the primary criterion of a man's worth, and patriarchy becomes a maudlin compensation for powerlessness (1992: 75).

Cole portrays 19th-century America as having adopted 'a hygienic utilitarianism that had little room for either the vicissitudes of old age or the glory of God' (1992: 78). Rejecting communalism and hierarchy as they had formerly rejected established churches and monarchies, 'Jacksonian custodians of order opted for an especially rigid code of moral self-government' (1992: 93): 'an equally repressive regime' (1992: 97). The body itself was part of this regime, subject in the mid-19th century to health-reform regulation recalling that of today. Longevity was 'the emblem and reward of an upright life' (1992: 98), and a diseased old age the punishment for sin. The desire for 'a rational, orderly and secure course of life' led to the conviction that

> God's laws of morality and health enabled all to live to a healthy old age, die a natural death, and enter the kingdom of heaven. Failure resulted from individual ignorance or lack of will … (1992: 110).

There were alternatives to this outlook, Cole tells us. Later in the century, more 'liberal and Romantic' pastors 'helped define Christianity as culturally female' as femaleness was then perceived – 'gentle, meek, forgiving, and humble' (1992: 129). But this too reinforced the dualism associating health with self-control, and infirmity with sinfulness (1992: 138; cf 230); self-help books offered advice for achieving both better health and improved spirituality (1992: 146). By the period 1890–1925, this viewpoint had inflated into a 'war on old age', supported by charlatans and quacks of every kind. By the 20th century, therefore, 'ageing had been largely cut loose from earlier religious, cosmological, and iconographic moorings'; it was now 'available for modern scientific scrutiny'; 'The founders of modern gerontology and geriatrics set about discovering the laws of normality and pathology as applied to senescence' (1992: 192, 194). Ageing was becoming 'seen as a problem', 'an unwanted obstacle' 'to be explained and regulated by scientific management' (1992: 211). A 'professional aging industry' began in the 1940s and grew rapidly after the 1960s (1992: 224f), precisely in this vein. For Cole, the rigid self-control of individualism undermined the capacity to appreciate depth and complexity. But today's attempts to counteract negative stereotypes of ageing bring their own problems. They fail to show 'tolerance or respect for the intractable vicissitudes of ageing' (1992: 233), its 'moral and spiritual frontier'; Cole's effort is to alert us to the demand for new combinations of resources of 'humility and self-knowledge', 'love and compassion' (1992: 243).

Such an account is not free from cultural pessimism, perhaps evaded in Lars Tornstam's exploration of 'gerotranscendence' through a shift in the focus of attention to relatively optimistic accounts supplied by older people themselves. Tornstam terms his position 'A Developmental Theory of Positive Aging', one that features 'what old people themselves say' about what it is to age well – specifically eschewing the projection of white, Western, career-oriented ideas onto older age (2005: 3). Tornstam's 'grounded-theory-like concept' (2011: 166) evolved from work in Sweden that attended to statements by older people who 'described ... transcending borders and barriers that had circumscribed them earlier in life'. They now enjoyed their lives, expressing 'great satisfaction' with them (2011: 168). 'Gerotranscendence' thus focuses on the heightened sensitivity Tornstam finds among some older people for 'transcendental sources of happiness' (2005: 59). 'The gerotranscendent individual ... typically experiences a redefinition of the self and of relationships to others and a new understanding of fundamental, existential questions' (2005: 3). His respondents feel that their identities have changed and developed in later life, moving away from self-centredness in the direction of deeper 'broadmindedness, tolerance and humility' and even a form of 'modern asceticism' (2005: 68–89). Important though this is to those who experience it, the influence of public discourses is felt here too: such insights may be difficult to express in the conventional terms of our Western, '"normal", paradigmatic world' (2005: 77). For example,

> The experience of nature evokes the feeling of being at one with the universe, which is called at-one-ment in the Eastern tradition. The increasing significance of these small everyday experiences of nature could therefore be interpreted as a way in which the barrier between the self and the universe is transcended (Tornstam, 2005: 59–60).

One of Tornstam's respondents says that whereas she used to feel that life was carrying her along like a river she could not control, 'today I feel like I'm the river' (2005: 6). Tornstam hopes that a similar state of mind is one many people could aim at; indeed, he offers exercises at the end of his book that are intended to support readers in learning to dispense with unnecessary, inhibiting social rules, imagining 'the landscape' of their lives as from the detachment of a mountaintop (2005: 197).

For Tornstam, the phenomenon he is describing embraces three dimensions. Its 'cosmic' dimension changes apprehension of time, so that past and present can be experienced together:

> The borderline between now and then is transcended, and this may also include a return to and reconfiguration of childhood. Like the layers of an onion, all ages are available at the same time, but when returning to the inner layers, to childhood, things are observed that could not be seen then, and reinterpretations are made of events and situations from childhood or other earlier periods in life. Such reinterpretations frequently include some kind of reconciliation, as was the case for the old woman who had been mistreated by her mother as a child, and who now understood her troubled mother in a new way and was able to reconcile with her, 20 years after her death (Tornstam, 2011: 169).

This goes together with a heightened 'feeling of being part of the flow of generations' (2011: 169), a diminished fear of death and acceptance of 'the mystery dimension of life' (2011: 170). The second 'dimension' Tornstam identifies concerns the self. Older people he talks to discover new aspects of their own selves, good and bad, as well as experiencing a decline in self-centredness and a capacity close to what Erikson called 'ego integrity', directed to a view of the world outside the individual (2011: 172). The third dimension deals with 'social and personal relationships': individuals become both more relaxed and more discerning in social situations, less 'cocksure' about right and wrong and 'travelling light' as far as material possessions are concerned (2011: 173). Like Jung, Tornstam speculates that some cases of depression and anxiety in older age may be linked to blockages in potential development (2011: 177); he deplores the assumption that it is only in the early stages of life that human beings develop and mature, and calls attention to the necessity of doing so continuously.

Coleman remarks that Erikson, given that he was writing in the immediate aftermath of the Second World War, was 'surprisingly sanguine' about the capacity of sociocultural resources to support individuals' efforts to become more attuned to 'the goodness of life'; he contrasts Erikson's apparent optimism about the benign effects of the social world with Tornstam's view of 'the active role of society in this process as solely negative' (2011: 6–7; cf 60ff). While Tornstam sees gerotranscendence itself as 'culture free' (Tornstam, 1989: 59), he does see its development as vulnerable to unpropitious cultural habits, languages, pressures and conventions (cf Sherman, 2010; Atchley, 2011). Dalby (2006) reviews a small number of independent, and not entirely conclusive, attempts to trace the development of gerotranscendence in a variety of cultural settings, suggesting that sociocultural impacts on capacities for it can be traced; they might include high degrees of materialism and perhaps secularity in a society, according to Ahmadi (2001). Dalby points out that Tornstam's approach does not specify that gerotranscendent individuals need to believe in a God; 'spiritual' themes of concern to the people investigated in studies he reviews include 'integrity, humanistic concern, changing relationships with others and concern for younger generations, relationship with a transcendent being or power, self transcendence, and coming to terms with death': topics 'not related to age per se, but to some of the challenges that age presents' (Dalby, 2006: 4). By 'integrity', Dalby means 'bringing meaning to one's past and present life', by which he seems to be indicating coherence of pattern rather than integrity in the sense of ethical rectitude; by 'transcendence', he means 'finding meaning beyond the immediate experiences of physical ageing and its associated losses' (2006: 9). He does not term these *universal* needs, though he clearly envisages a capacity for gerotranscendence as traversing cultures, offering a valuable form of significance to older people's lives.

Harry 'Rick' Moody too sees the project of creating meaning in later life as more than an academic issue. Like Cole, he associates problems in this field with the ideological pressures of modern capitalism (Moody, 1992). In *Abundance of Life: Human Development Policies for an Aging Society* (1988), he attacks the 'failure of imagination' (1988: 3) to be found in the fact that

> Our image of old age is commonly an image of decline and decay ... We offer old people help with their needs but do nothing to nurture the strengths that might allow people to solve their own problems. We ignore latent strengths and respond only to dependency or failure (1988: 2).

For Moody, responding to this predicament with a 'policy for lifespan development' demands courageous practical and political planning for how 'the unprecedented abundance of life' in the modern world 'could be mobilized for the benefit both of older people and of society as a whole' (1992: 5). 'If this point of view sounds utopian, consider the alternative' (1992: 5). There are radical sociopolitical problems to confront, including widespread anxiety about economic insecurity, a lack of social mobility combined with ubiquitous credentialism, unresponsive social institutions and an insidious loss of faith in progress (1988: 15–18). Resisting these means combining positions with a variety of origins and practical effects:

> In part, this message, which is the essential framework of this book, is deeply conservative: suspicious of professional imperialism, doubtful about the culture of modernism, insistent on the need for self-development within small-scale communities that have traditionally been sensitive to the human experience of old age. On the other hand, the thrust of the book is also radical: a critique of ideology and vested interests of the political economy, a call for grass-roots activism, an appeal for widened opportunity for the poor and the least advantaged elderly (1988: 11).

This by no means endorses what Laslett (1965) called 'the "world-we-have-lost syndrome"' (Moody, 1988: 26), which erroneously perceives older people as having been better off, better cared for by their families, before the industrialisation of the modern world (cf Hareven 1982). 'The finitude, fragility and mortality of the human condition' 'is unchanged by modernity'; what modernity has done 'is to seriously weaken those definitions of reality that previously made that human condition easier to bear' (1988: 27). Moody quotes Berger et al, pointing to the discomfort of 'the culture of modernity' with 'old age as an existential reality' (Berger et al, 1974: 185).

  Moody's work insists that 'such distortions express a dominant ideology of old age that itself contributes to the problem of aging in America' (1988: 122), an ideology all the more 'insidious' because it is unrecognised as such, and indeed is propagated by social science and social gerontology (1988: 123–4). This tends to involve an 'ideal of value-free social science', 'based on a systematic separation between facts and values', denying any role for 'human interests':

> Social science, presented in the guise of experts or scientific expertise, plays a central role in legitimating actions by policymakers and in setting the terms for public debate. But the structure of value-free social science also contains a hidden ideological dimension that supports the status quo in aging policy. In the behavioral sciences, for example, prestige and rewards go to investigators who make the greatest use of quantitative methods: statistics, survey

research, econometric data, and so on. But quantitative measurement favors investigation of only those activities already predefined by the larger policy system (1988: 124).

This directs attention to the ways in which ideology, methodology and policy are intertwined. Moody denies that a preference for quantitative methods in the behavioural sciences is 'methodologically neutral or value-free'; 'Quality of life in old age is ignored because single vision ignores what it does not see' (1988: 125). 'The result is a depersonalization, and the experience of old age itself begins to vanish from sight' (1988: 126). This analysis explains the blend of the theoretical and the practical in Moody's work; he wants to apply Freud's formula 'to love and to work' to everyone, including older people (1988: 128), and for him this entails a holistic, transformational approach to 'conscious ageing' (Moody, 2003).

The resistance to ideological pressure that this entails can, for him, draw strength from varied spiritual stances. Moody prefaces his 1988 volume with quotations from religious leaders: Christ's 'I came that they might have life, and have it abundantly,' and Muhammad's 'Richness does not lie in the abundance of goods but in the richness of soul.' Other commentators too link insight in later life with both spiritual stances and traceable effects on individuals or communities: Schachter-Shalomi stresses older people's 'service to the community' (1995: 5). McKee and Barber (1999) argue that wisdom may be developed in response to loss, potentially decreasing egocentricity and heightening empathy – that is, with an impact on others. Rothermund and Brandstädter (2003) support a 'mindfulness' approach to ageing, focusing on continual growth and change, with evolving criteria for what individuals think of themselves as obliged to do. But in the cases of Moody and Cole, critique is located within a theory of science and of the effects of political and economic ideology that makes theirs a radical contribution to the self-understanding of gerontological analysis.

Moody continues this work by engaging in direct efforts on a variety of levels, not least in connection with the lifelong-learning-related travel organisation Elderhostels, or in editing the website *Human Values in Aging* for the Gerontological Society of America. This speaks directly to readers, publishing 'items of interest about humanistic gerontology' (1 September 2012), as well as *Teaching Gerontology*. Items in these newsletters might include conference announcements for Jungian or Buddhist conferences on ageing, or the Sage-ing Guild founded by Rabbi Zalman Schachter-Shalomi, who 'envisions the elder as an agent of evolution, attracted as much by the future of humanity's expanded brain-mind potential as by the wisdom of the past'. For Schachter-Shalomi (an inhabitant, like Moody, of the small town of Boulder, Colorado), this heralds 'the next phase of human and global development' that will unite past wisdom traditions with contemporary research into mind and consciousness, together with ecological movements directed towards the future.[1] *Human Values in Ageing* also directs us to a chapter on humanistic gerontology by Ron Manheimer, published in *Valuing Older People* (2009). The 1 August issue includes a passage from Robert Butler, inventor of the term 'ageism', written shortly before his death at 83 and contributed by Andrew Achenbaum in connection with writing his biography:

> Probably at no other time in life is there as potent a force toward self awareness operating as in old age. Those who lead us through the valley of the shadow of death have the responsibility to help us deal with disillusion and help us hold a vision of the larger world that links us with others and with the universe.

Brief articles in this newsletter are both practical and theoretical, concerning different interpretations of positive ageing, or discussions on spirituality or creativity and ageing, or social security and medicine (18 July 2012), the pleasures of ageing (2 July 2012), or costs of residential healthcare (15 May 2012). Reflections are included from the work of luminaries such as Rabbi Leo Baeck: 'A spirit is characterized not only by what it does, but, no less, by what it permits, what it forgives, and what it beholds in silence' (1 June 2012); or, more tersely, 'Biologist J.B.S. Haldane put it this way: "The universe is not only queerer than we suppose, it is queerer than we can suppose." Wake up: we are engulfed in mystery' (1 February 2012). The same issue (1 February 2012) includes a quotation from Jung: 'For a young person it is almost a sin – and certainly a danger – to be too much occupied with himself; but for the aging person it is a duty and a necessity to give serious attention to himself.'

References to other websites include direction to the 'Eldering' website,[2] whose 'Eldering Principles' of 'Wisdom in action' are as follows: Responsibility, Completion, Respect and Compassion, Authentic Communication, Humility and Service. This website represents an effort to instil meaning into readers' lives, speaking to them directly and supporting practices of resistance against stereotypes:

As Elders, we own our circumstances and always have a choice in how we respond. Rather than placing blame or taking credit for our lives and the world as it is, we engage in responding in unprecedented and what might seem unreasonable ways.

... Elders appreciate and let go of the past to be 'present' in conversations. By completing our 'unfinished business', we free ourselves. We no longer have to be dominated by our moods. And we don't have to have the past limit and determine our choices and actions. This allows us to hear what is happening and see what is showing up in our conversations today, rather than superimpose our past experiences, expectations and moods on the current situation.

... As Elders, we treat each other – and ourselves – with respect and compassion. We are patient, trusting that everyone grows and learns at their own pace. Elders acknowledge that all human beings are whole, complete, competent and able to transform and transcend their circumstances – no matter how difficult they may be.

... We listen non-judgmentally to each person's perspective, experience and ideas and speak our 'truth'. We strive to be authentic in expressing our commitments in the world.

... Instead of reacting to our thoughts and feelings, we acknowledge our limitations and humanity. As Elders, we seek to work with others in collaborative ways, rather than persuading, manipulating or dominating.

... We care deeply and are connected to other people. Elders give people space to be who they are. We create new possibilities for others and leave it to them to choose whether they will modify, discard or make them real. We contribute the best of who we are in a way that helps others realize their potential and their grandest vision for themselves. We are valued for our contributions.

Communications like these urge older people to confront their ethical concerns; the implications of interpersonal views and practices are not topics of academic analysis but objects on which action is intended to be taken.

On a website intended for Certified Senior Advisers to older people, Moody specifically addresses the question of ageing 'and the Search for Meaning'.[3] He stresses that the 'subjectively experienced "world" of old age is different from the world of people who are young or in mid-life', quoting from the journal kept by the playwright and analyst Florida Scott-Maxwell during her residence in a nursing home. Finding that she has reached a 'place beyond resignation' she 'had no idea existed', the writer reflects:

> 'Age puzzles me. I thought it was a quiet time. My seventies were interesting, and fairly serene, but my eighties are passionate. I grow more intense as I age. To my own surprise I burst out with hot conviction. Only a few years ago I enjoyed my tranquillity; now I am so disturbed by the outer world and by human quality in general that I want to put things right, as though I still owed a debt to life (Scott-Maxwell, 1968: 32).

Moody refers to a survey by Burbank (1992) asking older people what gives meaning to their lives; nearly 90% describe their lives as meaningful, over half referring to relationships with other people and about 12% to service to others, as well as activities related to religion or leisure. Moody refers to the contention by Thompson et al (1990) that fear of poverty or ill-health are less threatening to people as they age than, as Moody puts it, 'loss of life purpose and boredom'; unless they are sick or depressed, they 'don't feel old'. Moody recognises that finding meaning happens for different people in different ways, but links it to what he terms 'self-acceptance', part of a set of 'recurrent, indeed nearly universal developmental tasks of later life'. Certified Senior Advisers need, he suggests, to learn to be responsive to talk of this nature, 'listening in a deeper, more attentive way' that is hard to achieve without both professional training and a proper understanding of ageing. 'More than getting facts', this 'requires overcoming stereotypes and asking deeper questions about values, about the meaning of life, about our hopes and dreams', helping older people to 'get past stereotypes to make truly individual choices so that they can fulfil their dreams for the second half of life'.

These practical interventions stem from Moody's conviction that gerontology itself should offer an 'emancipatory discourse' (1994: 27-28), both on social and on personal levels, lending practical as well as theoretical support to 'a positive idea of human development: that is, ageing as a movement toward freedom beyond domination (autonomy, wisdom, transcendence)'. This converges with Thomas Cole's insistence that analysing ageing in technical terms alone would amount to a moral and political stance that should be rejected: it relegates ageing to an impossible attempt to evade disease, instead of confronting 'conflict, mystery and suffering in late life' (1992: 237). For Cole, 'ageing' is an irreducibly moral concept. Writers like these are not only conscious of the extent to which social theories generate, endorse or rule out particular moral positions, they attempt to resist these effects on a multiplicity of levels.

Theories of 'moral economy' explore how social norms related to distributing economic resources prescribe obligations we owe each other within families or between generations (cf for example Kohli, 1986; Minkler and Cole, 1992); critical gerontology underscores the effects of public views on the legitimacy or desirability of certain ways of behaving, or, on a larger scale, ideas about power and justice, including justice between generations; these analyses are expected to generate efforts to influence public policy and practice. But Moody and Cole wish to confront distorted views of ageing on at least three other levels too: the influence of society-wide ideologies; the influence of these ideologies on gerontologists; and their influence on individuals' behaviour. In each case, they are prepared to endorse practices of resistance. It may be significant that these authors are writing in an American context, where ethical, religious and spiritual language retains more common currency than is frequent among academics in the UK and Europe. They do so in a context where there seems to be plenty of evidence and argument vigorously defending the significance of a meaningful, ethical approach to life – one stressing what Baars (2012) calls the *interhuman* condition. We should, therefore, interrogate some reasons for why these approaches do not appear to be succeeding in decisively affecting social views of ageing.

Notes

[1] http://www.uua.org/documents/hoertdoerferpat/elderhoodspirituality.pdf, first accessed 17 September 2012.

[2] http://ca.eldering.org/eldering/principles.

[3] http://www.hrmoody.com/Meaning-CSA.pdf (accessed 2 September 2012).

TWO

Diminishing older people: silence, occlusion and 'fading out'

The ambiguity of age-consciousness

There is striking evidence that later life can be a vantage-point from which fruitful developments can be expected, both for the protagonists and for others. This is not to claim that older age is always enjoyable, nor to deny the challenges and vulnerabilities that attach to this stage of life as they do to preceding ones; it is merely to stress that it is important. Hence gerontologists display and discuss compelling reasons for expecting vibrancy and insight from older age. Yet at the same time they note that common discourses and major social practices fail to support this expectation. This is not centrally a question about individuals' personal attitudes towards older people. Survey evidence indicates that these are often on the whole positive, and a variety of experiences by or in the company of frail older people suggest that members of other generations can take active pleasure in their company. The point is, rather, that such attitudes do not effectively translate into political and public culture and policy; they fail to allow older people systematically to feel senses of agency and self-respect, fading them into the background of everyday attention. In other words, major forms of social exclusion revolve around denying meaning to people and processes involved in ageing.

This predicament cannot be repaired in the absence of accepted public languages on a significant scale that accord status and interest to older people: that establish the compelling interest of what they do, feel and think, and pay adequate attention to it. In the absence of discursive practices of this kind, children and adults who are not yet 'old' find it hard to formulate why they should expect to gain from the views and company of older people. Nor do the common practices of contemporary social life encourage older people themselves to anticipate that they will have significant experiences to enjoy and convey, or to express this anticipation readily in words. Ancient rhetoricians emphasised techniques for bestowing 'presence' on salient parts of an argument, making it vivid and meaningful for those who heard it; arguments without presence will be ignored. Older people are regularly subject to this opposite effect: social 'presence' is denied to them, causing them in effect to fade out of public attention. Much of the meaning and insight associated with human experience is interactive, discernible between people rather than introspectively; if older people systematically lack social roles and interlocutors, their capacity for contributing to their own and others' lives is crippled.

According to Mike Hepworth (2000: 3), 'Ours is probably the most age-conscious period in human history;' and the *way* in which it is age conscious tends to be highly constraining. Ageism is a 'widely shared prejudice' (Moody, 2010: 12). Gerontological literature thus rightly emphasises the social impact of stereotypes of older age, but in order to understand the formation and impact of stereotypical attitudes, the construction of discourse itself needs to be explored, for which interdisciplinary instruments are indispensable. Media communication in particular is criticised for caricaturing older people (Miller et al, 1999). Fealy et al (2012) point to devices that 'other' older people even as they overtly try to valorise them. In the Irish newspapers examined by these authors, older people's identities were homogenised and their past experiences ignored; they tended 'to be represented as vulnerable, fearful and weak' (Fealy et al, 2012: 97; cf Pain, 2001). Behaviour that threatened this stereotype (which is implicitly joined to the assumption that vulnerability is a freak condition for humankind) was interpreted as deviant or anomalous. In addition, there seemed to be an implication that if older people were *not* vulnerable and weak, they would not need to receive their pensions.

Fealy et al were writing at a time when many older people in Ireland were engaging in political protest to defend entitlements to free medical support; even when journalists sympathised in principle with their stance, they seemed hard pressed to find any language within which to frame the issues in a non-discriminatory way. As Krekula also points out (2011, 2009), social interpretations of other people in terms of 'age coding' are extremely difficult to escape, irrespective of individuals' good intentions. This affects behaviour towards older people throughout public and private worlds. Without any conscious decision having been taken, older people working in organisations can receive less of the support that employees need in order to function well; they may be 'written off' in terms of future commitments. This activates what Dannefer (1987, 2003) terms 'the power of self-fulfilling prophecies', impacting at meso-levels of society as well as interpersonally: people who are not expected to contribute actually find it harder to do so. This chapter therefore examines some conspicuously meaning-related aspects of ageism that amount in effect to contempt for later life stages. These are connected to wider political features of contemporary discourse. Not least, the devaluation of ethical communication and a widespread misunderstanding of what human rationality can achieve make it harder to imagine what later life could offer.

Work such as Christina Victor's, or that of Hepworth and Featherstone, or Bytheway (1995), also highlights social attitudes that occlude the significance of older people's contributions to society. Victor et al (2009) comment on a generally 'negative perception of the contemporary experience of old age':

> There are many myths and stereotypes surrounding the experience of ageing and later life. For example, we readily conceptualise old age as a time of universal and inevitable biological decline that then manifests itself in physical and mental frailty (Victor, 2005; Mulley, 2007). Additionally we also perceive older people as neglected and marginalised by society; in more current policy parlance, we see them as 'socially excluded' (Victor et al, 2009: 203).

Mulley (2007) argues that in visual art, older age tends to be portrayed as uniquely unhappy, austere or frightening; like Wright (2004), he sees efforts to assist older people going hand in hand with denigrating them. Mulley discerns a trend to explore 'successful' ageing in contemporary films, though he contends that it is not powerful enough to overcome strong negative myths about older age that pervade medicine and geriatrics. The dichotomy noticed by Bytheway appears again: 'For some old people, ageing is indeed a time of loss and diminishing capabilities. For others, it is a time of social activity and fulfilment' (Mulley, 2007: 71). Few observers seem to take seriously the notion of fulfilment; yet if later life is not to be understood as a mere continuation of middle age, it suggests questions about values and meaning that have serious philosophical and political implications – as Moody, Cole or Tornstam recognise.

Victor et al argue that common myths and stereotypes are misplaced – that the subjective experience of loneliness, in particular, is reached by a variety of pathways and should not be attributed simplistically to the lives of the majority of older people (2009: 205), nor equated with living alone (2009: 209). They emphasise too that

> The focus of research examining the social relationships and patterns of social engagement of older people has focused predominantly on the pathological. This reflects broad social policy concerns with the disadvantaged, a concern about who will 'care' for the 'excluded' and the dominance of gerontological research in the UK in the 'humanitarian' tradition.... However, this focus has served to divert our attention away from the majority of older people who do not experience the pathological states of loneliness or social isolation and who are not socially excluded.... Few researchers have looked at daily life in old age and how people make sense of old age through the rhythm, patterns and activities of daily life ... (2009: 224).

The participants in their research, by contrast, 'spoke at length and passionately about their engagement in local activities' (2009: 224). Victor et al conclude that today 'Relationships with neighbours, family and friends are, for most older people, robust and enduring', with high levels of contact (2009: 225): they stress that we urgently need to know more about what older people offer those neighbours, family and friends. In a relatively rare concentration on just this topic, Gallagher (2008) explores how older people in Ireland contribute to a sense of local community, often through small-scale practical activities that, cumulatively, make their surroundings more habitable.

An American university's website on 'Social Gerontology and the Aging Revolution' summarises this debate when it claims that 'There is nothing inherently problematical about growing old. And yet in most nations of the world, old age is increasingly understood in "social problem" terms'.[1] Sinclair et al (2007), reporting that three-quarters of older people feel that age discrimination is an everyday occurrence, remark that ageist perceptions in a society preoccupied with youth make older people 'seem invisible'. The Archbishop of Canterbury, Rowan Williams, made an appeal for 'an end to damaging stereotypes of older people' the subject of a major speech prior to stepping down at the end of 2012.

> Too often we want to rush children into pseudo-adulthood; too often we want older citizens either to go on as part of the productive machine as long as possible or to accept a marginal and humiliating status, tolerated but not valued, while we look impatiently at our watches, waiting for them to be 'off our hands' ... We tolerate a very eccentric view of

the good life or the ideal life as one that can be lived only for a few years between, say, 18 and 40.... It is assumptions about the basically passive character of the older population that foster attitudes of contempt and exasperation, and ultimately create a climate in which abuse occurs.[2]

As Williams' intervention implies, the ways in which we envisage ageing are themselves social products (Gullette, 2004; Edmondson, 2013a). 'The ageing of societies' may be portrayed as a terrifying burden, characterised by new forms of 'risk'; in contrast, medical and scientific approaches to ageing may be envisaged as minimising risk, even risk free. Not all these discourses are popular in origin; they are also influenced by 'generations of gerontologists, geriatricians and other well-intentioned agents of care and control' (Gilleard, 2005: 162). From the biomedical perspective, ageing can be envisaged as a state that scientific measures can hope to alleviate or even cure; there is no need to attach significance to how we *think* about ageing, for it is simply a biological problem. This flight from idealism has unintended consequences. Now, 'We live in a profoundly ageist society', complains Thomas (2004: 3), constantly seeking 'pharmacists' miracles' to shield us against old age, or at least against its appearance.

Underlying ageist stereotypes and making them possible are, therefore, fundamental conflicts in principle that affect both how human lifetimes are conceptualised and the legitimacy of critiquing these conceptualisations. Public and personal interaction with older people tends to be larded through with the assumption that they should fade into the background, expected to have little to say that is of interest. These assumptions prohibit older people from laying claim to significant meaning in their lives, for themselves or for others. They are systematically (even if not always overtly) constructed as social and discursive subordinates, exemplifying a phenomenon examined in philosophical analyses of the impact of ideology and communicative power.

> As Habermas noted, such inauthentic communication is a basic means for imposing and maintaining relationships of domination ... The superordinate rhetor typically seeks to restrict communication to the denotative content and forbid discussion of the terms of the relationship that she has imposed (Brown, 1987: 89).

This form of domination is implicitly justified in terms of the pincer movement formed by the political and aesthetic movements of relativism, on the one hand, and neoliberalism, on the other. Each denies the value and relevance of what can be said about human striving; both undermine the validity of trying to offer insights into the lifecourse, opening the way for purportedly timeless practices of measurement and control. In comparison with these, the contributions embedded in everyday life so much valued by Victor and her colleagues are accorded a vastly inferior status.

This predicament has evolved owing to intertwined developments including the effects of positivism in the philosophy of science (Sayer, 2000) and the declining position allotted to ethical language (MacIntyre, 1981). MacIntyre argues that among 20th-century philosophers and in everyday life it became supposed that ethical language expressed nothing more than emotional preferences; this position deprived ethical stances of authority and interest. The social sciences too contributed to these developments, introducing the novelty of envisaging 'selves' as somehow subsisting independently of the social roles people fill. Refraining from 'essentialising' social roles was taken to imply that it did not matter how they were accomplished at all. It was no longer taken that people *are* sisters, brothers, mothers or fathers, say; they were thought of merely as *acting* as sisters or fathers, a change in perspective that unintentionally stripped out much validity and importance from the efforts concerned (1981: 32–3). Denying the significance of what people attempt in relational facets of their lives, for MacIntyre, helped to undermine the concept of the lifecourse itself, robbing it of its possible purpose – its telos, or underlying point.

Gerontologists such as John Vincent (1995), Stephen Katz (2009) or Bill Bytheway (2011) draw attention to associated features of 20th- and 21st-century social organisation that conspire to fade the meaning out of ageing: the aims and images highlighted in modern discursive structures as well as bureaucratic practices connected with them. For them, replacing images of disease and decline with those of 'independence, activity, well-being, and mobility' merely conflates anti-ageism with anti-ageing. Underlining 'successful ageing' can tend to disguise the fact that people are ageing at all (Katz, 2009: 16–17). The 'regimes of life course and technologies of expertise' that support 'the disabling bounds of consumer practices and neoliberal, market practices' need, Katz contends, to be undermined by reconnecting ageing with 'new and wide-ranging timelines' (Katz, 2009: 19–20). Like Riley et al (1994), Bytheway (2011) too urges resistance to the relentless chronologisation of contemporary life, with the unremitting references to birthdate and time that make us 'unwitting agents of the state' (2011: 106). Aware that these discursive failings affect gerontologists also, he reiterates Townsend's accusation that gerontologists too easily succumb to an 'acquiescent functionalism' (2011: 28) – one that fails to critique, or even be properly conscious of, ideologies of ageing. Bytheway warns us not to reduce the dynamic of later life to a false dichotomy: It 'is much more complex than either a general decline or some kind of end-of-life success, as promoted by competing gerontological theories' (2011: 218–19). This is not to deny that the social conception of the lifecourse must bring with it institutionalising effects and contribute to social order (Kohli, 2007), but to draw attention to negative effects that this particular order brings.

Bytheway points out that individuals' chronological ages have gained unprecedented salience through a concatenation of official documents, birthdays and time-related social expectations. Dates of birth, in previous centuries relatively insignificant to individuals or even unknown to them, now actually form our key forms of *identification* in bureaucratic systems of all kinds (Bytheway, 2011). That is to say, our selves have come to be defined and labelled through birthdates; birthdates form individuals' key distinguishing features as far as state or medical organisations are concerned, generating languages and practices that have become pervasive. Yet it is not long since dates of birth were a matter of some vagueness in the West, as they still are in some other parts of the world. When the British government decided to retain passport regulations after the First World War, making personal chronologies standard public knowledge, the move was criticised as 'dehumanization' (Marrus, 1985: 92). Agatha Christie in her memoirs (1977) recalls her husband, the archaeologist Max Mallowan, remarking that Polish fighters who were his colleagues in the Royal Air Force during the Second World War were strikingly unconcerned about their dates of birth and ages – 'Twenty – thirty – put whatever you want!' An Irish nurse known to the present author had wished, in the 1970s when she was aged 67, to work for six months in Australia. Suspecting that she would not be employed if she disclosed her age, she merely altered her passport, giving herself a birthdate ten years later. She carried out the job competently and returned home in due course. The fact that such examples seem surprising shows how deeply our cultures have adjusted to the official collection of personal data. In contrast to narratives of progress in terms of life-course health and survival, 20th-century states' bureaucratic practices impacted on the habits of thought of entire societies to accentuate the stereotypical perception and treatment of older people (Hareven, 1982; Katz, 1996).

Chronological age has come to function, for these practices, as a 'master' trait (Hughes, 1945; Becker, 1963), so that it has gradually become uncontentious on a global level – even if in complex configurations of ways – that older people should be constrained by stigmatising expectations (Kunow, 2010).

Yet psychologists like Peter Coleman concur with Moody and Cole in seeing the transmission of meaning and value as central to what we expect from older age. For Coleman, this expectation only makes the position of older people more complex. He outlines the 'double challenge' involved in ageing, given that social surroundings also age and change:

> Older people are expected to give witness to what has been important in their lives and what is of lasting value. They need to do this also for maintaining their own sense of identity. At the same time their own adaptation to new times and customs requires that they acknowledge and accept inevitable change (2009: 23).

For Coleman, traditional societies present less challenge in this respect, in so far as older people have the task of 'articulating and giving witness to the value choices that they have made in the course of their lives, and to the religious underpinning of these values' (2009: 23), in the knowledge that this will be helpful to younger people who also hold to these or similar ideals. This is not, he says, perceived to be the case in societies in which there is a large plurality of value choices that change all the time – even though, paradoxically, even in changing societies older people are expected to be resistant to vulnerability and doubt, in questions of meaning and religion. As a matter of fact, older people have, historically, often been spiritually innovative (Coleman et al, 2006). A number of founders of religious orders or contributors to new theological traditions have made their contributions in later life, not least St Theresa of Avila. Yet in the contemporary world a failure to take lifecourses seriously seems to operate even where it might be expected least, in the case of the churches and their practical theology, which might be anticipated to attend with particular sensitivity and energy to questions of life-course meaning. As Coleman points out for churches in the UK, the notion that older people might have something to offer *them* does not appear to figure significantly in their expectations. 'The spiritual dimension' of ageing is now neglected:

This neglect is the more surprising when one takes into account that the later stages of life raise fundamental questions about the purpose and meaning of life, for example finding justification for continued living in states of diminished physical or social functioning (Coleman, 2011: 1).

In former times, Coleman suggests, 'the ordinary wisdom' within cultures offered answers to such questions. This may overstate the unity of cultures in the past, which were often riven by dissent about religion, politics and meaning in ways at least as radical as they are now; 20th-century philosophers such as Rawls declined to discuss belief in the good life at all because of the death and destruction repeatedly caused by religious strife (not to mention other ideological conflicts). But Coleman's main concern is with the recent past, for example the contrast between generations growing up just after the Second World War and those growing up in the 1960s. He stresses the complex dynamics of matters of belief and the difficulty of expressing them succinctly in words (2011: 25ff, 57); together they make simple accounts of generational change seem crude. He also takes into account that individuals' beliefs themselves change over time (for example 2011: 21–2) and may be hard to characterise in univocal language. People who summarise their positions as Christian, for example, may not necessarily support 'orthodox Christian teaching' (2011: 31). Coleman's emphasis points in the first place to the sociocultural predicament approached in different ways by the other writers mentioned here: he depicts today's situation as one in which people may feel that they inhabit 'fragmented' societies, within which 'individuals often have to search for their own answers in relative isolation from each other' (2011: 1).

The answers they find deal, for Coleman, with questions about what beliefs to use as guides to 'what we value as goals and objectives in life': as in '"belief in my son", "belief in democracy" or "belief in God"' (2011: 1). 'These beliefs provide orientation and direction for our lives at difficult or unclear moments' (2011: 1–2). Coleman stresses that such beliefs can offer bearings in difficult times. He does not say, and surely should not be taken to imply, that the commitments in question go into abeyance when we are not subject to puzzlement or confusion. But the examples he gives are extremely mixed. They seem to allow for almost any type of position: 'belief in my friends', for instance, or 'belief in competitive sport'. Coleman himself addresses this breadth of interpretation:

Beliefs about the nature of humankind, its purpose and destiny, and its relationship with the world and universe within which it is embedded, are increasingly referred to as spiritual belief. Use of the word 'spiritual' seems to have lost its original tethering alongside religion and to have come to refer to a search for connection ... with and/ or belonging to whatever powers, forces or principles are considered to underlie the universe we live in. Spiritual practice is understood as the appropriate response to this awareness of connection (2011: 2).

In fact, Coleman remarks, the term 'spirituality' seems often to be chosen 'in order to avoid the negative connotations that surround the concept of religion' and its 'rules and regulations' (2011: 2).

On the one hand, questions about the insight and meaning appropriate to later life cannot be permanently evaded; not least, workers in the health services are repeatedly confronted with 'the practical relevance of dealing with issues of meaning and belonging in the face of suffering, alienation and death' (2011: 2). On the other hand, despite these recurrent needs, Coleman underlines problems in putting such issues into words. Perhaps '"meaning-based" needs' might be a 'more accurate and less ambiguous' expression to refer to 'the human experience of needing to justify continued existence in the face of the pain that life can bring', pointing to 'that aspect of human nature that goes beyond itself' (2011: 2). He quotes James Woodward as complaining that the term 'spirituality' is in danger of growing so 'vague and diffuse' that, 'like "intellectual Polyfilla"' , it can change shape and content so as 'conveniently to fill the space its user has devised for it' (Woodward, 2008: 69; Coleman, 2011: 3). Coleman remarks here that even the anti-religious writer Richard Dawkins is described, by Michael Hogan, as a spiritual writer, on the grounds that he is trying to offer 'crucial life guidance' to those he sees as in thrall to religion, making an effort 'to promote life-sustaining beliefs' (Hogan, 2010: 14).

Coleman, therefore, acknowledges that the search for meaning displays a diversity reflected in public language that itself is fluctuating and elusive. In his 2011 book he concentrates on exploring 'beliefs', 'whether religious, spiritual or neither', and what people say about how these beliefs 'support them in understanding and coping with life's challenges': this means, he says, 'belief in action', 'referred to in the context of people's daily lives' (2011: 4). This he specifically contrasts with an interpretation of spirituality 'as a normative development characteristic of subjective experience as persons grow older' (2011: 4). Thus Coleman's approach can be compared with those of, say, Erikson or Tornstam (see below), who do argue that as human beings grow older they have at least the potential to become more clearly attuned to the importance of what Coleman refers to as aspects of life that go beyond the individual. Like many writers who follow a broadly Jungian approach to human maturation that does stage a vehement resistance to the general silence imposed on later-life insight, Achenbaum and Orwoll (1991) also focus on increasingly transcendent attitudes in older age, in comparison with more worldly aims in earlier life stages. But Wink and Dillon (2002) suggest that this positive, maturational approach can be opposed by one stressing social and personal hardships, and the constraints faced in later life, locating spiritual growth (if any) in response to these. Coleman himself has suggested that in contemporary societies people can, perhaps paradoxically, feel isolated in their search for connectedness; the influence of social context is a matter of concern for him, but one he treats with tantalising brevity.

A significant feature of Coleman's work, here as in other texts, is its sympathetic interest in the doubts and uncertainties of older people, and reluctance to impose on them the expectation of some form of spiritual advancement. He argues that we need much more longitudinal evidence if we are to maintain that spirituality generally develops with age, while what data we have suggests great variation (2011: 8; women, especially, and contrary to public expectation, may question their beliefs more as they grow older (2011: 69)). Despite these hesitations, Coleman contends that belief will in the future become more rather than less important (2011: 9), both because it is becoming more often chosen than simply inherited and taken for granted, and because it is capable of contributing so strongly to people's 'overall sense of well-being' in later life (2011: 10).

Coleman's insistence on the dynamic nature of belief during the lifecourse in general, and the later lifecourse in particular, is significant. Potentially it could impact positively on relations between older and younger generations; Coleman remarks that younger people are reluctant to be told what to do, think and feel by people who regard themselves as having all the answers, and he is clear that many older people do not see themselves as authorities in this sense. However, his own investigation emphasises meaning-related quests particularly directed to bereavement, or embarked upon in order to cope with problematic experiences. Thus, much of his interview material is taken from bereavement studies and focuses on issues such as participation in war, the death of children or spouses or both, serious illness or disability. Chapter 5 explores religion's role 'as a coping resource in circumstances of bereavement' (2011: 79), particularly in cases where it is a spouse who dies. These investigations are not, therefore, primarily directed to exploring in detail how older people relate specifically *to others*, people in their own generation or in younger ones.

Coleman's own interest is not only in spirituality and meaning but also in religion, which he associates with 'a search for what is of supreme importance – "the sacred" – and the wish to incorporate it in one's own life, and that of one's family and community' (2011: 7; cf 2011: 162). This, he acknowledges, comes close to what some people see as the spiritual. He recognises too that non-religious viewpoints can fill similar functions; chapter 6, 'Coping without religious faith', by Wilkinson and Coleman, reports on case studies on older British Humanists, whose beliefs are 'centred on the power and capacity of human beings' (2011: 98), exploring four 'basic functions of a belief system' as identified by Dawkins: explanation, exhortation, consolation and inspiration (2011: 99). Thus, for example, one interviewee says,

> 'I know that people are suffering and dying all over the world, so I have tended not to make too much of my own suffering, my own problems … I believe that the human condition is universal and that I do not regard myself as being outside or more important than my fellow man. I mean, a lot of people find that concept difficult. They think, "Well, I'm a person and I'm important to God; you know, I'm a very important person." I have never been able to accept that …' (2011: 101).

In terms of 'explanation', humanists, on the evidence of this chapter, accentuate a natural-scientific account of how the universe came to exist, in the sense of privileging it as a narrative. (Religious believers, at least in Europe, characteristically also accept this account, but they do not require it to generate life-course meanings as such.) In terms of exhortation, they see human beings as obliged to create their own morality. In terms of consolation, interviewees are a little more hesitant: "'Everything – every plant and tree – is either growing or declining.… And really, when you think of the universe, you are such a microcosm that … in the space-time thing, it's nothing …'" (2011: 107). Wilkinson and Coleman (2011: 104) quote from a British Humanist on what makes his life meaningful:

'To my way of thinking, social really means global, and thinking in terms of humanity per se and not any particular nation or race or whatever. But, thinking of humanity, you could say that my aim would be to try to help towards the continuing survival and, if you like, refinement of humanity, the human species. So that's what I see as really the overriding morality. Actions should be based on that to try and improve the lot of humanity ...'

A number of those interviewed here refer to the facts of astrophysics, and to a feeling of oneness with distant galaxies, not least '"because matter doesn't change, or it simply changes its form"' (2011: 108). Interviewees find inspiration in voluntary work for others, in experiences of relatedness to others and to aesthetic or spiritual experience such as singing in a choir, or in the idea of scientific exploration. They may feel inspired by feeling 'an extra pressure' to use their lifetimes well and 'to live life more fully and morally' (2011: 107). Wilkinson and Coleman point to parallels between this set of viewpoints and a religious stance on the world (2011: 110); they are clear that the interviews they have presented do suggest an entirely liveable approach to ageing, though they are agnostic about how representative of atheists in general their sample may be. They conclude that

> individuals who have questioned life's mysteries and have found answers that appeal to them on many levels demonstrate an ability to cope well with the challenges of ageing, and this includes atheists and agnostics (2011: 111).

Their book does not deal only with relatively conventionally Christian and atheist believers in the UK and such well-documented societies as the Netherlands; it also examines the experiences of Christians in contrasting European social and cultural settings, and individuals in the UK who embrace faiths such as Islam, Hinduism or Judaism, as well as more eclectic groups. In the former case, it may be partly the need to locate in their settings examples such as Catholicism in the Italian province of Liguria that means that this part of the text focuses particularly on practice – about which people might have different opinions. Feast-days and farming form a highly visible part of this background, what people do rather than their efforts to say what they believe. One interviewee describes stories and prayers together with a grandfather:

> He would say the intentions, for example 'for all seamen', 'for all people in prison' ... because he had a kind thought for anyone who needed help, and he taught us to pray for them (2011: 134).

Another interviewee describes the hard life of former times, slaving to plant vegetables, maize and wheat:

> Otherwise what was there to eat for so many mouths all the year through? But when I think about the old folk! They were such an important part of the family – the real authorities! They were listened to, and always had a good word of advice to give you. And they were more religious than nowadays. You know, I think it was thanks to them that families stuck together so well... (2011: 135).

Though these interviews do highlight 'older people's close attention to deficiencies in religious organisations', Wilkinson and Coleman suggest that they also indicate a potential contribution to dialogues between secularist and religious outlooks in the future of the European Union (2011: 136–7) – as well as to the overall project of deepening discourse about the human condition (2011: 158–63). That is, they do not simply chart the effects of denying meaning; in redirecting attention to questions of meaning, their work suggests some possibilities for repairing them.

The struggle for language

Work by Outi Jolanki (2009: 261) deals specifically with ways in which certain types of discourse can be ruled out for older people, and others ruled in, by social and political conventions. Jolanki pursues the question of what ageing means to older people in Finland: 'What changes does it bring to the ways they see themselves and their relations to the rest of society?' Her results are revealing for an understanding of the lifecourse and the extent to which older people's contributions in terms of meaning and insight can be systematically underplayed. Not only, Jolanki argues, is ageing prominently associated with (declining) *health* rather than the acquisition of life-course insights, both for her subjects and for the public at large: health is 'a central preoccupation' in our notions of ageing, to the extent that 'questions connected with health contribute largely to the meanings bestowed on ageing itself'. Rightly, Jolanki sees that talk about everyday matters such as how people manage particular health conditions can lay bare 'profounder social attitudes' 'touching on what is desirable or undesirable for human beings': 'in a word, moral attitudes to ageing' (2009: 261). Her work is an important exposure of the way in which intendedly benign social concerns can have devastating effects on how the lifecourse is imagined – and thus, in effect, on how it *is*.

Jolanki's comments derive from a project in which 250 Finnish people aged 90 or more were interviewed. Those she deals with here all live independently; they have all come from the rural region around Tampere, but have moved to the town in the course of its industrial expansion at the beginning of the 20th century. Jolanki takes a discursive and rhetorical approach to these interviews, one that treats language 'as a central tool that constructs different versions of speakers' social worlds' (2009: 262):

> Talk about one's own experiences of ageing, or defining oneself as old or not old, is linked to self-definitions and the process of positioning oneself as a certain kind of person (2009: 262).

But this is neither necessarily conscious nor a matter of entirely free choice. 'Certain positions are often considered more proper, believable or realistic than others' (2009: 262), as well as implying normative dimensions about how one should behave.

Jolanki reports that respondents feel compelled to demonstrate how 'active' they are, and how independently they can manage their daily lives. Apparently they fear that unless they can do so, they might not be accepted as competent, adult moral agents. For example, a respondent aged over 90 'clearly questions' her interviewer's implications that her age might be expected to entail physical decline:

> With talk about dancing and going 'racing around' she produces herself as an independent, self-reliant agent who has an active social life [and is unwilling to see 'old' as determined by restrictions] ... We can see that the interviewee, in order to evade this kind of restrictive definition, associates herself with activities that are generally connected with young people (Jolanki, 2009: 264).

The discursive resources available to speakers such as this, in other words, compel them into a flight from ageing itself rather than allowing them to explore explicitly what may be positive, interesting or challenging about it. Jolanki reports that on the relatively infrequent occasions when they try to refer to older age as 'a time of mental and spiritual development enabled by, and born as a result of, long life experience', they need to furnish long and complex details in order to try to do so (2009: 269). This suggests that they need support against doubts: that they are unpractised in this form of discourse or not confident that it will be accepted. Jolanki writes,

> Cultural discourses are theoretical abstractions, which do not determine but rather offer resources for thinking (Holstein and Gubrium, 2000). Yet, they furnish us with ideas about the possible ways to define 'old', and the identities and positions that are seen as possible and proper for older people in a given society. The detailed analysis of older people's own talk given here shows how they use different discourses of old age to construct identities and to give shape and meaning to their own experiences of old age. But the analysis also shows that the identities offered within these discourses can be constraining and restrictive (2009: 271).

Jolanki concludes that 'there still seems little room in public discourse for seeing old age as something else, and something more, than an individual "body project" to keep fit and healthy' (2009: 272). Other forms of meaning are simply fading away.

Jolanki has explored ways in which 'active' approaches to ageing can occlude older people's linguistic freedom to discuss spirituality, ethics or wisdom. This is also a theme in the work of James Nichol (2009). Nichol, observing 'the continuing strengths of eldership as a formal public and family role' in indigenous communities, has worked for an extended period with a group of people 'born between 1940 and 1956' in the UK, with the aim of discovering if the term 'eldership' held any resonance in a British setting. All his participants reject this term, yet they do affirm 'a belief in later-life development and contribution' (Nichol, 2009: 249). It is notable that this group of creative, intelligent individuals have to struggle to locate language in which to express what they feel. Nichols summarises their views in terms of 'slowing down to find it', 'purple' eldership and 'guardianship' (2009: 249). He uses a process of 'cooperative inquiry' in order to let these meanings emerge; his co-participants lack access to a ready-made vocabulary to express what they want to say. Sometimes they refer to literature: Goethe's Faust, struggling to bring new things into consciousness, or the poem

'Warning': 'When I am an old woman, I shall wear purple ...' (2009: 254); for Nichol, they are 'resisting limitation and marginality with counter-cultural panache' (2009: 255). Guardianship, on the other hand, is for at least one of the participants about

> asking people, through a micro-example [erecting a wind turbine], to understand chains of cause and effect over a long period of time, to imagine their consequences and to take responsibility for the welfare of future generations ... rather than being in the thrall of a continuous present (Nichol, 2009: 255).

These insights definitely relate constructively to what later life can provide – both to individuals themselves as they age and to society in general. But they locate a genuine problem in terms of lack of recognition for this on a social level. One participant in the research, an artist, reports feeling 'patronised and dismissed' by a female arts administrator younger than herself; a man in the group says that he lives 'with a sense of being judged all the time', perhaps envisaged as '"some pervy old guy who lives on his own and rides a bicycle"'. The person in the group who feels calmest about these issues is a Quaker who is 'in fact a formally recognised elder' in a socially significant context (Nichol, 2009: 256). Unusually, this individual does possess access to a social setting in which being older is recognised as possessing positive potential.

Nichol brings together some of the interplay between vulnerability and creativity in his participants' experiences:

> Unable to see themselves in the roles that older people have had in the past and retain in some other cultures, ... inquirers nonetheless believed in continuing development in later life and that they had something distinctive to offer. The inquiry process, instead of delineating new models of eldership, powerfully revealed participants' vulnerability and confusion about ageing when the question became more fully present for them (2009: 258).

It would not have been possible, this implies, to plumb these participants' feelings using a simple interview method. When confronted with issues for which a common, current social discourse is not easily available, people need to work through them together over a protracted period in order even to begin to work towards means of expression. Simply constructing 'new models' straight off is out of the question.

Unease about ageing is only in part a new phenomenon; as Victor remarks (2010: 1–2), an association between ageing and ill health has persisted throughout recorded history (see also Thane, 2005). Anxiety about ageing can be related too to the age-old assumption that 'the body, especially the face, is a reflection of the self' (Featherstone, 2010: 193). If the face looks older, the self must somehow be decrepit also, even though older people comment repeatedly that their own experience of themselves is otherwise. Hepworth (2000: 40) explores repercussions of the fact that 'The "look of age" in human beings is, generally speaking, considered unwelcome and undesirable.' The decisive question here is whether there are *also* other reactions to balance out these prejudices and fears. Thomas Cole (1992), as we have seen, discerns a key discursive shift for the worse as the association between capitalism and industrialisation developed. This is not to deny that, before that time, there was also room for misconception about the purposes of the lifecourse, remarked on by commentators from the Old Testament prophets to Thomas More in the 16th century. More's *Utopia* is a radical deconstruction of his contemporaries' views on what made life worth living – fashion, status and power – and he was also aware that these misconceptions were woven into the entire social structure. But it was Adam Smith in the 18th century who pointed out, in *The Theory of Moral Sentiments* (6th edition, 1790), that the capitalist system itself is based on distortions that are indispensible to it. Beyond a certain point, possessing more objects and higher status does not in fact tend to make people happier, but unless they erroneously believe that it does, the system will collapse. Smith was aware of the strong influence of habitual practices on people's moral capacities; he was conscious of the need to evolve powerful conventions to counteract strong distorting features. Contemporary social and discursive practices, in contrast, now largely urge the significance of work and the career rather than the lifecourse. Questions of meaning have been thrust into the terrain of the problematic: broached chiefly in the context of crisis, in hospitals and morgues rather than throughout everyday life.

Contrasting versions of the lifecourse remained discernible as late as the Edwardian period, where conceptions of lives as moral journeys, stemming from the Victorian era and earlier, were still in evidence. This metaphor retains some appeal today, at least in the Netherlands: Dohmen's (2002) book on the art of living was conceived in the course of a conversation on a real journey, on a railway. But the image lacks the authority it formerly possessed. Much of the force of the journey metaphor derives from acknowledging the relevance of meaning *throughout* people's lives: on a real journey, it is essential to keep to the right course, return to it if it has been forgotten, or to have good reasons for finding a new one. This concept was remarked upon especially on occasions such as engagement or marriage, where much of the journey remains in the future. *Penelope's Irish Experiences* (Wiggin, 1902) ends with a serious moral reflection on the duties of husbands and wives to cooperate with each other and behave considerately throughout life's journey. The impact of constant consciousness of the ethical implications of everyday actions is highlighted by Agatha Christie (1977), who mentions the pedagogic custom of drawing a moral from the slightest event; she recalls her satisfaction as a child with the Edwardian emphasis on 'unworldliness', a now almost-forgotten virtue that was, according to her account, felt to be central in the lives of families like her own. Even in the recent past, therefore, remnants of public discourse still connected on-going daily practices with the temporal production of the lifecourse as a moral enterprise. But they no longer offer a living metaphor for common-sense guidance in daily dilemmas and disputes.

Social hegemony and age

The social construction of ageing is more complex than can be described simply as a concatenation of prejudices, although prejudices are by no means absent from it. Simone de Beauvoir's views highlight what would now be termed habits and structures that are pervasive throughout Western societies. In an often-quoted comment, she contends that

> The meaning or the lack of meaning that old age takes on in any given society puts that whole society to the test, since it is this that reveals the meaning or the lack of meaning of the entirety of the life that leads to that old age ([1970] 1996: 10).

For de Beauvoir, the way a society behaves towards older people uncovers the truth about its real underlying principles in a way few other features do ([1970] 1996). She argues that it is crucial for older people to 'go on pursuing ends that give their life meaning', and for this we need to break 'the conspiracy of silence' (1996: 2) that prevents them from doing so. Speaking of the US, she associates 'the convenient plan of refusing to treat them as real people' with 'the distorting myths and clichés of bourgeois culture' (1996: 2). So, while she mentions the poverty of many older people as highly significant (1996: 3), this is not the only key aspect of what she is saying. For her, ageing and class are intertwined; belonging to the exploiting or the exploited class makes a different to the experience and interpretation of ageing. But there are also profounder issues of meaning and value that confront the way life is lived in a society as a whole. We prefer to pretend that old age 'happens to other people', but

> We must stop cheating: the whole meaning of our life is in question in the future that is waiting for us. If we do not know what we are going to be, we cannot know what we are: let us recognize ourselves in this old man or that old woman (1996: 5).

In other words, while issues of class and social exclusion are crucial to understanding conditions associated with ageing, deeper humanistic concerns need to be addressed too. Indeed, unless they are addressed, issues of ageing and class will not be effectively approached either.

It was Robert Butler (1975) who first used the term 'ageism' to refer to the phenomenon of *standardly* seeing older people in negative terms: when images of older people and relationships with them are in general marked by neglect, distortion or fear, taking a variety of forms in different settings. The inattention to older people's spiritual needs on the parts of UK churches analysed by Coleman may be symptomatic of ageist assumptions about the futility of making efforts to connect with older generations; at a deeply unreflected level, it may simply not seem worth the trouble. Hepworth and Featherstone (2005) point to the deleterious influence of 'idealized representations of a consumer lifestyle' on all members of a society, but show that this involves envisaging older people in particular with special venom: they may be portrayed as 'frail, forgetful, shabby, out-of-date and on the edge of senility and death' (2005: 354). Gilleard associates modern forms of the 'generation divide' specifically with the need to sell consumer articles, starting in the 19th century – which he sees as marking the beginning of the end of a unified idea of the human lifecourse – and accelerating into the 20th century, whose valorisation of youth provoked a 'ghettoization' of age (2005: 156–7). Older people's reactions, habits and opinions are denigrated from the start, owing to the peculiarly pervasive nature of consumerism in tandem with the hyper-rationality and bureaucracy of the post-modern world (Katz, 1996; von Kondratowitz, 2009; Bytheway, 2011). When these conditions are exacerbated by resource-related patterns of power and influence (Moody, 1988, 1992; Phillipson, 1998), older people who wish to be taken seriously have, at best, the opportunity to try to prove that they possess traits that are *exceptional*.

There operate, in other words, descriptively elusive but practically effective social barriers to life-course-related discussion and commitment. This amounts to a form of hegemony that relies on a confluence of forces, from the dominance of economic rationality to the relativism associated with post-modernism. David Harvey's emphasis on neoliberalism's 'commodification of everything', extending to cultural practices and social relationships (2005: 169), suggests a systemic account of the decline in practices associated with respecting age or older people. This is not to imply that, historically, older people have never had reason for complaint when inhabiting different cultural systems in the past (Thane, 2005). But it offers contemporary reasons for the fact that older people and their status continually recede from the forefront of awareness. Public discourse about basic values of citizenship is systematically degraded (Harvey, 2005: 187); the sociality of meaning and the lifecourse is consistently brushed aside. This effect is redoubled by the fact that it does not apply only to older people as regarded from the outside, by those who are not (yet) old. Powell points out that Harvey's account needs to be expanded by an explication of the ways in which neoliberal discourses affect agents themselves (2009: 328); in other words, 'the configuration of the rational-economic individual as at the heart of neoliberalism's constructivist project' is 'a mode of governmentality, understood in Foucault's sense of techniques of governing which supervise the individual's conduct towards himself or herself', organising the 'conduct of conduct'. This form of governmentality entails, in other words, a systemic reluctance to acknowledge the significance of the human person. This suggests further answers to the question why, even after decades of effort by gerontologists, the standing of older people has not been transformed. Gerontologists are operating within larger social systems marked by views of rationality associated with that of Friedman (1970), with his 'simplistic' 'reductionist approaches' to modelling human social and ethical behaviour (Le Menestrel, 2002: 164). Post-modern stances fail to provide effective counterweights to such schematised views of human undertakings, seeing truth-claims as purely internal to the cultures that construct them (cf Jameson, 1991; McDowell and Hosteteler, 1998; Eagleton, 2003).

It is therefore not entirely surprising that efforts by older people to resist the negativity of their status and assert the meaningfulness of their lives can have results that, in the context of social attitudes to ageing, seem contradictory. Wilińska summarises her work on older people in the Polish University of the Third Age (U3A) as follows: 'The results of this study indicate that rather than resisting ageist discourses, the U3A simply rejects the idea of old age. The U3A characterizes its members as exceptional people who have nothing in common with old people outside of the U3A' (Wilińska, 2012: 290). Or Sally Keeling (2013) concurs with Komp and Carr (2012) in arguing that the 'shelf-life' of the discourse of the 'Third Age' may have 'expired': its effects are to exclude everyone who does not happen to satisfy its particular demands.

Similar tensions and lacunae are examined by scholars such as Clary Krekula; she sees the understanding of later life as undermined not just by the absence of appropriate discursive techniques but by theoretical errors in conceptualising the individuals involved and their activities. Even so, she argues that there is evidence for the emergence of efforts towards a newly positive discourse of meaningful ageing. With regard to older women, she argues that

> As the category of 'old woman' is composed of two positions, age and gender, one might expect that research on older women and on constructions of old age together with gender, are pursued in both these fields (Krekula, 2007: 155).

Nonetheless, within gender studies, she continues, older women 'tend to be left out'. Within social gerontology, they have been studied,

> but not necessarily with theories that have a potential for understanding intersections of age and gender, together with other central positions such as ethnicity, class, sexuality and disability (2007: 156).

Gender debates contain 'hints of an age bias' (2007: 158), whereas official writing on gender can contribute to 'the invisibility of older women' by implying that the 'normative' woman is one with small children. That is, the default human is a man, but if women are to be considered at all, it is women caring for children who are normative.

Krekula also takes exception to the convention whereby people 'over 65' are treated as either homogenous or 'simply non-existent' in official and other forms of statistical investigation (2007: 159). Moreover, she says, even though contemporary approaches to gender stress its social construction, social gerontology makes much less use of this approach, tending instead to study older women 'from a misery perspective'; old women are 'deviants from a norm', and the multitude of experiences arising from the intersection of age and gender with other categories are simply ignored (2007: 160). It is not enough, therefore, simply to add one disadvantage to another. An 'intersectionality' approach needs to investigate empirically how such predicaments interact. Yet, under some circumstances, multiple vulnerabilities can actually emerge as strengths. Women over 75 whom Krekula interviewed took this view, stressing what they saw as their own 'increased self-esteem and independence' (2007: 164).

Krekula's interviewees have won through to the capacity to perceive advantages in later life. Rather than being preoccupied with beauty they may have lost, as the prevalence of 'double standards of ageing' would adjure, they discuss the experiences and 'new values' they have gained. It is not that they are indifferent to their bodies;

> Their appearance is important and they use many unmistakably *negative words* to describe their bodies. They talk about wrinkled skin, about a belly that will not disappear no matter how much they exercise, and of muscles that have lost their fitness. At the same time, there is also an acceptance. These changes are *accepted as part of becoming older*. The body is also talked about with *pride*, for example, when dressed in beautiful clothes, and also as a *source of joy and pleasure* (2007: 165).

Sexuality and physical exercise too are valued and enjoyed, transmitting senses of activeness and strength. The 'misery perspective' is inadequate to deal with these women's experiences of their lifecourses, and they are straining to create the terms in which to express real insights. Among Krekula's respondents and in the predicament common to them, a new language of ageing is being sought. But languages cannot subsist independently of practices that sustain them. And while political interventions are necessary to instigate or support such practices, they themselves need to make discursive sense to their communities. With the conceptual practices currently available, this is difficult to achieve.

The crisis of ethics

If there are pervasive problems both in according adequate status to older people and allowing them to claim it for themselves, it is clear that we cannot see these issues as solely connected with personal attitudes to older people as such. They are affected by larger-scale problems in expressing meaning-related ideas in the contemporary world. Salient among these are difficulties in formulating views and adopting stances on ethics and wisdom: sets of ideas that have in the past always been key to making sense of human lifecourses. Simon Blackburn (2001: 4–5) emphasises that people still seek ethical narratives for their lives as a matter of everyday self-presentation: 'We hope for lives whose story leaves us looking admirable; we like our weaknesses to be hidden and deniable.' Yet even those eager to behave ethically for ethical reasons can find it difficult to say why they wish to do so. MacIntyre (1981) traces these problems to the dominance of implicit 'emotivism' in contemporary cultures and its effects in undermining the meaningfulness of moral debate. He claims that 'the language of morality' today is in a 'state of grave disorder' (1981: 2): we treat it 'simultaneously and inconsistently as an exercise of our rational powers and as mere expressive assertion' (1981: 10). Moral arguments are treated *as if they simply expressed emotional preferences*. In consequence of emotivism's considerable 'cultural power' (1981: 19),

> to a large degree people now think, talk and act *as if* emotivism were true, no matter what their avowed theoretical stand-point may be. Emotivism has become embodied in our culture (MacIntyre, 1981: 21).

This is not a problem confined to philosophy. A moral philosophy 'characteristically presupposes a sociology' (1981: 22); emotivist practices and assumptions colour a pervasive amalgam of meanings and assumptions that MacIntyre refers to as 'the ethos of the distinctively modern and modernizing world'. For him it 'is nothing less than a rejection of a large part of that ethos' that can 'provide us with a rationally and morally defensible standpoint from which to judge and to act' (1981: viii).

This 'modernizing world', MacIntyre underlines, enjoins commitment to sharp distinctions between facts and values, as Weber intended. Despite his own sincere evaluative commitments, and despite his association with exploring meaningful understanding in sociology, Weber saw 'Verstehen' as intrinsically incomplete. He claimed that the most complete form of understanding occurred between individuals discussing mathematics (1968, I: 5), and that even though one can reconstruct someone else's view of the world, one cannot debate reasonably about that person's choices within it. In this view, 'Questions of ends are questions of values, and on values reason is silent; conflict between rival values cannot be rationally settled' (MacIntyre, 1981: 25). This leads to a conception of politics based on 'negative' freedom, one that oscillates 'between a freedom which is nothing but a lack of regulation of individual behaviour and forms of collectivist control designed only to limit the anarchy of self-interest' (1981: 33). As a result, even people who wish to defend the status of ethical meaning in their own and in public life are at a loss to find the language that they feel would allow them to do so. Ethical approaches to living are defended by philosophers such as Kekes (1997) or Dohmen (2013), but the predominance of emotivism renders ethical reflection a mere matter of preference: if values are relative, moral debate is pointless. In a society where relativism reigns, as Eagleton (2003: 223) puts it, 'Discussion must at all costs remain on the level of the ready tag, the moralistic outcry, the pious rejoinder, the shopworn phrase', using 'well-thumbed tokens which serve in place of thought'.

We can illustrate this ethical predicament by examining the following example: a document written as a serious effort to reinforce the power of ethical behaviour in public life. Here, if anywhere, we ought to be able to find an expressed commitment to moral communication. Far from officially espousing indifference to morality, *Standards Matter: A Review of Best Practice in Promoting Good Behaviour in Public Life* (Kelly et al, 2013: 1) is a UK government policy document arguing that 'expected standards' must be 'embedded' in organisations in such a way that everyone takes responsibility for them. This report itself, despite its intentions, exemplifies ethical relativism in action. Its executive summary states that 'Standards of behaviour matter' (Kelly et al, 2013: 5), but is unable to explain why. It claims that it is 'disturbing' that 'questions continue to be raised' about key British institutions, particularly since 'inappropriate' behaviour may have been 'dishonestly covered up'; but the main drawback attributed to these actions appears to be that the situation 'has been especially shocking to members of the public, many of whom rate truthfulness as one of the most important ethical standards' (2013: 5). It is curious that the report does not assert that truthfulness *is* one of the most important ethical standards; it merely reacts to the fact that 'many' people think it is. Right and wrong are not referred to, only 'appropriateness'; the seriousness of misdemeanours is related to the fact that they give offence to people who do not like them. The report's summary conclusions (Kelly et al, 2013: 10ff) suggest continually reviewing current practices, showing 'leadership' in assessing ethical risks and evincing trustworthiness by exemplifying high standards. The report supports 'seven principles' of public life, including 'honesty' ('Holders of public office should be truthful': p 24). But its language throughout suggests embarrassment about supporting ethical behaviour *for ethical reasons*. It is as if Kelly suffered inhibitions about attempting to broach this topic: as if he feared ridicule or incomprehension as reactions to explaining what the virtues of 'best practice' actually are.

If contemporary discourse suffers from problems in using ethical language, it may not be surprising that an associated concept, wisdom, also faces difficulties in current academic debate – even though, like morality, it appears significant to *individuals* as they reflect on their lives and relationships. This is not at all to deny that forming moral opinions is a partly practical task (Gubrium, 1975/1997; Duncan, 2011); this process does not entail that people never take their opinions seriously – even if they can find it hard, under present conditions, to explain why they do. Thus, any edition of a newspaper is likely to contain uses of the terms 'wise' or 'wisdom', not least in relation to politics and large-scale social decisions, particularly with the intention of signalling that the items in question are considered important. Obituaries frequently refer to the wisdom of the deceased and his or her ability to guide and inspire colleagues and friends. Individuals are, if asked, prepared to discuss what they see as wisdom and answer questions about it (Clayton and Birren, 1980), or to acknowledge that it plays a significant part in social life – in quotidian 'social' and 'emotional' wisdom; common sense and international (financial) affairs; cultural criticism and exhortations to political change; 'alternative' life-styles; or grandparenting and intergenerational relations. Arber and Timonen (2012) note the significance of moral *exchanges* between grandparents and their grandchildren. People uncertain how to run political campaigns or how to bring up their children look for advice from those they see as wise and experienced. The desire to acquire or to practise wisdom is reflected today in sales of popular psychology or theology, or in conversation about life-course decisions to be taken. Even in societies where it is regarded as courteous to *treat* older people as wise, it may be understood that whether or not they actually are so is the outcome of growth and struggle on their own parts. Wise and insightful ageing has not generally been alleged to happen automatically, but is treated in everyday life rather as a goal to be attempted. Yet it is comparatively neglected in academic analysis.

In the ancient world, the idea of wisdom was a standard for assessing both lifecourses and societies: to become at least somewhat wiser was something people could reasonably be expected to aim at throughout their lives. But the discursive problems now affecting ethics apply to wisdom too, an entire concept subject to the 'fading' techniques of contemporary culture. Gabriel Marcel, writing on *The Decline of Wisdom* in France just after the Second World War, complained of a world obsessed with technical quick fixes and superficial illusions about youth, speed and efficiency. Marcel's views chime in this respect with those of other social critics of the time, such as Marcuse or Fromm. He claimed that

> the huge multiplication of means put at man's disposal, and of recipes for their uses, takes place at the cost of the ends they are supposed to serve, or, if you like, the set of values which man is called upon both to serve and to safeguard. It is as if man, overburdened by the weight of technics, knows less and less where he stands in regard to what matters to him and what doesn't, to what is precious and what is worthless (1954: 49).

In place of wisdom, he argued, we have the expert. Today, authoritative experts are likely to be economists, or the management consultants seen by MacIntyre as symptomatic of the contemporary world, and who rule explicitly that 'ends' are not subject to reasonable discussion.

The term 'wisdom' will in the main be used here to refer to the tradition, dating from Aristotle, Isocrates and Cicero, in which wisdom is seen in terms of interlocking ethical, emotional and social practices, both tacit and explicit, making possible responses to other people, to oneself and to profound problems of human existence; questions without predetermined answers. Because these practical capacities depend on a certain amount of experience, which needs to be built up over time, it has in the past been assumed that people capable of behaving wisely potentially form a significant resource for a society (Edmondson, 2005); attaining wisdom was traditionally considered one of the highest aims possible for a human life, and educational systems aimed at enhancing wisdom among citizens. For over 4,000 years of recorded human history, wisdom was thought central to confronting problems where solutions cannot simply be read off from accepted knowledge. Disparate traditions of wisdom reflect the different societies in which they evolved and to whose problems they were applied, but Aristotle or Cicero saw an especial need for wise deliberation in relation to questions where information is incomplete and fast changing, where we can never know enough to reach completely certain conclusions and where no recipes can simply be read off to tell us what to do. These dilemmas occur in contemporary life as often as they did in ancient Greece of Rome.

In the *Nicomachean Ethics* Aristotle specifies the relationship of wisdom to ethics: practically wise people need to be generous, courageous, concerned for the common good, practising these virtues for their own sakes. Ethics is not a matter of knowing principles or recipes, but of working towards what conduces to human flourishing. Thinking and knowledge are not enough to motivate people to action of this kind; they need to have characters and desires that make them want to do so. 'Getting the timing, the tempo, and the manner right requires a well-formed character, the right desires and beliefs embodied in habits (1106b36)' (Rorty, 1980: 380). These are habits of attention too; the wise person's 'having the right desires conditions his perceiving: they fix his patterns of attention; and what he sees activates the appropriate directly motivating desires' (Rorty, 1980: 381). In other words, someone with virtuous habits will be used to according 'presence' to the right aspects of the right considerations. While, roughly speaking, an action may seem to have been done for wise reasons – choosing a particular political policy, for example – whether it is really virtuous or not 'will be manifest in the *way* the action is performed' (Rorty, 1980: 380). This is a holistic conception that takes into account the element of time, specifically lifetime, in building up the capacity for constructive conduct. It does not split off reasoning from human concerns, but shows how it forms a part of social existence. Wise people and practices explicitly accept uncertainty as an ordinary part of private and public life, rather than aspiring to a super-rationality that is in effect irrational because it is incapable of being applied to real-life situations. This makes interpersonal and public life feasible, allowing for personal and political problems to be understood and tackled appropriately.

While thought imagined in over-cognitivised terms cannot accommodate sociality, wisdom can be seen specifically as social, situated in the midst of human interaction (Edmondson, 2012). Socrates himself practised wisdom not alone but in dialogue. He saw the point of his dialogues not as arriving at hard-and-fast conclusions, but as reaching an awareness of complexity that was some improvement on the unquestioned reactions his interlocutors had shown before (Woerner, 2000a). He envisaged the process of debate not as an abstract exercise, but as a lived experience intended to strengthen both the intellects and the characters of those concerned in it. (Rabbi Lionel Blue, in an interview with the author in London, remarked about the views of the early Rabbinical writers: 'The argument itself is holy': Edmondson, 2013: 203–4).

Under the influence of both Aristotle and Cicero, the holistic nature of deliberation was explored through ensuing centuries. For Cicero, in the 1st century BC, 'great deeds' are 'the products of thought, and character, and judgement'; 'far from diminishing, such qualities actually increase with age', in which older people can spend their time using 'wisdom and logical powers and judgement' ([1971]: 220–1). For Cicero, wisdom involves friendship and trust; he writes vividly of what it *feels like* to try to practise them, bringing experience, feeling and ethical reflection into reasoned concord. This had a great impact on European humanism, particularly in terms of the ideal of the 'whole man', a person who could resist blind obedience to authority in the service of the common good.

This desire is frustrated by a powerful model of cognition that insists that good thinking should be purged of feeling or ethics, and remain independent of human involvement: the view that it is carried out not by ordinary citizens in their everyday lives but by experts. This model cannot explain how political judgements can sensibly be made; it does not account for how we come to see the point of view of someone whose position is different from our own, or how to justify policies in public medicine or taxation. A rigid distinction between thought, feeling and interaction would make it impossible to describe these deliberations systematically or to find criteria for evaluating them (Edmondson and Hülser, 2012). Major traditions of wisdom, by contrast, take a more naturalistic approach to reasoning. They see wise decisions in daily life as synthesising thinking, feeling and morality; often, they result from social processes in which more than one person is involved. Yet, currently, 'wisdom' might be termed a concept that is 'interstitial': it often falls between cracks in academic analyses, even though its everyday usage is more persistent.

In the view of wisdom presented here, a person like Tim O'Flaherty in South Connemara was considered wise because of this ability to activate elements in a store of common knowledge between himself and his interlocutors. This process involved interlocking elements: himself, his interlocutor (the person with the problem) and the community that had laid down this store. Tim did not himself administer a wise solution; he quoted a proverb he chose especially because he diagnosed its likelihood to activate in his hearer both insight into the current predicament and the capacity to change. This was not knowledge he had invented, but knowledge he had come, through experience, to appreciate. The fact that it was common knowledge facilitated the style of this interchange, whose egalitarian nature made it acceptable in this social context; the fact that it was friendly and witty was part of what made it effective (Edmondson, 2013). Edward on Inis Oirr (Edmondson, 2009) or Seamus in North Connemara were, like Tim, people who were agreeable, generous, inventive and constructive. Wisdom, here, is not technical, but embedded in a social setting; how it is activated depends on what the people concerned are *like*, on their styles of interaction. All the men referred to here were genial, sociable individuals, who enjoyed other people's company and were open to new experiences. Tim O'Flaherty would take lifts up and down the coast road near his home purely for the sake of meeting new people; the local landlord, Lord Killanin, commented on what a worthwhile conversationalist he was. Edward, as an old man, was getting ready to attend the opening of the new quay on his island when he died. Thus wisdom seems to be associated with the personalities of those involved as much as with their particular opinions and beliefs. Also, it involves processes that specifically allow for time to develop. Seamus's interventions could take months or even years to mature, depending on how long their recipients needed to come to terms with their predicaments. As Rabbi Blue said in London, 'It takes all sorts of people together, that's my aperçu on the whole thing!'

This version of wisdom, it will be argued here, has potential traction for contributing to a counter-version of human thought and reasoning to support efforts by older people such as those described by Krekula. It has the capacity to recognise both the developing processes of everyday life (alluded to by Victor et al, 2009) and the role played in those processes by ethical reflections, while still taking both seriously. And there is already evidence that counter-models to the destructive duo, rationalism/relativism, are actively being sought. The contemporary popularity of Buddhism in the West may derive in part from the fact that it does reason about questions of meaning on a quotidian basis: how people can sensibly react to feelings of powerlessness, avarice, jealousy and so forth and how they can interact meaningfully with others. This has the social and political effect, moreover, of restoring significance to these experiences.

New linguistic conventions evolve in response to new shared predicaments; it is characteristic of environmental protests, for example, to need to struggle to evade the influence of languages that express constrictively bureaucratic or administrative aims (Treanor, 2010). Garavan (2008) describes the protracted process through which an Irish environmental movement painfully developed the language it needed to express local feeling for the land about which it was concerned. When the movement began, it struggled to free itself from terms whose conventional connotations were inadequate; it was only when they came to develop novel communicative terms and practices that the people concerned fully realised and came to respect their own views and feelings. King (2014) too describes the process of developing constructive practices that can emerge from intercultural contexts in which different views of life combine and affect each other, producing creative communicative syntheses. She examines a new urban area whose inhabitants come from at least 33 different countries – but where, through concerted efforts over time, genuinely practical forms of mutual understanding and wisdom have evolved. This use of the term 'wisdom', therefore, is hospitable to the idea of building up lifecourse-related meaning through lengthy processes of private and political interaction, and on interlinked social levels.

This chapter has examined some paradoxes and complexities illustrating the fact that, despite continuous efforts from gerontologists and others to defend the position of older people in society, and despite some genuine respect for older people as individuals, there persists a dearth of social symbols and discourses that can activate this respect on a social scale. This stems partly from prejudice and stereotype, but it is a predicament given force by wider political and cultural circumstances, especially those that reinforce problems in taking ethics and morality seriously, on the one hand, and conceptualising argumentation and debate, on the other – especially wise debate, to which older people might otherwise aspire. For movements, groups and individuals seeking innovative forms of discourse in connection with ageing, returning to these classical sources in a contemporary setting might prove startlingly effective. Molly Andrews says (1999: 309) that 'Years are not empty containers: important things happen in that time', 'the stuff of which people's lives are made'. She complains about the trivialisation of this fact, but to combat it, languages are needed that take seriously the serious developments in these lives.

Notes

[1]   http://www.trinity.edu/mkearl/ger-cul.html (accessed 4 September 2012).

[2]   http://www.guardian-series.co.uk/uk_national_news/10110861.End_elderly_stereotypes_Williams/.

THREE

Lifetimes, meaning and listening to older people

Gerontologists complain that older people's lifetimes and their insights are not generally treated as significant. Their own struggles to bestow impact on older people's views and understandings, by contrast, take place in a variety of ways with importantly different implications. In this chapter we shall explore this work, separating out some contrasting strands in work on meaning, as well as examining how they can be used in combination. Then, in the second section, we shall be able to interrogate some of what this implies for methodology in life-course studies. This will draw attention to further aspects of the need for interdisciplinarity, particularly in view of the need to overcome the atomism endemic in much contemporary work in the social and human sciences. Since many of these attempts have centred on concepts of social and political practice, lastly we shall interrogate some connections between meaningfulness and shared practices, investigating how practices significant for the development of lifecourses can be traced and evaluated. To the extent that the term 'wisdom' has been associated with specific forms of meaningfulness, we shall ask if any of these lifecourse-related practices can reasonably be described as particularly constructive or as wise.

Insight and the lifecourse in gerontology

H.R. Moody and Thomas Cole (1996: 247ff) have been tireless in drawing attention to a pervasive 'problem of meaning' in relation to older people and the process of ageing, urging the need for a forceful 'emancipatory discourse' in opposition to this crisis. Older people need to be freed to engage in conscious, creative ageing, clear that there are positive advantages to later stages of the lifecourse; but this is a counter-cultural cry to arms, one demanding active resistance to discourses in which it is taken for granted that ageist expectations simply make sense (Moody, 1993). As Dannefer and Settersten underline (2010: 10), ageist assumptions have become 'naturalised' in the social world: norms dictate often-inaccurate suppositions that certain sorts of conduct are appropriate only at certain ages. These suppositions 'are legitimated by the pronouncements of pop psychology and supported by some serious clinicians and scholars', hence 'widely believed and followed, and in some cases defined and sanctioned by the state, which makes them plausible and compelling'. This is despite the fact that 'the very awareness of "age-appropriateness" as a behavioral issue is socially and culturally constructed' (2010: 10; cf Dannefer and Kelly-Moore, 2009). When Phillipson stresses the seriousness of the 'absence of meaning' currently attaching to later life (1998: 14), therefore, he is implying that current ideologies and widespread social expectations fail to allot meaningfulness to this phase: not that individual human beings are incapable of it.

The previous chapter explored some respects in which powerful public discourses make it hard to express the kind of energy that critical, humanistic and cultural gerontologists in particular are seeking. These discourses distort the abilities of older people, inhibiting the meaningfulness of their lives even to themselves. Kunow (2010) draws parallels between older people and other groups whose identities are constrained or damaged, from women to disabled people. Yet this does not mean that everything we know about older people is permeated with negativity: there is recurrent resistance to ageist norms and stereotypes. Thompson and his colleagues (1990) portray the older people they interview as full of individuality, leading energetic and purposeful lives. These people do not fit stereotypes of rigidity, passivity, dependence or helplessness; they are vital, active, energetic and diverse, notwithstanding challenges attached to loss or physical discomfort. The term 'pointful' seems to summarise their lives, replete with practices that fill out and enrich their own and others' worlds.

Similarly, Michele Dillon stresses the importance of leading a 'purposeful' life, examining the various ways her subjects achieve this. Purposefulness, for her, includes practical activities such as running a local business or contributing to local environmental organisations, as well as spiritual efforts to find sources of insight that prove inspiring and satisfying to the individuals concerned. The term 'pointful' is offered here to underline the fact that the activities that are significant to people can sometimes be of modest proportions, like the prize-tomato growing to which Thompson and his colleagues refer (1990: 160); but they are activities and practices that make complete sense to the individuals concerned. Woerner (1989) links this type of activity with what some ancient theologians meant by the term 'eternity'. Such activities belong to the 'search for meaning' (Thompson et al, 1990: 245), though they may change as the circumstances faced by individuals alter throughout their older age (1990: 250). They are not as a rule bounded within concerns internal to the self, but are situated within networks that are meaningful to other people too.

Such accounts are not intended to offer an unbrokenly optimistic account of ageing. The Eriksons, writing with Kivnick, note well-founded fears among their interviewees, not only for their own health and mortality but also on behalf of their families and entire societies: the people they spoke to were conscious of moral failings in the public at large or the prospect of nuclear or environmental disaster. Yet they had progressed in the capacity for self-criticism, in tolerance and in the ability to recognise that positions they had in the past considered unacceptable perhaps were not. The authors mention the struggle for 'wisdom and perspective', in which negatives are not blotted out but brought into balance as the culmination of a lifelong struggle for wholeness. For them, this is a meaningful struggle in a double sense: it is meaningful *to* struggle, and meaning seems to be what it produces.

Frankl's account of meaning also refuses to deny the reality of horror in the world, but locates meaning in the struggle for love and for a kind of heroism that, at least sometimes, takes non-egotistic choices and attempts to encounter other human beings in an authentic way. But none of these writers believes that such efforts are independent of social structures or policies. Glen Elder, while he highlights the role of individuals' own efforts in shaping their lives, specifically argues for the key role of supportive social measures in making these efforts effective. *Children of the Great Depression* explores how meaning is created in the interaction between individuals, and between themselves and their changing life circumstances: meaning, here, is treated as a genuinely socially created phenomenon – as it is in many early US community studies too.

What can be supported by social arrangements can also be damaged or diluted by them; correspondingly, the potential of social constructions to *undermine* meaning is highlighted by Cole's (1992) account of the rise of capitalism's rigid individualism, the removal of later life from its cosmological setting and the reconstruction of ageing as a social problem. Tornstam's account of 'gerotranscendence', on the other hand, points to people – as it happens, mostly inhabitants of relatively equal and supportive societies – whose individual responses to ageing resist negative expectations, stressing instead the espousal of more 'transcendental' sources of happiness than they had embraced earlier in their lives. As Coleman does, Tornstam's subjects stress the significance of connectedness, to other people, their own pasts and the cosmos in general; like the Eriksons', they grow more tolerant, broad minded and humble with the passing of time. Perhaps it is Tornstam's subjects' Scandinavian setting that frees him to be relatively uninterested in sociopolitical contexts for ageing; for H.R. Moody in the US, this is impossible. His work stresses both the significance of individual meaning, with its potential roles within relatively small-scale communal life, *and* the importance of analyses in terms of political economy to support practical struggles for justice and equal opportunity. He enjoins resistance to 'insidious' conventional repressive ideologies, and to the myths of objective science that support them, in favour of establishing gerontology as 'an emancipatory discourse' (1988: 32).

These authors make clear that meaning is *important* to ageing. But in trying to understand more about what exactly is meant by 'life-course meaning' or 'living a meaningful life', we are confronted by a remarkable variety of work relevant to meaning and the lifecourse. Even the language concerned can be used in very different ways, for at least two reasons. First, meaning may be seen as something that accompanies human living, something not crystallised out even in pointed attempts to offer meaningful advice. Walter Benjamin (1936: 86) sees storytellers as offering counsel to their readers, but 'counsel is less an answer to a question than a proposal concerning the continuation of a story which is just unfolding', moreover a proposal dependent on the listener's receptiveness; for him, wisdom is 'counsel woven into the fabric of real life'. Thus some of those describing wise or meaningful lives might see themselves as describing those lives, rather than describing wisdom per se. Meaningfulness and wisdom thus depend on a *style* of interaction, residing partly in the way that interaction is perceived by someone else. This makes meaning both transactional and elusive. Second, there is genuinely much work yet to be done in this field: meaning is interstitial in the straightforward sense of being neglected.

Meaningfulness, for Moody and Cole, is nonetheless heavily inscribed into human interaction. For them, meaning is 'inherently relational' (1986: 250), and older people are 'centers of meaning and value'. This ascription has an ambiguity that is carved deeply into their account of the origins of interest in meaning. They ask how meaning is to be understood: as a psychological, philosophical, sociological or historical phenomenon. Each approach, they say, has contributions to make but also raises problems, partly associated with 'the diversity and fragmentation of modern experience' (1986: 250). However, they remark that '[i]n cultural anthropology, the question of meaning and the life course grew out of the use of biographical methods' (1986: 250).

In the last quarter of the 20th century, a widespread therapeutic interest connected the reconstruction of meaningfulness with biographical work. James Birren, a pioneer of life-course research, with his colleague Donna Deuchman (1991) taught autobiographical methods to groups of older adults who had encountered losses of partners, work or health, aiming to encourage them to retain belief in the meaningfulness of their lives, and their pride in their own lifecourses. Subsequently, Malette and Oliver (2006) among others focused explicitly on the use of Butler's (1963) 'life review' methods to support individuals' attributions of meaningfulness to their lives; but it is not clear that their approach retains the social dimensions to meaning stressed by Moody and Cole. Referring to Birren's original work in this field, Malette and Oliver describe their own attempts to provoke personal growth in respondents who can be encouraged to 'revisit and integrate' past events 'in order to live more fully in the present and prepare for the future' (2006: 30). They support the concept of 'conscious aging' in the tradition of Moody or Tornstam, quoting Moody's account of 'a spiritual process that draws its inspiration from religion, art, lifelong learning ... reflected in the field of transpersonal psychology and wisdom traditions in the great world religions'; increased spiritual awareness in this sense is 'a path toward greater wisdom' (2003: 139). Malette and Oliver conclude,

> Most of the participants came to realize, via reframing and/or instrumental reminiscence, that their identity is not limited to what they currently do or even what they did in their active working life. Many were at peace with this new awareness, which brought them even further towards an integrated and terminated review of many events in their past and current life. In that sense, our study found that LR [life review] promotes the compassionate re-definition of self (2006: 41).

Key for these authors was the extent to which respondents were able to achieve self-transcendence, overcoming 'hurt and sorrow associated with difficult interpersonal relationships' in order to live more fully in the present (2006: 42). The *relationality* of individual meaning seems to have subsided. Biographical methods may emphasise, like these, what it *feels like to be* a particular person; or they may emphasise *what the person was like*, which is potentially a more interpersonal question.

In some of Dillon's (2009) accounts of people's personal lives, meaningfulness is also associated with capacities for enjoyment – not least for Dave Allen, of whom we acquire a very strong sense of what he is like. Kalyani Mehta emphasises religious and cultural origins of meaningfulness for her subjects in Singapore, but they are not necessarily sanctimonious about following them; religious meaning can be associated with meeting friends for a game of cards. In her examples, one of the main results of religious meaning is that it makes older age *pleasanter to experience*. The same applies to the present author's observations in the West of Ireland. In a local nursing home in Connemara, a number of individuals from the local community gather once a week to play cards; this is in one sense the fulfilment of a duty, but it would be impolite and inaccurate to refer to it in this way or even to experience it as such. The point of card playing would be lost if participants did not like doing it, and it enhances their contribution to nursing-home life when they actually do enjoy themselves. They add meaning to their surroundings through what their presence is like, for those who participate in it and for those who just know that it is there.

A triad of approaches to meaning

In this section, we shall disentangle a number of basic meanings of 'meaning' and its associated insights that we can see reflected in gerontological texts. It is important to stress that these are forms of meaningfulness ascribed to older people in relevant literature; they are not directly prescriptions for developing meaningful lives in the sense dealt with by Peter Derkx (2013a, 2013b). The usages we shall chart here can be arranged in three groups, whose constituents are capable of being related to each other in different ways – and which are conveyed through cultural symbols and messages that bring them alive for those who engage with them. The first group is concerned with perceptions of types of connectedness between individuals and wider states of affairs, including moral or spiritual connections; the second with issues connected to the lifecourse as it develops through time; the third with wisdom and understanding the human condition. We could arrange these in a diagram that takes the form of three overlaid triangles, a nine-pointed star, to explore both how these different elements relate to each other and how they can interact, making it possible to refer to further layers or dimensions of meaning. The diagram itself would acquire new shades or hues if we located it in different contexts – emphasising gender-related or political issues, for instance – or in different life stages, for example comparing older age with youth.

The first version of meaning to be stressed can be interpreted in terms of vivacious engagement with life or 'pointfulness', especially vivid in the work of Thompson and his colleagues. Their book is rightly appreciated for its presentation of successive instances of people engaged in projects, living their lives with energy and for a variety of reasons: doing things in a *way* that communicates absorption and engagement. This is connected with the basic sense of being alive that people lack when they are depressed, when they complain that life 'has lost its meaning'. In contrast, we can recall the woman who describes her husband:

> Oh, he loved gardening. He'd do the best potatoes, he grew the finest tomatoes, and he had them ready every year, Fair weekend. Beautiful tomatoes (Thompson et al, 1990: 160).

In this example, meaningfulness is not associated with any particular reason or cause associated with the activity in question, rather with the sense of life associated with it. For this particular gentleman, it is not that he claimed that growing vegetables and doing it well ought to be regarded as supremely important by other people; it happened to give *him* a sense of purpose and value, a personal preference that could also be exercised and validated in the public setting of the Fair. Others might be indifferent to the value of gardening as far as their own experience was concerned, and their lives might gain meaning of this kind from different sources.

This is a type of meaning that tends not to attract much attention in contemporary work and can easily be under-estimated. In ancient writing, it was related to concepts of happiness or eternity, not least by the Roman philosopher Boethius (Woerner, 1989: 208). According to Woerner, Boethius envisaged eternity not in terms of everlasting time, or chronological time that continues without ever ceasing, but on the model of activities in which we are so engrossed that time ceases to have a meaning for us while we are engaged in them. Woerner gives the example of a woman who ran a small café or eating-house for lorry-drivers in the Rheinland in the 1970s. She so much enjoyed her own being in this cafe – bantering with her customers, preparing the food, clearing tables and keeping the place in order – that it was obvious she was entirely absorbed in it while she was there. For ancient philosophers, this type of sense of life was intimately linked to a feeling of connectedness to the world, as well as to the art of living and the kind of person one tries to be; it is this that links it to the other two approaches to meaning and insight in this first category.

A second sense of 'meaning' has become more popular in literature connected with ageing and is associated with spirituality, also a difficult phenomenon to define. Spirituality may be thought of in connection with religion or, in a broader sense, with the transcendent: as a consciousness of values or aspects of reality that extend beyond the individual and his or her immediate concerns (Orwoll and Perlmutter, 1990; Atchley, 2011). Michele Dillon (2009) uses the term in both senses. Some of her subjects have spiritual interests in a consciously non-religious sense, and her 'spiritual seekers' may or may not be religious in the sense of belonging to some recognised church; but their lives are oriented to a sense of deep connectedness in the world and an attempt to understand this further. Leceulle (2013) too associates spirituality with self-development; though Honneth warns (2004) that self-development can too easily become a tool masking crippling dependence on capitalist ideology, Leceulle argues that it can also offer positive potential for older age. Derkx (2013b) points out that a feeling of spiritual transcendence can be centrally important to individuals' feeling of value in life, but nonetheless 'ordinary' in the sense that it is not an esoteric experience beyond the reach of most people (cf Young-Eisendrath, 2000). Levenson and Aldwin (2013) associate transcendence with a capacity for transformational change in adult development that is stressed in major contemplative psychologies all over the world.

Terms such as 'spiritual' can often be used to cover a range of forms of 'meaning' associated with taking life and (human) connectedness seriously, as Dalby (2006) does in a review of 13 studies exploring associations between spirituality and ageing.

> Some common spiritual themes identified across the research were integrity, humanistic concern, changing relationships with others and concern for younger generations, relationship with a transcendent being or power, self transcendence, and coming to terms with death. These were not related to age per se, but to some of the challenges that age presents, and were mediated by cultural factors and individual differences (2006: 4).

In this article, Dalby supports the claim by Hill and Pargament (2003: 65) that 'Spirituality can be understood as a search for the sacred', though they are prepared to associate what is 'sacred' with some type of 'ultimate reality' or 'the transcendent' rather than, necessarily, a deity (2003: 65). By 'the transcendent' is meant 'that which is beyond or outside the individual life or material realm' (Dalby, 2006: 5). Dalby refers to the longitudinal study by Wink and Dillon (2002), which reports a significant increase in spirituality between late-middle and older adulthood, especially for women; in this study a concern for 'spirituality' is not necessarily associated with religious affiliation.

Ardelt (2002) suggests that older adults with 'intrinsic' orientations to religion are more likely to have 'a sense of meaning and purpose in life', as opposed to those whose orientations are extrinsic, and indeed that wise older people tend to experience particular satisfaction in older age (Ardelt, 1997). MacKinlay (2005, 2001) relates an orientation to transcendence with challenges associated with ageing, though not exclusively with ageing: challenges connected with overcoming disability or loss, and searching for final meanings, for intimacy with God or with other people, and for sources or habits of hope. She identifies themes of self-sufficiency/vulnerability, wisdom/provisional stances with regard to final meanings, relationship/isolation and hope/fear; but she does not insist that an association between religiosity and spiritual transcendence need be standard in these respects. None of these interpretations need imply a mind/body dualism, or a rejection of the significance of bodily experience, warned against by Gunnarson (2011). Gunnarson stresses that all forms of meaning in ageing are ascribed by and to people living in the physical and social world as bodies – and living, too, in time, as Baars (2012) underlines.

The third meaning of 'meaning' in this group illustrates a further sense in which references to life-course meaning may be made: to refer to taking morality, values and human relationships particularly seriously. The term 'spiritual' is often used to include this attitude also; thus, for Mehta (2009), spiritual questions include questions about moral conduct. She reports on people for whom the question how one should behave, particularly in the last years of life, is significant, and moreover susceptible of specific answers, depending on which culture one belongs to. Her enquiry has the important implication that in many cultures these are not regarded as specifically *private*, personal concerns. In many cultures ethics and politics are conjoined, as they were for Aristotle, and remained in Western culture at least until the end of the 18th century. In Mehta's cases, morals often also appear to be interpreted intergenerationally, dealing with questions how one should behave in order to set an example to younger people, for instance how not to shock, discourage or be a burden to them, or how one should get on harmoniously with one's immediate family and wider social group. Older people interviewed by the present author in the former East Germany often see the moral point of their lives strongly politically and in relation to the public sphere: how can they contribute to political life for the common good? Ethics and politics, of course, are pointful activities themselves. They may be 'spiritually' meaningful in the transcendent sense referred to here, but equally could be pursued without overt reference to transcendent feelings as such.

We have noted interpretations of meaning stressing connectedness, including attributions of pointful, spiritual and moral connectedness; we now move on to meanings connected with the development of the lifecourse through time. The fourth meaning, or group of meanings, associated with 'meaning' in this literature concerns issues connected with personal development, identity or what Adler termed the 'tasks of life'. When H.R. Moody terms coping with the tasks of life particularly important, he seems to mean facing up to challenges likely to be encountered during a lifecourse; learning from life. Such challenges might be practical, personal, psychological or developmental, social or political, featuring crises or choices in which we set our personal priorities, or in which these become clear, and in which we either expand or limit our personal capacities. There can be expected to be strong links between this version of meaning and meaning as identity, to the extent that learning in this way contributes to answering the question, who am I? But meaning in this sense need not be an exclusively private issue; the question of identity is connected with fitting in with others' practices or expectations, or taking one's place in a larger picture (Whittle et al, 2011). Moreover, as Charles Taylor emphasises (1989), if one is not recognised as a certain sort of person, with certain sorts of priorities and aims, it becomes difficult or impossible to sustain one's own sense of identity. Recognition itself is in part a structural and political issue, as Moody is aware; it may be denied to individuals or groups as a result of disputes over the distribution of power or resources; and if people lack the resources to pursue the priorities they value highly, it is not easy for them to be the kinds of person they want to be. This is a question central to work by, for example, Gilleard and Higgs (2000), who pursue the question of what older people do when, unusually in historical terms, some of them do have access to abundant resources that allow them to traverse the boundaries of the conventional selfhood allotted to older people.

This form of meaning may also be taken as a 'spiritual' issue if progress in the development of identity is thought of in these terms, as it is by Michele Dillon's 'spiritual seeker', Kate Ward. She says, "'I would do almost anything to allow myself options to grow and to develop ...'" (Dillon, 2009: 61). For her, identity-related progress is strongly spiritual in a transcendent sense. Wink and Dillon (2013: 183) also offer another example of a 'spiritual seeker':

> Melissa benefited considerably from psychotherapy. In particular, she developed insight into the passivity and lack of assertiveness that had contributed to her troubled

interpersonal relationships. The ... psychologist who interviewed her when she was in her early 40s described her as someone who is 'almost excruciatingly honest and direct' and who refuses to let herself 'off the hook' over emotionally difficult issues such as her relationship with her parents. Melissa herself said that, 'Psychotherapy literally changed everything I'd ever thought. I had to rework and undo everything I'd ever learned.'

It need not be the case for everyone, however, that developmental progress should be consciously spiritual in this sense. Positive psychologists emphasise the ways in which human beings characteristically develop during their lives, but this development is not compulsorily understood as transcendent. It tends to become so in the work of, for example, Erik Erikson, who sees life as a journey in which overcoming an interlocking series of obstacles does conduce to a type of spiritual completeness bordering on wisdom. But even for Erikson, it need not be the case that attempting to meet life's challenges demands conscious focus on the self in the ways practised by either 'Kate' or 'Melissa'. These women think deeply about broadening their own capacities and sensibilities, but it is possible to do so while concentrating on the problems and people concerned, rather than on one's own agency in confronting them. Thus, developmental approaches to life meaning may be consciously self-focused or not, wisdom oriented or not, and transcendental or not.

Non-transcendental approaches to life tasks can be perceived in views on the meaning of ageing taken by writers such as Kohli and Meyer (1986), in relation to ways in which the lifecourse itself has become institutionalised, not least in terms of the economic, educational and bureaucratic ordering imposed on individuals' lives (see also Mayer, 1986). Riley, in contrast, explores how 'social structures are reorganized around the stages of life and, as self-development becomes a dominant value, the ageing process is transformed' (Riley, 1987: 8). While structural constraints are clearly crucial, they are less often discussed than is self-development, at least *until* a certain age; it seems far from certain that older people are popularly included in an equation of the lifecourse with development. (An exception is an 80-year-old psychologist speaking to the author in Germany in September 2013; he said, 'We change and transform ourselves every day, at any age'; cf Andrews, 1999.) As a position influenced by developmental psychology, we might compare some of the work of Elder (1999: 5), when he explicates 'the meanings of age' in terms of 'life-span concepts of development' 'such as transition, coping, and adaptation', and remarks that these concepts themselves brought 'a perspective on "timing"' to his study.

A fifth interpretation of life-course meaning concerns the feeling of having pride or otherwise in one's own lifecourse. The older people with whom James Nichol worked (2009) showed a sense of living their own lives, a sense of where they had got to in a trajectory they experienced as being their own. This is the sense, perhaps, that is encouraged by reunions of various kinds, and summarised in German by the question 'Was ist aus ihm geworden?' (a version of the chilling question, 'What has become of him?'). Reunions compel participants to show what they have gained from life, in terms they think colleagues will or should appreciate; they may be avoided by those who believe themselves to be at a disadvantage in this respect. James Nichol's participants were remarkable for attempting to work out their own positions vis-à-vis their own lives, rather than demonstrating that they have 'done well' in terms of social expectations for people of their age, gender and class.

This use of life-course 'meaning' is relatively rare in gerontology but perhaps commoner in everyday life. For example, Yan and Ku (2013) present evidence in which older Hong Kong residents looked back at their lives, feeling proud of their lifecourses, primarily because they felt they had withstood well-known challenges in Chinese history, including the Civil War and devastations associated with subsequent events; these individuals had saved enough money to buy apartments to live in with their families and had educated their children to high levels. Their lifecourses, in their estimation, had been good; they accorded them positive meaning. By contrast, Domínguez-Rué (2013) deals with the way novels can thematise *spoiled* lives: lifecourses whose promises of success and happiness have been foiled by malicious individuals, or apparently successful lives that are revealed to be shams, in which brilliant fronts conceal crime or deceit.

This contrasts with a sixth, broader aspect of meaning in the gerontological texts we have been examining, 'generational' meaning: that is, the place of individuals or numbers of individuals within the flow of generations, or in the flow of humanity through time. This is not a use of 'generations' with necessary connections to having children or grandchildren; it indicates orientation to a common future and what one can contribute to it. Thus it also seems to include meaning in terms of developing a sense of fitting in to a bigger picture. Respondents interviewed by Coleman or Tornstam describe coming to perceive themselves as standing in relation to the universe, achieving a sense of perspective. Some describe this in terms of a feeling of 'humbleness' and being in some way appropriately insignificant, in the sense of not being over-impressed by the importance of one's own concerns, instead feeling part of the web of life on earth and simply doing one's best as person, independently of public recognition. This connects to what Erikson called 'generativity'. John Kotre (1996) opposes it to 'a growing unwillingness or incapacity on the part of [American] citizens to identify with the future', observable in his view from the 1970s onwards. This is the willingness

> to be interested in offspring and willing to sacrifice for them, to leave the site of one's life in better shape than it was found, to feel that one has something of value for succeeding generations (1996: 1).

It is therefore the inverse of cultural narcissism (1996: 2); Kotre makes it his project to explore, through 'life-storytelling', the life histories of people who do show generativity of this kind.

> Connections must be found between what is past and what is present, between what is latent and what is manifest in an individual's history. Connections must also be found between histories, and ... between a group of histories and the larger context of fertility (1996: 3).

Erikson expects this type of generative desire to be integrated into the personality only towards the end of life, and terms it 'wisdom'. Kotre (2004: 39), on the other hand, suggests that it can also be manifested among very young people, quoting from a 23-year-old woman mentioned in one of his earlier works:

> 'I'm not sure if I will have children, but I want to make a difference in a child's life even if he or she is not my own. Maybe, if I'm lucky, I can say that I changed someone's life for the better. Maybe there's a term for being my age and being concerned with the legacy that I hope to leave' (Kotre, 1999: 158).

In this chapter Kotre argues that this type of generativity can be attributed not only to individuals but also to whole societies, which are capable of maintaining cultural arrangements supporting inhabitants' moral and psychological developments – or the reverse. He contrasts the Virginians with the New Englanders in 17th-century America, claiming that while the latter began as a distinctively generative society and declined, the former moved in the other direction. 'It's not just a matter of whether cultures are generative, but when' (2004: 39). This contention is clearly of relevance to social and political decisions, not least environmental decisions that crucially involve trade-offs between immediate and long-term benefits. Anthony Giddens (1991) suggests that the narcissism of contemporary culture will be overcome only when individuals become able to perceive (or are forced to perceive) that they must unite to avert global disaster. Life-course meaning of this kind thus has pressing links with political positioning, on the one hand, and meaning in terms of the capacity to make *wise* decisions, on the other. For Moody (2014), it needs to become key to ageing in the 21st century that older people press for protecting the global environment: this would be a generativity that would enable their grandchildren to live, and to have somewhere to live.

Though this wish to feel joined with and to benefit coming generations often has clear implications for the environment, it applies to the work of teachers and artists too. Some older artists known to the author feel despondent because they believe future generations will not care about their work, which to them seems to invalidate it. By contrast, the German artist Jonas Hafner, in his early seventies presented the entire contents of his atelier to another artist; he likened this to giving it to an apprentice, specifically passing on his experience and teaching. At the same time, he is conscious of cultural problems in the contemporary world that make many people unreceptive to art. Thus he feels it is appropriate that one of his sculptures, a giant crucifix, should remain in its current location, disregarded and overgrown by nettles beside an old barn, to await a more propitious reception by generations of the future (conversation, Bernried, September 2013).

This brings us to three more interpretations of 'meaning' in relation to ageing and whatever insights it might bring, all connected in various ways with the attainment of some form of understanding or wisdom. Shulamith Shahar points out that, throughout history, older people have been regarded 'as part of the symbolic order of the world and society' and not only as participants in them (2004: 1). This yields a seventh sense of meaning in relation to age. Older people themselves carry sociocultural messages for other generations (a fact readily recognised by the older people in Mehta's research) – perhaps particularly vividly when they are seen in terms both of other people's 'journeys' and their own. This can bestow a certain value on older people in general, in so far as they not only convey cultural associations to other generations but also communicate messages about pointfulness, morality and purpose. Nhongo (2008) argues that it is a significant culmination of the lifecourse for older people in Africa to be able to enter the phase when they can be regarded as socially symbolic in this way. When they are deprived of this possibility by being trapped in middle age by the need to care for grandchildren, because their own children have died of AIDS, this compounds their suffering: it spoils the natural and expected pattern of their lifecourses.

On the other hand, the process of ageing itself may be accorded a social meaning. This is exemplified in the ancient idea of life as a development or journey which may be replete with possible pitfalls, or lead to a triumphant end – perhaps in the moral sense of 'spirituality', but also perhaps in terms of good or bad fortune or success. This version of the journey, therefore, is less intimately associated with self-improvement than in, say, Erikson's more specific version. It is, though, associated with the notion of some type of overall telos in terms of what a human being might aim at – in contrast with the notion of a career, which appears to be taking over from the journey, and whose implicit message is that the only aspects of a life journey that individuals should be concerned about are those that affect their employment or professions.

Dannefer's account of contemporary ageing acknowledges the significance of how older people and ageing are situated within broader understandings of the way society works. Thus he outlines 'a symbolic approach that encompasses age norms, meaning and values', including 'age norms' and the 'age-related expectations' that go with them (Dannefer and Kelly-Moore, 2009: 405). He enquires how these expectations become sedimented into social structures, especially as a result of social policies 'that have bureaucratized and increasingly institutionalized the life course'; for him this results from still 'earlier changes in the meaning and status of age': increased survival times and heightened technological domination of society in particular (2009: 405). This shows that 'the very concepts of age and life course are themselves historically contingent as culturally relevant and plausible constructs' (2009: 405). The shapes taken by these contingent phenomena cannot be understood without concern for the interplay of social structure and social interaction as it works out in individual lives, as well as 'in the symbolic understanding of age and the life course' (2009: 406). Similarly, Elder on occasion uses 'meaning' in connection with what he terms 'normative expectations' (as does Riley, 1987): for instance, 'We found that accelerated transitions have their greatest effect on a subjective sense of being old or older when they possess general meaning on "becoming old"' – as when one becomes a grandparent at a relatively early age (Elder, 1999: 10). In all these cases, the meanings attributed to particular life stages are connected with the ways in which the society concerned conceptualises what it is to age.

An eighth version of 'the meaning of life' implies an understanding of, or a feeling of familiarity with, 'the human condition'. This issue is beginning to be explored more often in gerontology by innovative scholars such as Peter Derkx, Jan Baars or Joseph Dohmen (see Baars et al, 2013; Baars, 2012; Dohmen, 2002). 'Understanding the human condition' may refer to a kind of lifetime experience that is relatively low key: knowing how to encourage people to perform a task effectively, or knowing when to expect others to keep their promises, and how to react if they do not. It is also associated with lifetime-related questions such as how much one can expect to achieve during the course of one's life, or what sorts of impact it is possible to make on the public world. It includes questions about how we should regard the past and the authority or otherwise of tradition, how possible it is to live an authentic life, what is of permanent value and what is worth investing effort in. For this reason questions about the human condition may be associated with the idea of an art of living; the lifecourses of iconic individuals such as Nelson Mandela may be interpreted as showing what it is possible to achieve in a lifetime, in terms of the human condition and individuals' contributions to it.

These questions are also associated with sociological, political and philosophical work on the nature of contemporary society, for example Weber's assertions about the iron cage of bureaucracy or Bauman's analyses of 'liquid modernity'. Hannah Arendt, in her book *The Human Condition* (1958), dissected what she saw as key contemporary changes away from an emphasis on the public sphere of active meaning and action contributed by citizens to the public good, in favour of the pursuit of individual economic interests and privatised individual introspection, regulated by bureaucracy, on the one hand, and the manipulation of public opinion by elites, on the other. For writers such as these, the nature of modernity imposes new facets on the human condition that alter the blend of opportunities and constraints individuals face in living their lifecourses.

Lastly, we have already seen intimations that 'meaning' may be associated in various ways with 'wisdom'. Two of this author's American interview partners, a woman in her forties and a man in his seventies, spontaneously associated wisdom with leaving a legacy. But wisdom is a concept interpreted in a variety of ways, of which Erikson's disinterested generativity, or Tornstam's 'at-oneness' are only two. This concept is explored in more detail in the next chapter, which stresses contemporary work in relation to wisdom and ageing, as well as the classical sources from which much of this derives. As in the case of all the versions of meaning we have enumerated here, there are many versions of the wisdom tradition and models of wisdom. We cannot ask simply what wisdom 'is', or what phronetic virtues such as courage or tolerance 'are': each appears differently across a range of interpretive contexts.

It is important to underline the fact that the word 'meaning' is a multivalent word: it may refer specifically to the types of content attributed to life-course meanings, as in the usages just commented on, or it may refer to modes of *conveying* meaning – communicative, linguistic or symbolic meaning in general (Figure 2).

Figure 2: Talking about meaning

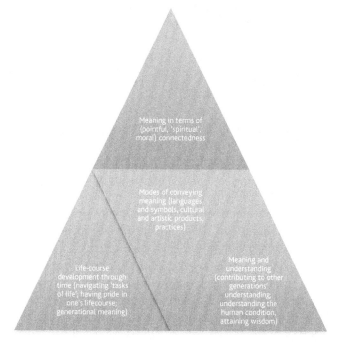

Meaning in terms of (pointful, 'spiritual', moral) connectedness

Modes of conveying meaning (languages and symbols, cultural and artistic products, practices)

Life-course development through time (navigating 'tasks of life'; having pride in one's lifecourse; generational meaning)

Meaning and understanding (contributing to other generations' understanding; understanding the human condition, attaining wisdom)

(Note that this figure does not include specifically prescriptive approaches.)

Meaning may be conveyed through everyday cultural practices, or it may be analysed in cultural productions, including artistic ones: broad categories that interact with each other in a continuous fashion. The nine major types of meaning surveyed in this chapter are reflected upon in art or literature, and conveyed through cultural symbols and practices, Geertz's 'webs of significance', in a fluid dynamic that reflects changing expectations and capacities. Hence Bytheway (2011), for example, comments on the changing cultural meanings of birthdays, or of bureaucratic practices such as recording age; Twigg (2012, 2013) explores the different cultural messages inscribed into particular forms of dress, and the impacts these messages may have on individuals concerned. In the case of dress, 'meaning' in the sense of cultural implications may be readable by a wide section of the population – even though individuals may be uncertain whether they themselves have read accepted messages correctly. Dress can be a part of embodiment that contributes to individuals' personal narratives of past, present and future as they interrelate with immediate and wider settings (Weber and Mitchell, 2004).

On the other hand, cultural interpretations may be limited to particular groups, perhaps prized particularly because they are so. A Scottish lady in her seventies known to the author was particularly fond of a neo-Georgian silver-plated teapot bought from the London firm of Maple & Co., which for her was emblematic of the propriety and family practices important to respectable people in Edinburgh in the first half of the 20th century. To pick up such a teapot was to be reminded of the details of these attitudes and practices, and to feel an affinity with the other (now older) people who also knew them at first hand. For this particular lady, the teapot also conveyed a form of life-course meaning; to use it was to feel reassured that the trajectory of her lifecourse was marked by objects with 'solid' worth, appreciated by people like herself, redolent of their hopes and fears, and emblematic of a tried and trusted approach to dealing with life. Such cultural items enrich the 'meaningfulness' of the inhabited landscape, reflecting back the messages with which they have been endowed. This meaningfulness is not necessarily put into words, partly because symbolic objects express such meaning more eloquently than their users can – though it does underline how serious it is to compel older people to 'give up the possessions of a lifetime' late in their lives (see Rowles and Bernard, 2013: 4). The role of such objects, with the personal or shared narratives they convey, is one of the foci of 'memory studies' (Kattago, 2015): they do not all mark purely private experiences, for often their function is to plot the conjunction between the individual and the social, with the wider significance Herodotus sought: preventing human events from being obliterated by time.

Individuals and groups enrich each other's lives by making such cultural symbols present to each other; while the disappearance or transformation of such cultural meanings can denude the landscape for the individuals formerly familiar with them, making life significantly lonelier for them. But Phillips et al (2011) point out that cultural meanings do not all rely on shared memories and continuity of interpretation. On the one hand, these authors give a nuanced account of what it is to read off messages about one's own lifetime from familiar environments; but cultural meaning, like linguistic meaning, can also be virtually society-wide: the older people they study also make use of cultural messages to interpret *unfamiliar* urban settings. Built environments can activate common aesthetic knowledge with the effect of making novel surroundings negotiable.

The major uses of 'meaning' we have now examined can allow us to interpret much gerontological work on insight and ageing, but the fluid nature of the topic means that this often requires disaggregating combinations of two or more usages. Thus Tornstam himself, for instance, sees 'gerotranscendence' as tracing meanings on three different levels, but in fact he combines more versions of 'meaning' than three. He mentions a 'cosmic' dimension accompanying a heightened 'feeling of being part of the flow of generations' (2011: 169); this is the sixth of the versions of 'meaning' we have just identified. Tornstam associates it with the issue of transcendence when he associates it with a diminished fear of death and acceptance of 'the mystery dimension of life' (2011: 170). The second 'dimension' Tornstam identifies concerns the self, stressing that the older people he talks to are discovering new aspects of their own identities; this was our fourth aspect of 'meaning', connected with 'tasks of life'. Tornstam says that 'The gerotranscendent individual ... typically experiences a redefinition of the self and of relationships to others and a new understanding of fundamental, existential questions' (2005: 3). This both reflects his respondents' acquisition of enhanced senses of personal 'coherence' and underlines the fact that their journeys are not *simply* journeys, but cast light for them on questions of transcendence and ethics. This appears to be a spiritual significance in our second sense, and the reference to ethics brings in the third sense too. Tornstam's own next dimension of gerotranscendence deals with 'social and personal relationships': individuals become both more relaxed and more discerning in social situations, less 'cocksure' about right and wrong and 'travelling light' as far as material possessions are concerned (2011: 173). These are ethical developments in relation to living well, also falling under the third aspect of meaning we identified here. His respondents feel that their identities change and develop in later life, moving away from self-centredness in the direction of deeper 'broadmindedness, tolerance and humility' and even a form of 'modern asceticism' (2005: 68–89).

'Gerotranscendence' is thought of as bringing all these approaches to meaning together, focusing on the heightened sensitivity Tornstam finds among some older people for 'transcendental sources of happiness' (2005: 59). In the view of Peter Derkx (2013b), human beings commonly have needs not only for moral connectedness and justification (the feeling that one can regard oneself as doing roughly the right thing in life) but also for stimulation and enjoyment. But for him, it is unconvincing to argue that 'gerotranscendence' is a 'natural process moving towards maturation and wisdom' (Tornstam, 2005). Derkx sees it, rather, as a normative suggestion, one that is for historical and cultural reasons more likely to find favour with some cohorts than others. He quotes the finding by Braam et al (2006) that the 'cosmic dimension' is the most empirically robust of Tornstam's findings: a heightened feeling of unity with the universe, new perspectives on time, life and death, and a growing feeling of affinity with past and, especially, future generations.

For Derkx, appealing to people to live with this type of consciousness in mind potentially supports the balance they might strive to achieve between what Arendt calls natality (Arendt, 1958: 9, 177–8) – a constant preparedness to start life again with new hope and energy – and acceptance of their own limitations and those of the human condition. Derkx sees these stances as making sense in terms of the meaningfulness of people's lives and also their enjoyment of them. His own treatment of meaning (Derkx, 2013a) centres specifically on exploring reasonable prescriptions for the meaningfulness that people can attribute to their own lifecourses, the meanings 'of' their lives.

The question of whether meaning, in any of the senses here, should be linked with enjoyment is one that is incompletely explored in much contemporary work, obscured on occasion by concepts such as 'quality of life'. For ancient philosophers, such as Aristotle or the followers of Epicurus, or for Confucius or Buddha, as well as for Christian philosophers such as Aquinas, enjoyment is a reasonable and necessary part of finding life meaningful. For them, this is an aspect of experience that itself heightens meaningfulness – perhaps, among other things, by welding together subjective experiences with their wider social contexts. In his work on friendship, Cicero quotes what he says is 'a celebrated saying' used among older people:

> If a man should ascend alone into heaven and behold clearly
> the structure of the universe and the beauty of the stars,

there would be no pleasure for him in the awe-inspiring sight, which would have filled him with delight if he had had someone to whom he could describe what he had seen (*De Amicitia* 23, 86).

This quotation acknowledges that the capacity to attribute meaning is related, on the one hand, to connection to other people, and to enjoyment, on the other.

Some approaches to listening

In order to listen to and interpret what people say and do about their lifetimes, two major methodological issues must be confronted. First, much that is conveyed in these connections tends to be expressed obliquely rather than directly; second, much relies on meaning that is as much shared as it is individual. Direct language may be used reluctantly, or may simply be lacking, in communication where actions may count as loudly as words. According to cultural custom and personal predilection, people may or may not attempt to frame views and feelings connected with insight and lifecourses in overt terms. Symbolic gestures may play a large part in this type of communication: symbols not only express what they do more eloquently than individuals might, but they gain much of their eloquence from the very fact that they are shared. The older people in Gallagher's (2008) study of older people in their communities in Ireland, for instance, are reticent in terms of trying to put words on perceptions of meaningfulness. Yet they derive significant parts of the meanings of their lives by creating community, doing so through small actions in their daily lives. Coleman too (2011: 7) comments on the reluctance or difficulty people may experience in expressing their views on belief and meaning. This has implications both for gerontological methods in general and for the evaluation of practices, addressed below.

This is not to say that direct attempts to use univocal language in research on meaning are never useful. It is possible simply to ask people whether they feel that they experience meaning in life, as does the 'Meaning of Life Questionnaire' used by Steger et al (2006: 93). The authors describe asking American undergraduates to rate their agreement with the following ten statements: 'I understand my life's meaning,' 'I am looking for something that makes my life feel meaningful', 'I am always looking to find my life's purpose,' 'My life has a clear sense of purpose,' 'I have a good sense of what makes my life meaningful,' 'I have discovered a satisfying life purpose,' 'I am always searching for something that makes my life feel significant,' 'I am seeking a purpose or mission for my life,' 'My life has no clear purpose,' and 'I am searching for meaning in my life.' But the purpose of this scale is to gauge, for use in psychological counselling, how respondents' psychological health should be assessed; it is not designed to tell us what these statements actually mean to their readers. Steger et al (2008: 199) assert that 'empirical research on this construct is sparse', even though its association with well-being is often attested (see also Ardelt, 2002). Their own account may seem open to imputations of circularity:

> We define the search for meaning in life as the strength, intensity, and activity of people's desire and efforts to establish and/or augment their understanding of the meaning, significance, and purpose of their lives (Steger et al, 2008: 200).

However, these authors' main interest is distinguishing between searching for meaning and feeling that one has attained it, and examining the association of either with measures of psychological well-being. This they assess through responses to statements such as 'When I look at the story of my life, I am pleased with how things have turned out,' or 'Most people see me as loving and affectionate' (Steger et al, 2008: 205). They conclude that people conscious of still searching for meaning 'feel little control over their environment and feel dissatisfied with themselves and their relationships', whereas 'people feel greater presence of meaning when they understand themselves (e.g., self-acceptance), the world around them (e.g., environmental mastery), and their fit within the world (e.g., positive relationships ...)' (Steger et al, 2008: 208). Perhaps, they suggest, it is the 'sense of hanging between an unhappy past and an unknown future' that accounts for the lower well-being of those who feel they are still searching for meaning; factors such as the capacity to tolerate uncertainty, they suggest, may also play a role in well-being (Steger et al, 2008: 222–4).

Approaches such as this are based on the assumption that, at least within a speech community in which such issues are customarily verbalised, it is possible to talk intelligibly about the impression that one has discovered meaning in one's life, and to do so using language that is largely comprehensible, irrespective of immediate context. Decontextualised language – 'that is, language in which the transmission of meaning depends on linguistic rather than situational information' (Hamers and Blanc, 2000: 120) – is in fact both widely accessible and locally intelligible, at least to some extent. Most people are culturally multilingual, in that they are able with more or less skill to produce linguistic and behavioural repertoires appropriate to different types of social setting – at home, at work and so on. In societies where bureaucratic enquiry occurs regularly, they have also learned to attach some degree of meaning to terms used in administrative forms. Language used in surveys necessarily attempts this type of neutrality because it aims to make sense over a number of different contexts; the more an enquiry deals with topics that are appropriately addressed using neutral languages, the easier this is. People confronted by decontextualised language tend to feel obliged to respond in its own terms, often without being aware that they are doing so, but in the nature of the case without communicating subtle and informative accounts of what they take it to mean.

In contrast to the use of univocal language for relatively well-defined purposes, life-course insight is often not verbalised directly by the people most concerned. In many (sub-)cultures, life-course meaning may be discussed reluctantly, if at all, or conveyed ambiguously: allusively, ironically or playfully. Someone who was not only attached to his allotment but communicated his understanding of life through his style of tending it might be unwilling to discuss this in terms of significant meaning in his life, even though this attribution might be made by other people in his circle of acquaintances. These aspects of communication have implications in terms of philosophical anthropology; for example, they attribute more significance to shared communicative practices than do methodologies assuming that individuals have the final say in what they mean. Some social-scientific methodologies see interpretation in terms of excavating to individuals' (psychosocial) intentions in the second of utterance; this is a principle, however, that was already disputed in the 19th century in the context of hermeneutic approaches to the interpretation of texts. Hannah Arendt (1958) extends this dispute to the meanings not only of people's utterances but of their entire lives, arguing that the meaning of any person's action does not exist except as and until it is narrated after the fact by others. Thus Tim Adams (2014) argues that Hamilton's (2014) account of the dying visit to Berlin made by his friend Nuala O'Faolain amounts to 'a profound statement of the idea that the essence of our lives exists not within us but in all the accumulated perceptions of those who have known and loved us'.

It would be rash, therefore, for investigators to assume that their own assumptions or communicative conventions normally neatly match those of the people whose lives they are examining. Cultural routines need to be functionally ambiguous in order to work relatively effectively for disparate participants; it is no wonder that ethnomethodologists describe social interaction as an 'accomplishment' in which meaning is created and conferred by participants' efforts (Turner, 1974). One of the features of this accomplishment is to make everyday interaction seem natural and complete to those who carry it out, disguising or mitigating the possible misunderstandings involved. Engaging in social interaction depends on activating the fiction that all participants have identical understandings of what is going on; people who converse may take it that they are being completely understood, even though this is seldom actually the case. Social scientists need to abandon this fiction for their own parts, while still preserving the effort to understand, consciously equivocating between comprehension and incomprehension. Thus they need to be cautious, exploratory and modest, not taking for granted that the cultural patterns being used around them are easily accessible.

Approaches to life-course meaning that try to follow these strictures include forms of reconstructive ethnography that investigate habit and convention, and the meanings that go with them, in order to make explicit some of the shared forms that structure what people communicate, even though they are seldom aware of them; they include humanistic approaches to empirical research, with their implications for moral cooperation between ethnographers and respondents (Gubrium, 2011; de Medeiros, 2014); they include the use of multiple methods in exploring long-term social processes and life-course narrative. Narrative analyses have a significant capacity in their ability to incorporate long-term aspects of sociality: how people, processes and deeds *are taken to impact* on others and on a variety of settings *over time*. While narratives are sometimes understood as predominantly individual methods of expression, they are eloquent purveyors of the impacts of sociality, in ways that might be more difficult to achieve using methods that focus exclusively on quotations from individuals' own speech. Methodological approaches to exploring age-related meaning need to navigate among contrasts between univocal and multivocal communication, contrasts between more individual and more widely shared forms of communication and contrasts between meaning as intended by the utterer at the moment of utterance and what an utterance, action or practice is taken to mean by others. In all these cases, speakers and actors select, activate and sometimes alter the means of expression offered by the cultures in whose terms communication is being made. Locales with 'their going concerns', 'such as nursing homes, courtrooms, and support groups', 'ordinary households and friendship groups' 'shape the self we live by' (Holstein and Gubrium, 2000: x). This does not *reduce* individuals to performers of their cultures. Not least, they extend their own repertoires in response to unfamiliar people and predicaments, and, as classical rhetorical theorists recognised, *choose* among materials with which their cultures present them, even if 'Inventiveness and diversity are always tamed by the social arrangements within which selves are considered and produced' (Holstein and Gubrium, 2000: 3). Nothing said here implies that individuals do not exist; but they exist in ways that are less simple than some methods in the behavioural sciences might imply.

Reconstructive ethnography: exposing communicative forms

In the effort to develop ways of listening for the sociality in what is said by, to or about older people in the course of leading their lives, it is useful to draw on the philosophical and ethnographic understandings of meaning developed during the 20th century. These turn on the Wittgensteinian emphasis that discovering what a piece of natural language means, or what a gesture or habit means, is predicated on discovering how it is used in the setting in which it occurs. Social-scientific explorations of settings add to this account by emphasising change as well as continuity; to the extent that settings change, meanings are in constant motion. At the same time, meaning is both social and public, for to make sense to other people it needs to belong to languages that are to some extent shared, even if this sharing is seldom complete. Geographical, professional, class-related and other forms of subculture impose local differences within their communicative spheres; individuals must search among these as they seek forms of reasoned communication that will function intelligibly in the contexts they happen to be in – what ancient rhetoricians referred to as commonplaces (Edmondson, 2013). People as they encounter each other bring with them repertoires from the multiple spheres of which they have experience; while these spheres are unlikely to overlap entirely, social exchange is made possible by activating conventions, or excerpts from sets of conventions, that do coincide. Individuals thus become practised in understanding cultural encounters by seeking out what seems to be familiar communicative behaviour, gravitating towards spheres in which they can elicit and provide responses that seem to make sense to the other actors involved. This means that only some aspects of what is said and done by the individuals whom gerontologists encounter in unfamiliar social worlds will be comprehensible to them. Reconstructive ethnography (Edmondson, 2012b) seeks sensitivity to aspects of communication not covered by simple linguistic comprehension; it entails actively seeking awareness of what might otherwise be routinely blanked out as unintelligible, to gain an impression of the shared reactions and practices that shape the social worlds people inhabit, and that express stances vis-à-vis human beings and what can be expected from them.

This is a methodological issue, but it is one with substantial implications for gerontology. Local practices, in conveying meaning, influence how their practitioners envisage their own and others' life-courses: the practical reasoning they employ and the everyday morality they accept as making sense. Practices covering what can be said and how, in what social circumstances, are in themselves communicative. They convey expectations in terms of philosophical anthropology and ethics: what people can reasonably be expected to do, and how they ought to do it. Answering questions like, say, 'What does it mean to be old in working-class Lyons?' with descriptions of practices, quotations, anecdotes and other information showing 'how to go on' in that part of French society is incomplete without some account of *why* those practices are taken seriously. Penetrating to these implicit guides to understanding life is challenging; communication would not work in the everyday coordination of action without powerful mechanisms to moderate the impact of discordant viewpoints and hence in part to disguise them. Since many communicative processes take effect below the level of conscious attention, it can be hard to notice them until the observer's communicative expectations happen to be flouted – in what might be termed 'xenisms' (Edmondson, 2013a), from the Greek word for 'strange'. When people speak or act in a way that does not seem to make immediate sense to the observer, this provides a clue that they may be making communicative assumptions the observer does not share.

About 15 years ago the present author heard a discussion of the appointment of a schoolteacher in Connemara: local speakers were annoyed that someone from an adjoining county had been chosen when a local person was on hand to fill the position. What was striking about this discussion was not that the speakers preferred the local candidate or felt loyalty towards her, which would have been readily comprehensible, but that they clearly considered it *irrational*, and to that extent blameworthy, to bring a schoolteacher from another county to take up this position. On what criteria might this judgement have been based? Applying an 'abductive' approach to the hermeneutics of this interchange suggests that it lacks one starting belief fundamental to 'universalist' Western appointment criteria: that job applicants are in principle interchangeable except in terms of their qualifications. This amounts to a striking cultural difference. It is not that the adage 'treat equal cases equally' is not being applied, which would be irrational; in this setting, the two cases are simply not regarded as equal, and it is up to the observer to reconstruct the reasons why not. Again abductively, we could speculate that if the speakers see it as reasonable to take work positions to be embedded within the environments where they operate, it would follow as a matter of course that it might be both unreasonable and wrong to introduce strangers to carry them out – any more than one would precipitately remove a local farmer from his land and introduce someone from the other side of the country to tend his farm. This interpretation does in fact seem compatible with other observations of beliefs and behaviour in this area; and it bears on expectations about people's lifecourses, treating them as reasonably implanted within known environments and subject to unreason if detached from them.

Inferring to the reasons that could make sense of a xenism in this way reveals an entire 'web' of meanings, to use the Geerzian phrase. It would in fact be strange if just one instance had its own specific meaning in a discursive setting like this one, for the example needs a wide system of assumptions to account for it: for example, one accentuating the relational side of work relatively more than in other interpretive systems and the technical side relatively less. Such differences can be felt particularly forcefully when one does not merely research, but lives, among people whose conventions are to some extent unfamiliar. Learning how to perform them correctly entails learning to enact a whole way of life. In the rural West of Ireland, as in rural regions elsewhere in Europe, it is a common practice to stop on the road if one passes a neighbour, and offer a lift. This practice succinctly expresses solidarity and readiness to be helpful within reason, without committing participants to a relationship that might be intrusively personal. (Helpfulness, too, can function in specific ways in a new setting, since there need to be limits to helpfulness in order to protect people from unjustified calls on them (Edmondson, 2000a); the implicative networks of roughly equivalent concepts will not be identical across settings.) For the newcomer, it may require occasionally painful learning to discern what topics and styles of conversation are appropriate while the lift is being given: public ones, connected with matters of common concern such as the ripeness of crops. This does not mean that this neighbourly interaction need be standard and routine, in fact it would be bad manners to participate in it in a standard and routine manner. Individuality can be bestowed on the occasion through humour, irony and wit; these are shared sources of enjoyment that downplay elements of egocentric display. In urban settings, comparable features can be found in interactions such as assisting neighbours with household tasks connected with plumbing or electricity. Practices such as these convey meaning and may be highly significant to the people who engage in them; but they are unlikely to be *mentioned* as sources of important interaction, for their most salient aspects are seldom reflected on at all. Reconstructive ethnography attempts to unpeel what interactions and practices are *for*, what is going on when people engage in them, and what underlying assumptions about the (interpersonal) world they reveal. In everyday life, people are compelled to engage in practical reconstructions of this kind, usually without formulating them as such; in new professional circumstances, for example, insecurity may be felt in trying to follow unspoken conversational conventions, which also convey their own views about what is locally regarded as significant and right in relation to human beings and human interaction.

As Peter Winch argued in response to observations by Wittgenstein, these practices can be discovered by 'learning how to go on' (1958: 123) in a particular social world – even though not everyone with indigenous knowledge of how to behave in a certain setting is necessarily able to describe it. To 'go on' in a new social setting it is important to learn what *counts as* being, say, friendly, or what counts as expressing disapproval. Some things cannot readily be said at all in certain circumstances (Edmondson, 1984). When the author was learning Irish in Connemara, she wanted to express admiration for a child's prowess on the accordion, asking how to say, 'I'm impressed.' The reply was that that was not the sort of thing one would or could say in this part of the world. This does not mean that one cannot make children feel appreciated in rural Ireland, as Nancy Scheper-Hughes (1977) assumed was the case. Coming to Ireland from the much more verbally expressive setting of California, Scheper-Hughes took it that people who feel affection tend readily to express it in language, so that what is not said is not meant. In fact a laconic 'Good girl,' addressed to the child, might quite effectively convey affection, acceptance and support in this setting as long as the child was sufficiently attuned to her own culture (though generational change ensures that this is not invariably the case). Ironically, it may be harder for ethnographers to notice different usages in local forms of a language they share, in this case English, than in foreign languages, where they are more alert for differences.

Thus there are lessons to be learned about the opportunities and constraints associated with shared habits from the way language and behaviour are employed in particular cultural contexts, and from the implications of specific usages. In the rural West of Ireland, both English and Irish languages are used to cajole, to joke, to get work done, to coordinate people, to tease, to insult, to conjecture. Linguistic and interactive conventions do not accord pride of place to expressing private, internal views about other people and the world; their lack of shared prominence conveys that they are not, and perhaps should not be, considered overwhelmingly interesting, not even by oneself. Some years ago the author was present as a group of women discussed what they considered the extremely rude behaviour of a neighbour's nephew. The young man had attended a mass in the village, and afterwards had debated with the priest about an aspect of the sermon. The women gave no evidence of being at all interested in what either the priest or the young man had thought or said, but seemed definite that the young man's intervention was discourteous and out of place. The tenor of their remarks suggested that the priest was doing his job as best he could, on his turf, and it was not correct or polite to object to it: perhaps as if someone had been invited to a meal and then criticised the host's cooking. This by no means implies that it is thought incorrect in this context to complain *about* a priest, which people often do (sometimes for reasons that may also seem in need of interpretation, as when it was taken amiss that a priest had wished to repaint the chancel in his church, but had taken a bucket and stepladder and done the job himself). It certainly was not implied that the young man ought to have agreed with the priest or was not entitled to his own opinion. But he should not, it appeared, have taken his own views so seriously as to express them in that time and place and in that way (though very possibly the priest, who is required to operate across a range of different meaning-conventions, did not mind at all). It was the elevated status the young man accorded to his own views that was thought inappropriate and unmannerly. Again, this is an abductive interpretation that chimes with other observations in the same cultural context. It had the implicit addendum, one that sits well with further aspects of the egalitarian reticence in this part of the world, that views as such are less significant than their bearers might believe.

Given the subtlety of such cultural differences, and the long accretion of observations needed in order to suggest and explore abductive conjectures, even relatively successful cases of understanding other people tend to be partial, in everyday life as well as in gerontology. Further, different cultures and subcultures, as well as different relationships, expect and reward different types of practical understanding. In the smallholding communities of the West of

Ireland, as in many other settings, interpersonal understanding itself is based on performing common work activities, knowing where the other person's behaviour fits into regular patterns of local life, being familiar with the other person's habits; language as such is treated as a less central or direct means of self-revelation than it may be in other places (Edmondson 1998, 2000b). In German middle-class culture, by contrast, a much more problem-oriented, causal-historical approach to understanding another person is expected, emphasising just the type of individual subjectivity that appears intrusive in Ireland. These differences not only give rise to methodological challenges, they are relevant to 'meaning of life' questions themselves. These are less likely to be discussed overtly in rural Ireland, and more likely to be expressed through longer-term behaviour patterns. Friendship, for example, is likely to be a constituent of what makes life meaningful in both contexts, but has different connotations in each. An older German woman expressed disappointment because Irish people, seemingly so open and welcoming, showed no interest in developing what she saw as friendships with her. A possible explanation for this experience was that she had a different conception of friendship, revolving for example around the verbalisation and dissection of personal problems and feelings, practices that did not function to indicate friendly closeness in this new setting in the same way.

This discussion has emphasised the importance of practical discourses: what is available to say and do in a certain setting, what can easily or convincingly be said and done, and how this can be understood by newcomers. Burkitt (2002: 222) refers to Aristotle's concept of techne as 'the knowledge and skills handed down from previous generations and developed by those who inherit this legacy': what we are discussing are the forms of techne involved in producing everyday social life. The examples used here show how shared conventions are both enabling and constraining: if local conventions represent people in later life as either authoritative or otherwise, it can be hard to change this quickly. If ageist discourses have become routine in a given society (Moody, 2010), this may stem less directly from individuals' intentions and reflections than from the structures of meaning that are available to them.

Knowledge of local conventions even among users may be incomplete; people are often slightly unsure of how things are done, even within their own immediate cultural surroundings, and individuals differ in sensitivity to such questions. The concept of 'habitus', 'our second nature, the mass of conventions, beliefs and attitudes which each member of a society shares with every other member' (Scheff, 1997: 219), is overdrawn if it implies social homogeneity, for conventions, beliefs and attitudes are variable and fluctuating, like weather systems (Edmondson, 2000b). Thus it is not always obvious even to participants how to accomplish, say, the communication of appropriate gratitude for a present. What one family takes for appreciation the next will see as gushing. Moreover, while communicative conventions are not usually changeable at will, sometimes they change much faster than expected, like the capacity to extract extra work from employees in organisations that was introduced by the advent of email. Needless to say, such changes are sometimes highly contested. It is impossible to be a doctor without engaging in practices that are comprehensible as a doctor's practices, satisfying expectations held of doctors in the society concerned. Variations in assumptions about what these expectations imply become more apparent when change is mooted: for instance, in debates about whether doctors in hospitals should wear ordinary clothes and whether their authority would be undermined if they did so.

Examples like these show that practical discourses imply their own philosophical anthropologies, with their own corresponding ethical overtones: (usually unformulated) assumptions about what a human being is, how people can be expected to relate to each other, how it is sensible to estimate what they may be doing. This can be illustrated in the following instance involving a xenism in the author's experience as a new inhabitant of the rural West of Ireland. When her dogs invaded neighbouring gardens and overturned compost heaps there, she wished to visit the neighbours with apologies, but was strongly discouraged from doing so by someone familiar with the district. This prohibition seemed hard to understand and was furnished with no explanation; it took a considerable time to amass enough experience to interpret it. With time she encountered several instances illustrating a local tendency to abstain from trying to explicate minor differences verbally. This makes sense if we take it that, in this setting, intentions about action are not expected to be largely explicit and verbalised; in the present example, to do so would actually be considered manipulative, an effort to cause the neighbours to think the speaker a responsible owner when she had proved herself not to be so. The only option, a long-term one rather than immediately achievable, was to train the dogs to remain in the place intended. This illustrates a more general observation that intentions in this part of the world are expected to be manifested over time rather than all at once – in terms of what people do once a week, or habitually, rather than in terms of what they say immediately about their views. Subcultural discourses derive from levels down to which we must excavate; this would be an apt misapplication of the analogy with 'rhizomes' to describe proliferations of subterranean connections without clear structures (Deleuze and Guattari, 1976) – especially in a part of the world in which invasion by bracken roots from neglected land threatens to become ubiquitous.

To understand practical meaning involves practical engagement by the ethnographer, who must not only be present during enough everyday interchanges to collect experience of them but must also allow his or her own conceptual framework to be altered by the life-course practices involved. This involves abandoning the assumption that the observer is entitled to determine what local meanings are, or how language and behaviour should be employed. Ethnographers need to project as little as possible of their own conceptual apparatus onto their surroundings; this implies submitting to a certain social vulnerability in the face of other meaning-worlds. Ideally, they would allow themselves to be stripped of their own immediate repertoire of linguistic and emotional reactions to other people (like Vincent Donovan among the Masai (1978)). This is disturbing to experience and not simple to achieve; it causes its own problems even in writing field-notes, since records of 'what happened' will normally be shaped and contaminated by the writer's original conceptual framework. Solon Kimball, working in Ireland in the 1930s, seems to have tried to circumvent such a problem by trying to record mainly quotations, words people had actually said. As far as possible he actually became an Irishman in dress, manner and speech – to the extent that his colleague Arensberg, meeting him after several months' absence, 'nearly failed to recognise' him (Byrne et al, 2001: xlvi).

The fact that cultures are not homogenous or complete, but dynamic and changing, adds to the challenges involved in building up hermeneutic capacities. Views of appropriate or ethical life-course behaviour within a setting will develop, and their interpretation may be subject to contention even among native practitioners. For example, the question of what can be taken to be private to an individual, and what is legitimately a matter of public enquiry, is key to delineating local notions of personhood and identity, and ultimately questions about lifecourses and what should be expected or aspired to from them. Some rural areas have been described in terms of 'squinting windows', framing them as involving the constant censorious monitoring of other people's activities. But in the rural West of Ireland it is not considered unduly inquisitive, if you see someone walking along the road, to speculate about where the person is going and why. In other contexts of practice, this would count as intrusive. An alternative explanation seems more convincing: public–private distinctions are applied somewhat differently here. Activities performed on the public road count as public, so it is not impertinent to enquire about them. Similarly, if one meets people on the public road, one greets them as fellow members of a community; appropriate conversation concerns matters of common interest rather than one's own private affairs. This allots a larger part of one's identity to common ownership, as it were, than is the case in a city, where people are permitted to be anonymous as they go about their daily business; but it by no means entitles neighbours to speculate on what others do in the privacy of their homes or to criticise their private opinions. In the present author's observation, these rural distinctions apply in other regions too, for instance in Finland or Austria, but they are beginning to become archaic, replaced by more individualistic Western interpretations of privacy.

Another case of cultural change concerns funerals, markers par excellence of life-course meaning. Irish funerals are deeply impressive for their large scale and relative conviviality. When a death takes place, everyone knows how to behave: to attend the deceased person as he or she is laid out in the funeral parlour or at home, to say prayers and perhaps to drink tea or even eat with the family; the next day, the funeral takes place in the church, and afterwards if possible those at the funeral will walk along the road behind the coffin to the place of burial. It is still common, in the countryside, for one's neighbours to dig one's grave. When the coffin is inside, hay is thrown down to muffle the sound, and the earth shovelled rhythmically back, the thuds it makes blending with the cadence of the rosary recited by those around. If necessary, the gravediggers will jump down onto the coffin to ensure that it is lying level, and stamp it down. When the earth is even again, they will roll back the turf they have removed to dig the hole, restoring the ground to its previous appearance.

This ceremony is all the more striking and moving for being so familiar, a genuinely solemn memorial to the person who has lived. Attendance is based on the generally behaviourist assumptions of rural Irish culture already mentioned. To attend a funeral and to say prescribed words such as, 'I'm sorry for your trouble,' *is* to sympathise; to be present is to give comfort. Consolation, it follows, is less a matter of subjective thoughts connected with one's relationship with the deceased, or words or gestures individually chosen, than of one's suitable participation in the funeral itself. This involves observing the tenor appropriate to the occasion rather than devising spontaneous and original feelings of one's own. This is bound to be the case, since one is required to attend funerals not only of people one knows but of relations of people one knows, but it has the comfort of freeing those involved from the burden of choice about titrating their behaviour to achieve a socially defined ideal.

Funerals are significant for marking the fact that a person has lived; they may or may not be expressions of personal, individual loss and distress. However, this aspect of the practice is not usually reflected upon overtly and it is vulnerable to change. It is now possible to hear younger people complaining of the obligation to attend funerals of people whose death does not make them personally sad. In a way they are missing the point of their own cultural conventions, applying expectations from one setting (say, here, American or UK conventions) to another. These new expectations are much more individualistic than the local ones; if they continue to be applied, the cultural practice will have changed. In the US or the UK, people are often at a loss what to do in the case of a death, whether in their own circle or outside it; they expect to have to devise appropriate reactions to it by themselves, rather than taking recourse to a set of meanings whose very force derives from the fact that they have evolved over time for this purpose.

Conveying meanings in texts

The sociality of meaning is not limited to language and behaviour in social situations, for texts are social phenomena too. We shall briefly explore this issue before moving to three major responses to key challenges raised in connection with the sociality of meaning: temporal, narrative and practice theory. Gerontologists approaching lifecourse-related questions need not only to negotiate between both tacit and verbal accounts in different contextual settings, but also to communicate their accounts in a manner intelligible to their readers, which poses issues of its own (Edmondson, 1984; Richardson, 2000). Matilda Riley points out that societies differ in how they deal with older age, and impose expectations and languages in accordance with these structures (Riley et al, 1972). Accounts of utterances or behaviour cannot be read unproblematically and 'themes' be discerned within them, just as if they had been written in decontextualised language. Even *recording* spoken language is a complex and profoundly challenging issue (Ross, 2010). Atkinson (2005) complains that many sociologists treat subjects' recorded remarks as privileged paths to their subjectivities, and write as if these subjectivities were automatically sociologically significant: slices of the social world, susceptible to direct perusal by readers. Linguistic accounts, Atkinson rightly contends, are produced in a variety of circumstances for a variety of reasons that need to be explored in the context of 'socially shared undertakings' (2005: 6). But their presence *in texts* can fulfil other communicative functions than the provision of evidence in a straightforward sense; they may well be there to teach the reader how given concepts and practices work in unfamiliar cultures.

Given that understanding what other people say and do in everyday life as well as in new cultural circumstances is problematic, conveying interpretations in terms the reader can also understand brings another layer of difficulty to the process (see Asad, 2010). Records of interviews in published texts, for example, often function tacitly to convey impressions that the author has acquired about the workings of cultural practices that he or she considers key in the overall argument being made. Interview extracts are not normally the most 'typical' responses the author has observed, but those that express most succinctly, forcefully or interestingly the points that he or she considers important (Edmondson, 2007). In fact, texts about the social world follow a plethora of unformulated conventions to spur their readers to fill in for themselves some of the contextual detail they need in order to understand what is being conveyed. Even though descriptions of settings may be relatively sparing, they can interact with quotations in order to convey a picture of a social world, a place where particular interactions can be anticipated: less a 'model' than an imaginatively heightened portrait of an inhabited place, in whose terms inhabitants' behaviour can be grasped as making sense.

The textual conventions involved have evolved implicitly, often in opposition to acknowledged social-scientific methodology (Edmondson, 1984). Writers tend to follow relatively conventional lines in offering context-descriptions, and standardly justify their quotations as 'representative' without elaborating on what it is they are intended to represent. In practice, the opposite may be the case – the particularity and multivocality of interview extracts can be a major reason for using them. Far from merely 'framing' and 'illustrating' arguments made by authors, context-descriptions and quotations can play a major role in helping to *constitute* them.

Reading the interaction between setting-descriptions and quotation involves imagining what the actors involved are like, what it is reasonable to expect of them; readers judge if it is likely that they will react as the author presupposes. To this extent, whether readers accept the text's reasoning depends partly on whether they broadly accept that (these) people are likely to behave as the author suggests. But readers' positions also need to be changed to some degree, as they learn how to interpret social reactions new to them. This depends on spurring them to extrapolate from their own experience, leading them to imagine new forms of behaviour (Edmondson, 1984). Showing why given forms of sociality in a given setting are important, what to expect of them and what is most relevant to interpreting them anticipates and conveys much of the author's argument itself. Often, this is accomplished by getting readers to imagine situations with which they are familiar and extending their horizons to apply new expectations in the same setting, or to extend familiar expectations to new circumstances. Arguments of this kind may be implied throughout a text in the kinds of description and quotation furnished for readers to digest. Textual communication in general is multifunctional, but the presence of quoted evidence plays a special role in encouraging readers to extrapolate to processes and practices whose presence is not directly described – and for which direct evidence may be hard to get. Instead, they are to be imagined by the reader.

An account by Ryan et al (2012) in *Ageing and Society* interrogates processes during which older people and their immediate relations come to the usually reluctant decision that the older person should enter a nursing home. Through examining this account we can become aware of some of the ways its textuality operates to convey multilevel types of meaning to readers. This paper does not contain much descriptive detail in itself; the quotations bear the burden of the narrative, and can be expanded by the reader's imaginative engagement, so as to make the authors' conclusion convincing and effective. The quotations both activate readers' interpretive capacities and pin down the resulting impression, assuring us that it is real: we can come to feel that the authors are not, or not merely, speaking 'for' other people, but that those people are also speaking for themselves. The fact that respondents have spoken given sentences in a given time and place has an inescapable rhetorical effect: it is reassuringly definite. The presence of quotations in the text thus quite legitimately adds to the verisimilitude of the authors' picture offered and the overall argument this picture helps to convey. Textual accounts of settings would not be intelligible if they did not indicate what sorts of worlds their subjects move in; even such brief accounts communicate much more than appears at face value. They are efforts to respond to the challenge of writing about sociality without being taken to imply a false homogeneity, taking account of the multiplicity of perspectives in the world the authors describe, but doing so with the pivotal assistance of the reader.

This article is explicitly intended to deal with decisions arrived at over time; it also aims to explore concepts of 'home' in connection with the debate on supporting older people's wishes to 'age in place'. It begins with a discussion of 'rurality', which is relatively sparse, discussing population densities and referring to the debate in the academic literature about what rurality really means. This is succeeded by an introduction to the study: to the extent that, in rural areas, elder care is particularly strongly expected to take place within the family, what happens when older people for whom relatives are caring do enter nursing homes? The first really descriptive segment of the paper, on its sixth page, is provided by quotations from relatives:

> 'She had lived in Enniskillen for 60 years and she always loved "The Glen". She loved the country';
>
> '"The Meadows" was one of our first priorities. We heard so much about it and we were very pleased with it';
>
> 'I suppose we suggested "Brook Lodge" because it is right beside my mother's home. That was the only home we ever considered really';
>
> 'Over the last two years she always said if there ever comes a time that I'm not able to look after myself, put me in the "The Cloisters". She had even said this to some of her daughters' (Ryan et al, 2012: 6).

At once readers can visualise these older people at least in outline, going beyond what is actually offered in terms of evidence on the page to create images of sociality extrapolated in part, unavoidably, from their own experiences of caring and of older people, modified so as to envisage them as taking place in a rural space – for whose actual specificities the article supplies very little evidence. These quotations are able to give rise to a second type of interaction, blending the familiar (to us) and the unfamiliar, what we know *from our own lives* with what is distinctive for us about the interactions in question. From the start, we are encouraged to imagine the older people identifying with the places in which they now find themselves.

Fresh quotations may activate other aspects of readers' experience, eliciting the capacity to imagine reluctance to place a relation away from home:

> 'He got a bit ill and the doctor came up. He said to me Kate it's going to get worse. He said it had to come to an end. I said I would be alright. He said to me that I wasn't too well. It was getting to me but I wasn't giving in to them. He said that it was going to kill me. The social workers and the doctor encouraged me all the time what to do. I didn't think I would take a heart attack out of it ...' (2012: 9).

Here, the reader can empathise with a relation who needs to be given permission, as it were, to give up caring on her own; the quotations are taken from different interviews, but it is as if they form a narrative of their own account.

> 'I came down to see Jolene who is the Manager and she took me round the whole place. Before I got to that stage it already had been recommended by several people' (2012: 9).

Lastly, quotations show us both relations and inhabitants coming to terms with the new arrangements:

> 'A lot of people love the country and they see the silage being made up and the cows down the field. The girls bring them out for a walk in their wheelchairs or whatever when the weather is warmer' (2012: 10).

Either the older people themselves or their relatives do have acquaintances in the nursing homes:

> 'When my mother was admitted and I looked round and I seen five people she would have known as residents who were in that home. I knew one of the nurses that I worked with previously in the hospital ... it was a big help' (2012: 11).

The authors conclude by making the theoretical point for which their quotations have, in effect, argued: they wish to extend the meaning of 'home' itself.

> This study confirms the importance of 'home' for older people and their carers. The findings suggest that as circumstances change, the definition of 'home' becomes rather fluid. This was particularly evident where home was not just the place of residence but also the wider extended community where the older person resided (2012: 14).

Underlying this account is the sense that for the older people concerned and their families, remaining in a district they associate with home rather than being cut off from it maintains the *meaningfulness* they attribute to life. We can read this text as emphasising not just that the older people in question *have the view* that this is home for them:

they know how to interpret whatever occurs here, how to respond to its symbolic aspects, and this fact itself adds to the homeliness of the setting. This extends even to the nurses at the nursing home, who 'lived, shopped, worshipped and worked with patients who were also their neighbours' (2012: 3): they could be interpreted as familiar neighbours as well as nurses, subject to the same cares and considerations as oneself. This need to accomplish interpretation was shared by the older people's families too: 'Carers took comfort in the knowledge that the home was recommended by friends and acquaintances' (2012: 9).

The physical setting of the home was likewise a source of familiar meanings. The older people concerned experienced rural activities and surroundings as meaningful; not just any rural surroundings, but those that were intelligible to them because they understood the point of what was happening in them. They knew how people were likely to spend their days, what was likely to be going on among them, and why; they could read the symbols, priorities and habits inscribed in those places and activities. Practical issues too belong to this concatenation of familiarity, not least because they generate the feeling that any mistreatment of residents could be detected and corrected by local people. 'For older people in this study, there was simply "no place like home"' (2012: 12), in the extended sense covering not only someone's domicile but the area in which they feel confident and to which a 'sense of self' is 'inextricably linked' (2012: 14). We can infer both that for something to be meaningful includes its capacity to *carry a message* as far as the perceiver is concerned, and that people's very selves are bound up with the need to live in a place that speaks to them in this way. They want to live in a setting in which they can read off practices with which they are familiar and of which they approve; and readers need to imagine what this is like.

The attention Ryan et al give to cultural issues concerning meaning has the practical potential to make older people's entry into nursing homes easier and more tolerable (2012: 15–16). We can extrapolate from their work that, ideally, what offends individuals' imputed life-course meanings should if possible be avoided: a person who understands the point of seeing the cattle moving up and down the land should not be confronted instead by a three-lane highway with alien ethical and practical connotations. This is not to suggest that all meanings are crucial to the ways people envisage their identities or lifecourses, but more are than may be apparent. An elderly farmer in a nursing home of this writer's acquaintance derived life-course meaning from being able to get up and answer the doorbell when visitors called: this activity allowed him to visualise himself as a person at work, contributing purposefully, which made sense to him of his life. His relations, who did not perceive this significance or did not value it, moved him away to a cheaper home in which no such possibility was available, and where he soon died. What is at stake here is sometimes addressed sociologically in terms of issues such as the need for independence, familiarity with setting, closeness to family and friends, or in more general terms such as 'quality of life'. But the text by Ryan et al encourages us to bear in mind that operating in terms of meaning is also key to reading one's surroundings as habitable.

Reading texts in this way depends on the reader's willingness to reflect on practices that are important to those involved because they are associated with being a certain sort of person, with particular interpersonal commitments. These may include issues as small as whether one offers a biscuit, or cake, with a cup of tea, or nothing; whether the cake should be bought or home made – all these symbolise sets of attitudes to home-making, hospitality, to other people, in ways that may be common to local cultures, as well as having personal associations with a person's own life ('My mother and my grandmother always made corned beef just like this, without adding extra spices'). Small daily customs are seldom as small as they appear; in the West of Ireland, a woman commenting on how some families neglect their older members said, 'They wouldn't even give them a biscuit with their cup of tea!' She was referring to custard creams, which would be quite acceptable in this part of the world. For an older lady in Kensington, the biscuit would have to be of a 'home-made' or other 'special' variety for it to carry a similar message of kindness and concern.

Thus, many practices combine local and personal meanings, as when it was said of a certain Irishwoman in the priest's eulogy at her funeral, 'No-one came into that house and went away without eating.' This draws on local customs about hospitality to indicate the unfailing degree of welcome extended by this particular woman. Practices carry valencies that may stimulate insight and moral connectedness – or the reverse. Insight and ethical stances are conveyed as much through the uses of everyday meanings as they are through deliberate discussion. Loneliness, for example, may be connected not only with the lack of a fulfilling partnership or not seeing enough people, but also with being cut off from a symbolic environment that speaks back to individuals of the setting they would wish to inhabit. The lack of the appropriate symbolic setting can inhibit people from operating the kind of moral, interpersonal language and behaviour they would need in order to convey insights acquired through the passage of a lifecourse.

Time and narrative

Given the centrality of time and change to understanding social processes, it is remarkable that social-scientific theories and methods remain relatively atemporal in character, treating time on the whole unsystematically (Rau and Edmondson, 2013), even though societies and cultures change continually, if erratically, over time. Interactions between changing sociocultural settings and individual changes in the process of ageing can be central to intergenerational tensions; the chronologisation of age that has itself caused so much social change in the 20th century (Cole, 1992; Katz, 2009; von Kondratowitz, 2009; Bytheway, 2011) will have affected generations in different ways. Baars (2012, ch 1) argues that even if lifecourses today are 'destandardised' and 'individualised' in important senses, this has induced a greater rather than a lesser dominance of chronomatic, clock time, literal measurements of the time that has elapsed since our births. He excoriates a 'causal' account of time, the assumption that being, say, 65, automatically causes one to be a certain sort of person or in a certain sort of position. This is, for Baars, associated with the accentuation during the 20th century of gerontological and social negativity about older people (much of it associated with the various guises of the Kansas City study, source of the 'disengagement thesis') that culminated in society-wide 'gerontophobic shame' (Moody and Sood, 2010). Being older was an embarrassment and 'being' became reinterpreted as 'being busy' (Baars, 2012: 66). The media in particular disseminate cultural narratives about ageing (Baars, 2012: 193ff) that turn on the misuse of temporal concepts in this way.

On the level of interaction, time-sensitivities and time schedules that clash with others', or with tempos that are culturally prestigious, can have special impacts on older people, causing them to be thought of as 'slow' or out of touch. Tim Jackson points to the 'paradox of well-being' that centres on issues of production and consumption vis-à-vis the allocation of time. People work and consume heavily rather than spending time on less resource-intensive activities such as exchanges with family and friends, and apparently do so voluntarily (Jackson 2009; Ryan, 2009). This impacts on older people, not least in that friends and relations may have less time to spend with them, albeit for reasons they themselves may regret. According to Ryan (2009), individuals retain the possibility of choosing what cultural habits to support, even if opting for new approaches to time might mean adopting an entirely 'alternative' life-style. But Goodin et al (2008) point out that levels of temporal autonomy and the distribution of control over 'time' as a resource vary both within and between countries, in ways that reflect distinct welfare and gender regimes: differences in time-use patterns are subject to significant impacts from public and social policies. For Goodin et al, these impacts are so profound that freedom and social (in)equality can be measured directly in terms of differences in access to 'discretionary time'. Studies underline negative impacts of stress and harriedness on mental and physical well-being, arguing for more temporal autonomy and time diversity, as well as the need to 'reclaim' 'quality time' and combat time poverty; this supports the view that high-quality temporal environments are fundamental to human well-being (for example Gei⊠ler et al, 2006; Goodin et al, 2008; Mückenberger, 2011). The perception that older people have privileged access to leisure time (Gilleard and Higgs, 2000) is itself a potential source of intergenerational friction.

Despite all this, even time-use research itself often provides only quantitative 'snapshots' of human behaviour at certain points in time. Bytheway (2011: 28) argues convincingly that research that lacks a longitudinal dimension fundamentally misconceives what human experience involves. But ethnography's own time-consuming nature can have the unintended effect that ethnographic accounts 'preserve in aspic' the versions of social settings they produce (Clifford and Marcus, 2010; contrast Taylor's (1995) conscious avoidance of this phenomenon). Repeat studies are relatively rare. In narrative psychology (White and Epston, 1990; Pearce, 2013), by contrast, it is specifically accepted that meaning must be *expected* to change from day to day, even the meanings people attribute to their own accounts. Respondents are explicitly asked how they feel about what they have said on previous occasions, and how what they feel has developed and changed. In this context, meaning is specifically treated as built up and changing dynamically, not least in interaction between people. Memory itself is understood as at least in part a shared public performance that evolves in real time (Sutton and Windhorst, 2009): not only do individuals prompt each other to reconstruct memories, but their settings, full of places and artefacts encountered on previous occasions or symbolic of previous interactions, themselves embody and (re-)activate memories. It is not assumed that meaning is fixed on the day of the interview, as many social-scientific methods tacitly tend to imply.

In an effort to repair misconceptions based on misconceiving time, Jan Baars proposes an analytical and descriptive approach featuring 'triple temporality', which aims to intertwine chronological measurement, personal experience and the 'narrative articulation' of ageing as living *in time* (Baars, 2012: 4; cf Baars, 2007). For Baars, the radical vulnerability of the human condition is 'interhuman', characterised by 'humane responses' (2012: 201–3) that entail both sensitivity to this vulnerability and the capacity for an Arendtian embrace of 'spontaneity, creativity, and the openness of the future' (2012: 205). He supports Heidegger's position that living in time is an existential engagement (Baars, 2012: 159–60), and, like Nussbaum, he stresses the key role of compassion in understanding human predicaments and their meaning. Baars rightly emphasises Cicero's account of ageing as the culmination of a life well lived, a period in which the older person cares for other people as well as him- or herself. This is not older age interpreted as staying young (2012: 123); Baars wants us to reflect on time in connection with older age as a valuable period of life in itself. Cicero argues that 'Serene leadership' (Baars, 2012: 114) might be attained if one has lived one's life appropriately and made the appropriate kinds and degree of effort, aiming at the 'harmonious culmination of the human life course instead of its decay' (2012: 116). This entails, of course, educating for a whole life rather than for a career (2012: 124). Rightly, Baars stresses that this type of wisdom has not been expected to arrive automatically, but is an aim 'to love and search for' (2012: 125).

For Baars, narrative identity is part of this process of development through life. If we want to know what sort of person someone has been, we tell a story; if we disagree with the implications of that story, we tell another one. Even though, as Charles Taylor emphasises, these stories are embedded in master stories extant long before we were born, this does not mean we are brainwashed into conformity (2012: 176): for Baars, telling, or acting, stories must be a creative process, and one for which we take responsibility. For him it is significant that MacIntyre and Taylor embrace the idea of life as a journey, which has connections with the Bildungsroman and its exploration of characters' progression through successive levels of life (2012: 177–8; cf Cole, 1992). Whether or not they show life as a whole is a different question, taken up in psychology in the notion of autobiographical memory and the narrative self (cf Birren and Schroots, 2006; Baars, 2012: 183). Baars does not take this view; he emphasises the surplus of meaning in stories and lives, which are both inevitably ambiguous, incomplete, in need of revision: the individual 'as such' is ineffable (2012: 185–7). But for him stories show, too, something of the role of the past in shaping the future (2012: 189f). For Baars, to understand this is key to an art of living, together with accepting the fact of finitude. He contends that it is not mortality so much as finitude that is crucial to understanding the human condition, the consciousness that human plans are destined to remain, at best, unfinished.

We can find an illustration of these views in Hugo Hamilton's *Every Single Minute* (2014), which employs the details of two days in Berlin – a brief time – to give an account of the writer Nuala O'Faolain as the person he knew: 'She liked to imagine that every day was the first day of her life' (2014: 8). The book blends small symbolic features – her red canvas shoes, the transparent plastic container she used as a handbag – with O'Faolain's own passion for the details of other people's lives:

> She loved meeting new people, for example the hotel staff. She got into conversation and made friends with them right away, asking them questions, personal questions like do you believe in ghosts? Do you have a boyfriend? What do you think of Lady Gaga? And they always responded truthfully, out of courtesy (2014: 9).

Hamilton and O'Faolain share a passion for the incompleteness of life, for the importance of not being in control (for instance, not understanding how to open an electronic car door (2014: 13)) – and for narrative detail: they argue bitterly about recounting events from the past and whether this reveals or distorts the person one now is. Hamilton is afraid O'Faolain is trapped by dwelling on and in her past; she believes he is trying to deny his.

> She said you can't possibly stop yourself from looking back.
>   I agreed with her. You can't avoid coming across things in your life that are pointing backwards, objects that surface in front of you, while you're not looking, while you're trying to delete things that cannot be deleted. Photographs, for example. Little bits of evidence that turn up where they don't belong in your life any more.
>   What are you talking about?
>   Just when you're trying to move forward, that is.
>   Rubbish. I'm talking about the truth, she said. Not hiding anything ... She could no more stop telling her story than she could stop breathing (2014: 62).

For Hamilton, it is not narration in the literal sense of telling stories but the experience of living within the process of O'Faolain's death that has allowed him to come to terms with other people's deaths, particularly his parents': 'It made me feel as if I was actually taking part in my own life for the first time' (2014: 44). This Baars might term living *in* time, with the vulnerability that is both its precondition and its effect, and the possibility of wisdom it allows. This entails relinquishing the idea of certainty, as Socrates stressed (Baars, 2012: 219), abandoning the aim of controlling reality in the way encouraged by much of modern science (2012: 145). Baars unpacks developments in modernity with their own implication for philosophical anthropology, one that makes this progress in sensibility much harder to achieve. Though 'the modern rational subject sees itself initially as the foundation ... of science, ... as modern science expands, human beings end up being part of the "subject-matter" of science' (2012: 146). Leceulle and Baars (2014) oppose to this pseudo-rationality the suggestion that narrative gerontology should take on a culturally-critical role; for them, this presupposes strengthening moral discourse on self-realisation. While Hamilton and O'Faolain are implicitly arguing about what it means to be a person, they agree in embracing a narrative conception of human beings, exposing and exploring the complexities and contradictions that lie within this position.

This is a debate Baars could only applaud. His association of resistance to time and narrativity with modernity can be contrasted with attitudes to time in the West of Ireland, a place that retains strong traces of traditional behaviour. As has already been explained, trying to convey attitudes *instantly* by the use of language is regarded with scepticism here; it is taken for granted that this takes time. Heard within this context, the reluctance of farmers in the West of Ireland to embark on precipitate change is not necessarily equivalent to conservatism (Edmondson, 2000a). Irish farmers are in fact relatively quick to change their policies or techniques if they consider it reasonable. Their verbal expressions might, in effect as a form of shorthand, refer to the past – 'That's not how things were always done.' But responses like this can be intended to refer to the fruits of experience, rather than offering a literally historical reason for action. Subsistence farmers cannot afford to take unnecessary risks, for they possess few financial bulwarks in case of disaster; in farming, there is only one opportunity a year to grow a particular crop, and if this is botched, illness or even starvation can threaten. But these farmers' concerns in making such references are not always literally to show respect for past traditions, rather to preserve their crops in the *future*. Time is not treated casually in such agricultural settings, as is sometimes assumed; it is a scarce resource, often pressured because every opportunity must be taken to respond to what the weather ('aimsir', or 'the times' in Irish) allows. This was acknowledged by one lady in her nineties visited by this author in a nursing home: her valedictory remark was, 'Thank you for your time.'

Rather than taking for granted that everyone has plenty of time, she was well aware that time is not to be ignored.

Conveying narratives itself takes time, as Ricoeur points out, as well as combining different dimensions of narrative time itself. For Ricoeur, 'the ordinary representation of time' as 'that "in" which events take place', or '"within-time-ness"', is already different from chronological, linear time (1980: 170). Then there is 'historicality', placing 'weight on the past', and finally, 'temporality';

> My third working hypothesis concerns the role of narrativity. The narrative structure that I have chosen as the most relevant for an investigation of the temporal implications of narrativity is that of the 'plot.' By plot I mean the intelligible whole that governs a succession of events in any story. This provisory definition immediately shows the plot's connecting function between an event or events and the story. A story is made out of events to the extent that the plot makes events into a story. The plot, therefore, places us at the crossing point of temporality and narrativity: to be historical, an event must be more than a singular occurrence, a unique happening. It receives its definition from its contribution to the development of a plot (1980: 171).

For Ricoeur this contrasts with 'linear time, defined by a succession of instants' (1980: 171): mere instants succeeding each other are quite different from systems of significance. These, in their turn, are not merely imposed on events but stem from the fact that we are deposited among them (Ricoeur is referring to Heidegger here) in ways that matter to us. Being in time is thus already radically different from merely measuring it (Ricoeur, 1980: 173). Diurnality is fundamental to human beings (see also Woerner, 2000), 'But a day is not an abstract measure; it is a magnitude which corresponds to our concern and to the world into which we are thrown' (1980: 173). Stories deal with this experience of being within time, but they add a strong directedness that must lead to an 'acceptable' conclusion (1980: 174). This develops within time that is very public, since it must evolve in a way whose directionality can be perceived by the audience: 'To tell and to follow a story is already to reflect upon events in order to encompass them in successive wholes' (1980: 178). The sense of an accepted ending is imposed upon mere succession (1980: 179), and for Ricoeur this ending imposes its own unity on the events that precede it.

For Richardson (1990), the 'narrative turn' has brought great advantages to social-scientific enquiry:

> Narrative displays the goals and intentions of human actors; it makes individuals, cultures, societies, and historical epochs comprehensible as wholes; it humanizes time, and it allows us to contemplate the effects of our actions, and to alter the directions of our lives. Narrative is everywhere ... (1990: 117).

This is not intended to imply that narratives can be recognised everywhere as looking identical to each other; de Medeiros (2014) shows that different genres not only shape narratives differently, but do so with contrasting potentials for insight. This can be key for their impacts on others as well as on themselves: McAdams places the construction of life-narratives at the centre of individuals' personal identities, including their moral and political commitment, and links particular types of life-story to the capacity for generativity (see e.g. McAdams, 2006). Here Andrews (2014) contributes a much-needed focus on the interactions between age and imagination in narrative. And while Ricoeur takes the view that meaning is conveyed primarily through narrative, this is not to assert that the social world is composed entirely of *completed* narratives. In Buddhism, the view is often taken that we should resist over-hastily attributing narratives to our own or others' lives, for this can become an attempt to impose unjustified forms of control on the complexity of events. An excellent portrait, for example those by Rembrandt, may rather seem to ask the question what has life made of a person, what he or she is like, or in what predicament to be found: it provokes questions about a narrative rather than insisting on one.

The question what narratives may be taken to convey is discussed exhaustively in the philosophy of art, especially in the context of 'cognitivist' theories asserting that we gain knowledge from art and literature, perhaps even in a way that is unique to works of art. Nussbaum (1990: 235) quotes Booth's claim that the stories great writers tell enable readers to live 'a richer and fuller life than they could manage on their own'. Thus Berys Gaut (1999) gives examples of learning morally from art. In *The Crying Game*, for example, we are invited to identify with a certain character, who undergoes moral development in the course of the film; our identification brings us with him, so to speak, so that we learn too, in this case to broaden our conceptions of sexuality and love. In *Letter from an Unknown Woman* we may identify with a character who seems at first beguiling but who makes a series of egregious moral errors, behaving much more manipulatively than she wishes to imagine; in the process of following this development we can come to be able to criticise ourselves for making similar mistakes. It is clear that narrative is needed for the learning Gaut describes to take place. The identification must be first established and then extended; we need to see what the character does and then to find out enough about her actions to perceive their lack of perspicuity, so that we can react appropriately to the judgements we make about the conduct involved.

Eileen John (2000: 426) argues that 'the experiential knowledge of sympathy' she gains from reading Woolf's *To The Lighthouse* 'contributes' to her 'learning something general about the concept of sympathy'. This sort of learning is not just learning about something, but learning to do or be something – perhaps to become more morally sensitive. 'Sympathy', say, is a complex body of practices implying acting according to different judgements and with different feelings in contrasting sorts of case. Learning about it involves learning more of the unspoken conventions by which it is applied, and how these differ in different cultures and predicaments: learning to do them, not just in some abstract sense to know about them. But this form of learning can take place when we look back at the narratives of our own lives, too. William Randall stresses that

> 'our lives' are experienced and understood by us not as strings of raw events but as stories; as vast, open-ended texts; as flesh-and-blood *novels* that are unfolding over time, continually thickening with potential for meaning

and to be examined as such with proper hermeneutic attention (2011: 22).

This is not intended to mean that lives are narratives 'about' forms of reality somehow separate from themselves. Gubrium and Holstein (1999, 2009) make clear that social narratives are not just about life and action, they *are* life and action – challenging though it may be to convey this textually. Nor should the role played by words in narrative be exaggerated or distorted: 'Narratives reduced to transcripts are flat, without practical depth or detail': they need to take account of 'the setting's discursive conventions' and the resources it offers, not least about 'what is *not* uttered or storied as opposed to what is communicated' as the process unfolds (2009: viii; my italics). On the one hand, participants' 'varied horizons of meaning' (2009: 72) warn us not to take settings as homogenous, for they bring to them different strategies and projects. On the other, these projects need to function as intelligible within their social settings – just as organisations, for example, bestow sets of meaning or 'gestalts' (2009: 192ff) that participants must habitually use to make sense of developments within them to themselves and to each other. Narratives involve practices that are counted as at least adequately intelligible, at least within their immediate settings, and practices convey narratives; these are closely interlinked forms of sociality.

Meaning, insight and practice

The operation of sociality is of explicit significance for gerontology, where the shared nature of what happens between people has been a key feature from the start.

> The general principle of 'linked lives' is an explicit part of life-course frameworks (e.g., Elder and Johnson, 2003; Settersten, 2003 …). This principle simply states that the course of an individual's life is intimately shaped by the needs, circumstances, and choices of others. Despite the recognition that individual lives simply cannot be understood in isolation from others, the irony is that we analyse lives as if they are somehow purely individual. Yet most of the things people struggle with, hope and plan for, and feel pain around are tied to relations with others (Dannefer and Settersten, 2010: 14).

Elder, who mentions specifically that he was influenced by the Chicago School (1974/ 99: 114ff), was particularly concerned to trace interactions and influences between individuals, as well as between them and the changing features of their social settings. Previously, the ethnographers Arensberg and Kimball, working in Ireland in the 1930s and pioneers in exploring the roles of older people in their families and economies, had been trained in America by their supervisor Lloyd Warner to perceive the 'basic unit of analysis' as 'the relation rather than the individual' (Kimball, 1979: 793).

This mode of perception was particularly congenial to their work because semi-traditional Ireland was a highly relational society (Edmondson, 1998, 2003); the two sociologists were interested in sociality in a society that valued it. Many features of the style used by Arensberg and Kimball to depict sociality have remained current;

145

they are not dissimilar to the approach used by, say, Mumford and Power, writing about the East End of London in 2003. Arensberg and Kimball preface their account of County Clare communities in the 1930s (1940/2001: 4–30) with statistical information on the chief products of the county, also describing individual encounters; but the details they describe are specifically related to 'the organization of habit' (1940/2001: 263) – for example, how 'the woman of the house' would come down first in the morning to light the fire (pp 35ff.). Taking relationality seriously means reading such instances multivalently. These authors draw inferences about the woman's position as composed of a complex blend of serving the household and commanding it. She *must* light the fire, which is a chore; nonetheless, she is the one *in charge* of lighting the fire – which is symbolically and practically at the heart of the household's activities through the day. In other words, they refer to what are now termed practices, and treated as increasingly significant in the attempt to explore sociality itself. This meaning cannot be shown merely by displaying what the practice looks like, even when it is made clear that it is heavily temporally loaded: it is a practice that happens, and can be relied upon to happen, on a regular basis, *and has implications for other practices, values and feelings too.* Readers must be induced to make the hermeneutic effort of understanding practices like this one as socially embedded and constituted, *imagining* the layers of complexity involved over and above the information supplied by the authors.

'Practices' attempt to take proper account of 'the routine accomplishment of what people take to be "normal" ways of life' (Shove, 2004: 117), recognising the dimension of time in that they deal with on-going, recurring forms of behaviour, and at the same time acknowledging the dependence of that behaviour on shared expectations and interpretations. Schatzki (1996: 89) terms a practice 'a temporally unfolding and spatially dispersed nexus of sayings and doings', one equipped with sets of rules, taken-for-granted understandings and affective structures. In place of the concept of rule, which has fixed and game-like connotations not always appropriate to social action, the term 'topos' (Edmondson, 2012) may often be more useful. Topoi are taken-for-granted inferential supports in a social setting among which individuals *choose* in order to accomplish intelligible behaviour. As Burkitt (2002) points out, the works of classical philosophers such as Aristotle are crucially productive in considering what practices are. The term as used in social science is not precisely the use of 'practice' employed by philosophers such as MacIntyre, who includes in-built criteria of excellence to the concept (see, for example, Breen, 2012); for him, practices are about doing things *well*. Sociological usages are more preoccupied with conceptualising sociality, treating what people do as a matter of course less as expressing an attitude than as *constituting* one.

As it does in the work of Bourdieu (1980/1990: 62), stress on this concept represents an attempt at a genuinely social form of analysis, in contrast to methods whose implications are more fundamentally atomistic.

> In contrast to conventional, individualistic and rationalist approaches to behaviour change, social practice theory de-centres individuals from analyses, and turns attention instead towards the social and collective organization of practices – broad cultural entities that shape individuals' perceptions, interpretations and actions within the world (Hargreaves, 2011: 79).

Thus Alan Warde uses 'practices' to distance us from the assumption that society is primarily made up of individuals taking choices and expressing emotions. He points out that 'It is the fact of engagement in the practice, rather than any personal decision about a course of conduct' that explains much behaviour (Warde, 2005: 138). People *find themselves* behaving like bikers or like bankers, rather than deciding overtly to do so. This is not a version of everyday life that describes the brainwashing of 'cultural dopes'; Warde's account of practices allows for change, both from the inside – as practitioners contest and resist routines and conventions, and as they improvise new doings and sayings in new situations – and also from the outside, as different practices come into contact or conflict with each other. Similarly, the version by Shove and Pantzar (2005) sees practices as congeries of images (meanings, symbols), skills (forms of competence, procedures) and materials, together with forms of manipulating materials such as technology, dynamically integrated by practitioners through reiterated performance. Practices, of course, are not essentially permanent features of social landscapes; they come into being, alter their forms or disappear in the course of processes of social change.

Practices are key methodological instruments in gerontology because they assist in conceptualising the sociality connected with ageing, not least in tracing relationships between spoken and unspoken aspects of meaning (cf Turner, 1994). Some practices, or aspects of practices, can relatively easily be made verbal and if necessary challenged, when they use similar ideas and conceptual structures to others that are overtly employed in everyday life in their settings. Hitchings (2012) contests the claim that people can never talk about their practices and that they necessarily exist at an unconscious level. The office workers he worked with came to enjoy talking about routines such as dress on which they had formerly not reflected; also, he interviewed older people who were well able to discuss practices associated with keeping warm in winter, even though they worried that these habits might be perceived as 'fuddy-duddy' by others (2012: 64). Practices such as using rugs to keep warm instead of turning up the heating can be developed consciously, and for intelligible reasons that can be verbalised and debated. Hitchings (2012: 65) therefore challenges the idea that people should standardly be seen as the mere 'carriers' of practices depicted by Reckwitz (2002: 250), reproducing sequences of mundane actions quite unreflectingly. To see people as simply 'carrying' practices is extreme, as the notion of the topos shows: palpably, they often choose between them for comprehensible reasons.

But many of the practices that confer intelligibility on behaviour do subsist at a deeper level, for example meta-patterns of reasoning like those mentioned here in relation to the West of Ireland, or many of the 'gestalts' analysed by Gubrium and Holstein (2009). These are often not amenable to overt debate even if practitioners did become conscious of them. On the one hand, to debate them would spoil their social spontaneity and genuineness, and in doing so undermine their validity as practices making routine social life possible. On the other hand, meta-habits that shape thought and interaction are genuinely hard to verbalise – even though they often embody significant social and political attitudes. Not all are easily amenable to conscious examination, and many people are highly resistant to reflecting on them too. Sometimes it might be excessively cumbersome, obstructing the performance of the practice; as in some of the everyday habits involved in diagnostic processes. Medical practitioners might try whether a patient will see things differently when less exhausted, for example, enacting a series of attempts to restructure circumstances for the patient without explicitly considering it (Edmondson and Pearce, 2007).

Practices often are used unreflectingly, therefore, and we follow so many practices in our everyday lives that it would be impossible to verbalise them all. People follow practices when preparing meals, for instance routinely putting parsley on the potatoes or lighting candles on the table; these practices may convey and reinforce symbolic values about which practitioners may never have thought outright – like the use of the silver-plated teapot referred to earlier in this chapter. The complaints box in a nursing home in Bavaria regularly visited by this author contained references to meals and food more often than anything else, but the writers found it impossible to verbalise exactly why they found offences against their preferred practices so distressing. But food-related practices have eloquent communicative value, acting as signals about much other behaviour that is or is not appreciated in the setting in question, and in doing so bringing with them cascades of further commitments. Wearing a tie or lighting a candle are not trivial as social gestures, just because they bring in their train entire sets of attitudes and behaviour that communicate much of a worldview concerning how life should be lived. They bring with them a penumbra of meta-habits; the character of its penumbra may be the main reason for supporting the habit, but this may be hard to make explicit.

Institutions themselves support specific cultural practices, and practices to which values can be attached. Peter Blau expressed this by attributing to them 'emergent' properties that are not solely properties of individuals. In Blau's observation of tax offices (1956), individuals working in competitive teams tended to behave competitively, but the same people, shifted to cooperative teams, behaved much more cooperatively. This illustrates Warde's (2005) contention that following a practice need not depend on consciously taking specific decisions, as much as on fitting into a way of doing things. Green (2013: 196–7), trying to unravel the concept of an 'unnoticing environment' in Winterbourne View hospital, points to practices making it less likely that negative aspects of patients' treatment will be noticed and commented upon. These include compelling families to visit their adult children only in 'designated visitor areas' and not encouraging them even to see the wards where their children live. This makes it more likely that residents' personal needs will go unnoticed, not because the staff in the hospital in fact all maintain similar beliefs and values, which observation would suggest that they often do not, but because it is made practically and discursively most viable for them to confine their behaviour within certain parameters. This may in turn, over time, support changes in belief, in negative or positive directions. In the case of a different organisation, Hargreaves (2011) tracks the progress of basic environmental practices introduced into an office – partly because these practices are expected to lead to others that may be more elusive, such as becoming more conscious of environmental issues.

The search for interlocking patterns of behaviour goes back to the interests of W.I. Thomas in the early years of the 20th century (Elder, 1974/99: 7): how do people respond, as time goes on, to changing events in the social structures in which they find themselves – and how do we notice the occurrence of these changes? Elder points to what might be now termed the disruption of practices as a prompt to observing changes from older to newer patterns of behaviour:

> Crisis situations are a fruitful point at which to study change since they challenge customary interpretations of reality and undermine established routines. The disruption of habitual ways of life produce[s] new stimuli which elicit attention and arouse consciousness of self and others. Control over events becomes problematic when old ways are found lacking as means for dealing with social demands and satisfying basic needs or standards. Situations enter the crisis stage when they are interpreted or defined as such by a group or individual, and thus constitute a problem which calls for novel solutions and lines of adaptation.

The early Chicago School and other community sociologists tried to avoid treating societies as static, seeking techniques for achieving this even in the absence of repeat or longitudinal studies. Elder's suggestion here in some ways parallels the sensitivity to 'xenisms' described above: he seeks anomalies or disruptions so as to infer what 'habitual ways of life' have been disrupted.

Green's (2013) work on 'unnoticing' environments points to the role practices can play in bringing about worse rather than better outcomes for intergenerational care in institutions, and their capacity to generate further practices that can cause a negative spiral, spawning further unsupportive behaviour and attitudes. Practices can be supportive or destructive, conducing to cooperative conduct or undermining it. Thus it is reasonable to suppose that some practices can be termed insightful, wise or instructive, even independently of the intentions of individuals involved. Moral theorists such as Aristotle or Adam Smith specifically emphasise the significance of both habituation and sociality to the human capacity for ethical behaviour. They do not see moral conduct as normally based on once-off decisions, or even as primarily intelligible in terms of specific decisions, but as associated with dispositions to act in certain ways (see Sherman, 1989). These dispositions are schooled by everyday habits and practices: regarding other people as beings with claims to honourable treatment, or supporting cooperation and honesty rather than their opposites. Such habits and practices evolve over time in social life. For Aristotle, not even the practice of independence and autonomy can be reached alone, for to achieve them one must live in a society that supports these values and renders them intelligible and possible (O'Rourke, 2012). This in principle supports the theoretical claim that wise or ethical institutions not only can but need to exist. Religious movements or universities, say, are founded with the intention of putting in place practices supporting wisdom and insight, even when participants do not think directly about these issues. Social rituals such as funeral practices or festivities may also function to this end in everyday life.

Wise lifecourse-related practices might be exemplified in rituals accompanying going to school for the first time in Germany (in Ireland or the UK, this takes place much earlier, at four or five, and is not attended by the same celebrations). When German children start school at about six years of age, each child is given a Schultüte, a colourful paper or cloth cone, brightly decorated with ribbons and stickers, full of sweets and other small presents and treats, and enormous in size: nearly as long as the child him- or herself. This long-standing practice dates from the early 19th century; it may be associated with celebrations in local churches or communities to mark the fact that children are beginning their school lives. Children are given gaudy satchels to take to school, and the entire event is presented as both fun and important – associating education, at least at the beginning, with enjoyment – and also, perhaps, with 'openness to experience'. 'Openness to experience', particularly strongly associated with wisdom by Staudinger et al (1998; see next chapter), is formally enjoined by the practice of 'Wanderschaft' among German carpenters. For three years, except in emergencies apprentices are not permitted to come closer to home than 50 kilometres, in order to absorb new ways of understanding and practising their craft.

Irish funeral customs, already described in part above, may also exemplify wise practices. When someone dies in the West of Ireland, all friends and acquaintances know at once what is to be done: the practice is a public one. It is important to attend the 'removal' if one cannot attend the funeral mass, for example because of work commitments. Here, people form a queue, often containing hundreds of people, outside the private house or funeral parlour where the deceased person is lying in an open coffin. If the ceremony is held in a private house, there will be food for the visitors to eat, usually brought by neighbours, which saves the deceased's family from having to prepare food themselves and itself expresses solidarity. Family members stand aligned round the coffin, so that sympathisers can shake their hands and make suitable brief remarks; they may touch the dead person's hands briefly, or even their face. After this it is considered appropriate to wait, chatting to people one knows, until the coffin is closed, followed by prayers from the officiating priest. When it has been brought to the church, the coffin will be laid on trestles for the night, with more, relatively brief prayers. It is hard to over-estimate the comfort to a family that practices such as this provide, partly because they *are* practices. They are familiar, they remove from relations the burden of making decisions about what is appropriate or otherwise: people know what to do, and the public nature of the event itself conveys significance on it. It is important, simply, that the person in question has lived and died. This practice is independent of decision, choice and intention: it marks the significance of a human life, and the person's life in the community, irrespective of what anyone happens to think. Grandeur and routine are blended in following a practice that is bigger than any individual's particular views or feelings.

It is possible to misinterpret practices, to misattribute to them expectations from other settings, especially when they contain tacit inferential forms unfamiliar to outsiders and possibly surprising to them. In semi-traditional Ireland, 'meitheal' was the set of practices by which farmers helped each other in operations that demanded many hands, for example getting in the harvest or bringing turf back from the bog. From the vantage-point of a more urbanised setting, this may be sentimentally recalled as the free and generous offer of mutual aid between country people; in reality, this could not be quite the case (Edmondson, 1998). Certainly it seems to have been possible to draw on a topos such as 'It is good to expect help from your neighbours,' but expectations about how much help could be expected from whom were not infinite. This might not have been verbalised in detail by people who gradually built up familiarity with what they could take for granted in their own localities; not all cases of entitlement or obligation to help could have been anticipated in advance, and in any case to specify them in a quasi-legal manner would have negated the feelings accompanying the practice and helping to make it supportive (Edmondson, 2000b). But it seemed reasonable to expect help in recognised enterprises, such as farming, which are of public concern, especially if your need is not your fault, for instance if it intrinsically requires several people for its execution or if you are a woman or orphan and cannot do all the heavy work of a farm. The entitlement to help would not operate if, for instance, you merely decided to paint your bathroom a different colour.

Appreciating this particular practice depended on encountering the xenisms that showed this author how it could be interpreted. For example, when she tarred not only her own drive but part of the common road, her neighbour expressed genuine surprise rather than pleasure: 'It wasn't your duty.' It seemed from this remark that the neighbour expected help (particularly help that was expensive or otherwise demanding) to be regulated by custom, rather than approving of it as a spontaneous gesture. More experience in the district showed the importance of this expectation, for example in providing food at 'stations' or celebrations of house masses. If one householder provides unusually elaborate hospitality, this puts cumbersome and stressful expectations on the next one. It is nonetheless hard entirely to avoid puzzlement about who can expect how much from whom. Friends of the author seemed disconcerted by elderly neighbours who habitually walked into their house, expecting to be driven to the shop or pub; were they or were they not entitled to expect that car-owners would drop all other activities to do them this service? The importance of tacit reflection on borderline cases became clear only much later. One neighbour had rendered another a service, but a couple of years afterwards he expected return assistance that appeared out of all proportion to the original good deed. 'Meitheal' in such instances might operate to indicate not only what could be asked of others, but also how much they could reasonably ask in return. Its practical uses included not only coordinating practices among subsistence farmers who could seldom afford to hire regular help, but also indicating the amount of assistance neighbours could be expected to give each other so that they did not fall into unsustainable aid debt. Mutual help was often very considerable by modern standards but could not be indefinite.

The question how much to give can be acute, given the burdens of subsistence farming in a harsh landscape, which entails considerable pressure of time and resources. Meitheal could not be an entirely sentimental arrangement; it does not show the bottomless, even extravagant (flaithulach) generosity sometimes attributed to it by people who associate the idea of helpfulness with practices imagined from other settings inappropriate to this one. This is not to deny that in societies featuring meitheal, generosity and cooperation were valued, nor to deny the wisdom with which this system regulated both support and obligations to support. But this case illustrates the importance of not transferring webs of expectation wholesale from one context to another.

Webs of expectation can add up to formal or informal institutions, which can have wise or unwise effects without compelling all their practitioners to become personally wise. Thus Marilyn Strathern (2000) supports organisations such as Cambridge colleges that, in her view, institutionalise practices augmenting trust and good judgement – features with significance for participants' conceptions of their lifecourses – rather than forms of depersonalised control that undermine them. Elinor Ostrom's (1991) work on local systems of resource management shows that practices all over the world, passed down by local people in local traditions, are preserving resources more sustainably than centralised systems may do. Sometimes even these practices may become considered irksome or unnecessary and happily abandoned; other habits may seem to observers to be of little importance, but possess implications for practitioners that are not at first apparent. An older lady, reluctant to move house to join her son abroad, said, 'The butchers there don't even cut the meat properly!' For her, such practices seemed to be associated with conceptions about doing things thoroughly and behaving dependably that were associated with what she expected from human beings as such. They were important to her not just because they belonged in a setting she was used to, but for the ethical attitudes she felt they conveyed.

FOUR

Languages for life-course meanings

Life-course meaning: insight and wisdom

Through most of recorded history, insights gathered in the course of a human life, or over the history of a people or society, have been associated with the idea of wisdom. This term has been interpreted in ways that vary along key dimensions, such as the capacity for judgement associated with wisdom, or the question of what sort of person can be expected to be wise. In work associated with ageing, commentators over the centuries have associated wisdom with a capacity for tolerance, for accepting uncertainty and for contributing to the common good. Ancient writers such as Aristotle or Cicero approach the concept with realism, pointing out that developing wisdom demands both hard, continuous effort and a degree of material well-being and good fortune. Nonetheless they treat wisdom as, in principle, not impossible to achieve. This chapter explores interpretations of 'wisdom' relevant to the lives of older people today; not in the spirit of imposing blanket expectations, against which Haim Hazan (2009) rightly warns, but in the search for language that works in opposition to the denigration of older people that makes it impossible even to perceive their capacities and potential.

Any reading of a newspaper will produce a range of uses of the terms 'wise' or 'unwise', not least in obituaries but also in connection with any difficult field, from child-rearing to wealth distribution or foreign policy. These daily usages have been relatively unsupported in the academic world, even though, in reflection on insight and meaning in work relevant to gerontology, ideas associated with wisdom arise more often. Frankl uses the term 'wisdom' in connection with love as the goal of life (1964: 36). Erikson describes a possible final life-stage as one of wisdom (for example, 1986: 37, 72). Moody urges older people to embark on 'a path toward greater wisdom' (2003: 139); MacKinlay (2005) refers to a search for enhanced wisdom as an aim for later life. The US 'sage-ing' movement is associated with arguments by Rabbi Zalman Schachter-Shalomi (1995) about the special role of wise older people in interpersonal life and in dealing with problems concerned with how to live in society. Particularly in 'positive psychology', which aims to explore and support constructive human capacities rather than concentrating on pathological ones, beneficial aspects of ageing began to be explored strongly in the closing decades of the 20th century. Robert Sternberg in the US or Paul Baltes in Berlin argued that ageing should not be understood primarily in terms of decline, and that among the abilities preserved into older age, or even enhanced in it, could be found the capacity for wisdom and wisdom-related knowledge.

Contemporary views on wisdom in the field of psychology build on ideas developed in societies in the past (Holliday and Chandler, 1986), where, despite variations in conceptualising wisdom or estimating the likelihood of achieving it, the *aim* of enhancing wisdom during one's lifecourse was assumed to be intelligible and significant. Holliday and Chandler criticise 20th-century theories of human development as excessively child and youth centred, abandoning concern for the latter two-thirds of a life span. (Despite his attention to later-life wisdom, even Erik Erikson's (1986) developmental account of the human lifecourse locates the first six stages in approximately the first two decades.) Holliday and Chandler (1986: 12–13) argue that the proverbs and folk tales of surviving wisdom literatures show that at many stages in the past, people of wisdom – often older people, or people with special kinds of life experience – have been thought to offer significant resources to those around them. It was not expected that older people would automatically become wiser (Edmondson, 2005); past debates on wisdom are seldom merely naïve or simplistic. Rather, the idea of wisdom was seen as offering a goal for developing and changing during the lifecourse that was independent of direct involvement in types of work that depended on physical fitness. As a resource for enhancing their status, it might supply a potential protective feature for people in later life – either singly or as a group. Material dating from as early as the third millennium BC shows that older people could, in principle, be expected to have something to contribute to society even if no longer physically strong.

There is no succinct, broadly accepted definition of wisdom as such (Jeste et al, 2010); the term is always deeply embedded in its cultural context, and its meaning cannot be assumed to be identical in all its uses (cf Rorty, 2004). But contemporary debates continue to overlap with ancient ones and consciously draw from them (Birren and Svensson, 2005). Margaret and Paul Baltes begin their account of 'successful' ageing (1993: 2) by rehearsing Cicero's arguments in *De Senectute* for the view that ageing can offer an opportunity for positive growth and change. They support Cicero's view that, while older age may be accompanied by illness and decline, it is an intrinsically variable life period and should not be seen only in terms of vulnerability and pain. Potentially, older age is a significant phase of life, to be valued in its own right. For Baars (2012: 114), a key addendum to this account is that Cicero adjured us to love and care *for others* in our older age as well as for ourselves. However, for Cicero in *De Oratore*, wisdom was a demanding achievement, based on knowledge encompassing almost everything concerning human affairs as well as the practical skills needed for effective communication. For millennia even before he wrote, older age had been considered a time that at least in principle offered the possibility of accumulating insights and growing wiser; not everyone achieves distinction in these respects, and there was considerable debate about whether it is acquired (if at all) only through experience, or can be taught as well. This debate remains current today. Among others, Staudinger and Baltes (1996) mention the influence of mentors in enhancing wisdom; Jordan (2005: 181) rightly points out that some social practices, not least those associated with the isolation of older people, may actually limit it.

An attempt to communicate how to become (more) wise over time was made explicitly in 'The Wisdom of Ptah-Hotep', as early as 2,500 years before Christ; the term 'hotep' indicates a type of peace and balance reached at the end of the day (Jacq, 2006/2004: xi–xii). This text sees wisdom not as innate but to be learned; it can be passed down, or at least stimulated, through written communication. The text offers practical advice at court, but also exhorts to humility, schooling one's own temperament. This is a complex work that combines advice on the art of good listening – what would now be called 'active' listening – with strikingly critical reflections on the social distribution of wisdom. The very first maxim dictates that anyone aspiring to wisdom should remain modest, taking counsel 'with the ignorant as well as with the scholar'. Good discourse is as rare as 'green stone', yet may be found even 'among the maids at the grindstones'. In view of its status and gender implications, this is a remarkable comment.

Though discussion of wisdom from its earliest beginnings recognised the complexity of the topic, it largely envisaged wisdom as something to be aimed at, both by individuals and by societies. Wise societies might be expected to contain and support wise individuals, even though the relationship might not be an easy one. Denning-Bolle (1992) shows that ancient Mesopotamian wisdom could be thought of as mischievous, culturally subversive; the Old Testament reveals that the wisdom of the prophets was far from routinely welcomed in the cultures they criticised. Audiences do not enjoy being recalled to principles from whose practice they have slipped. Similarly, wisdom has perennially been associated with concepts of the common good (Stange and Kunzmann, 2008), a feature retained but not explicated in detail by contemporary authors such as Sternberg (1998) or Baltes and Staudinger (2000). This means that, far from being essentially anodyne, the concept has a connection with political debates about what the common good demands, divisive as these disputes often are. Individuals regarded as wise, or who have commended particular policies as wise, have repeatedly encountered vicissitudes or ill-treatment, often the fate of those who seek to hold the powerful to their avowed ideals. But in principle, wisdom as a life goal has been accepted as a defence against assuming that older age contains nothing of value and can safely be despised. Hans Küng (2006) argues that this view is still valid today, indeed that wisdom is not just a personal achievement but sums up what an entire society can aim at: 'The cumulative wisdom of the elders refers to the art of living embodied in the thoughts and actions of a given society's exemplars.'

Wisdom in its different guises has repeatedly, though not invariably, been associated with tolerance and a broad concern for justice (Baltes and Staudinger, 2000; Edmondson, 2005; Jeste et al, 2010). This too has political implications, not least in casting doubt on rigid hierarchies and dogmatic prescriptiveness. As far as the ancient Middle Eastern world is concerned, the biblical commentator Joyce Hertzler is not alone in commenting on the 'socialistic' contributions of the Old Testament, which inveigh against the injustice of the mighty (1936: 279) and take the part of oppressed people. Translations of the Old Testament demanding that 'rulers of the world' should behave justly have a misleading impact on modern ears. They may sound to us like plaintive reproaches against those in power; in context, the terms 'rulers' or 'kings' refer not only to political rulers but to *everyone* (Clarke, 1973). All human beings are to be considered 'rulers of the world' in the sense intended here and have an obligation to justice and compassion.

Kathleen Woodward (2003) sees wisdom, at least as it sometimes appears in contemporary discourse, as involving quietism, passivity and acquiescence to the status quo; hence she objects to the idea that older people – in particular, older women – should be expected to be wise. Contested ideals are often co-opted into dominant practices, and there have undoubtedly been ideological usages in which wisdom was presented in this way – for example, to 19th-century servants, adjured to accept their lot in 'wise' recognition of social hierarchy. But this does not represent the historical scope of the word, which has been employed exceedingly variously in the course of its evolution (Curnow, 2010, 2015). Wisdom in the ancient world might embrace a study of 'the whole order of things', wisdom as the ability to heal, wisdom as a Pythagorean way of communal life, or wisdom as the attainment of divine insight or even divine status (Curnow, 1999: 25–9).

Accounts of wisdom in the past were in many ways more complex, detailed and questioning than those readily available to us now. They were connected with debate about the human condition and the subtleties of communication, or about individuals' capacities to control their fates; they also explored the nature of participating in wise processes of deliberation, the dispositional habits of wise people and the tenets connected with leading wise ways of life. Deliberation is rarely dissected in 21st-century accounts of wisdom, partly owing to misconceptions about what reasoning about human affairs involves (Edmondson and Hülser, 2012). Contemporary academic research emanates from disciplines with separate sets of conventions about what reasoning is and how it should be carried out, many of which are marked by a sharp distinction between supposedly rational cognition and all other forms of mental activity. Thomas Dixon (2003) argues that this ultimately destructive bifurcation results directly from the professionalisation of the disciplines in the 19th century. He sees accounts of human thinking and feeling before that time as far less inimical to one another than they later became. The most extreme version of this separation is the view popular among economists that rationality can be exhaustively represented in terms of quasi-mathematical models, whereas feeling is irrational. If this were true, it would mean that sensible discussions about the important issues of life – from love and friendship to raising children to war and peace – simply could not be held at all. When debating social and political matters is caricatured as an exclusively abstract cognitive process in this way, ideas about reasoning and rational thought become artificially dissociated from ideas about meaning and wisdom, upon which they can no longer gain any purchase. An alternative, and more realistic, philosophical interpretation is to understand emotions as potentially 'suffused with intelligence and discernment' (Nussbaum, 2004: 1), subject to rational criticism as belonging to deliberative transactions. If this were not the case, it would be impossible to ask people for reasons why they were angry, sad, ashamed and so on.

Aristotle's account of practically-wise people and practices unites reasoning with personality, virtue and social interaction in a way that is hospitable to this line of thought. His analysis, in the *Rhetoric*, of what it is to debate about urgent public affairs under conditions of uncertainty can be read as accepting that reasoning itself has emotional, personal and social aspects: these are not irrational adjuncts of reasoning, but part of the process of deliberation (Edmondson et al, 2009). His account of practical wisdom describes the cultivation of a temperament that generates feelings and reactions permitting good judgement, specifically connecting this with the capacity to deliberate well on whatever leads to or disrupts a good life (Aristotle, *Rhetoric* I,9, 1366b 20ff; Aristotle, *Nicomachean Ethics* II,3, 1105b 5ff). Judging wisely includes avoiding inappropriate recklessness or suspicion, remaining hopeful or cautious where apposite, in ways suited to the situation at hand (*Rhetoric* II 14, 1390a 29ff; Woerner, 1990). Someone behaving in a practically wise manner could also avoid the misjudgements to which people are susceptible in the particular time of life he or she had reached, for instance (according to the Athenians of Aristotle's time) impetuosity in youth or, in older age, the bitterness that can emanate from repeated loss or disappointment. There are limits to independence, however; habits of character nurtured within a particular polis can be expected to affect their inhabitants. Under oligarchies, for example, people will have become habituated to arguing in ways that differ from those under aristocracies. In this sense, Aristotle's account is markedly less individualistic than many contemporary versions are. He does not envisage wise people as self-made and entirely self-directed individuals whose lifecourses and concerns can be considered quite independently of those of their societies. His account is also more dynamic: it is concerned with movement towards decisions in changing, fluid circumstances, rather than the attainment of fixed, decisionist ends. In such circumstances, a person of practical wisdom would be able to find the right words and arguments to assist others in the process of deliberation (Rorty, 2011).

For Aristotle, the characteristic mark of human beings consists in their ability to debate on what is rightfully to count as good, just and exemplary and their opposites, and to organise their lives accordingly: to use human reason, logos, for the social and political sharing of values in everyday life (*Politics* I 1253a 14–18). For him, a human community is primarily created by communication about what can justifiably be counted as ethically or practically valid. This implies that what makes us human is precisely our capacity for wisdom (Woerner, 1999). To attain this, not only do we need to cultivate the good habits that derive from our societies: we cannot even be autonomous without the support of a community of people in whose terms autonomy makes sense (O'Rourke, 2012). Aristotle's account of practical reasoning treats it, in turn, as directed towards the workings of the polis. It specifically tries to make constructive sense of public deliberation – in law-courts, parliaments and public celebrations – where we must aim for the best decisions in the circumstances, even though we are obliged to deal in uncertainty: we never have what would ideally be enough information, and the situations concerned change swiftly and constantly. Yet debate in these conditions is not a second-rate form of argumentation, for political discourse is debate about our lives together as humans; in principle, this is the noblest form of debate we could possibly engage in (Aristotle, *Rhetoric* I 1, 1354b 24). Thus Aristotle embraces the humanity of deliberative processes, analysing discourse that is potentially wise as subject to time and judgement, including features that are creative, emotional and social, and at the same time as reasonable and as logical as is appropriate to the case (Woerner, 1998). In this model he explores interactions between the character of the speaker and the needs, reactions and contributions of hearers, as both take the communicative risks needed in a joint search for solutions that are as wise as possible in the conditions at hand (Edmondson, 2012).

Searching for solutions and deliberating about them are activities that are profoundly connected with understanding the point of what is, or ought to be, going on in the dilemma at hand. Schwartz and Sharpe (2010: 7) use the term 'telos' to describe the 'proper aims or goals' of a practice, just as 'the telos of doctoring is to promote health and relieve suffering; the telos of lawyering is to pursue justice'. These are not aims in that they are results that come after an activity or when it is completed; you do not work as a doctor for 30 years and then, at the end, look to see if the promotion of health begins to show as a result. Promoting health is something that gives sense and purpose to what you do as a doctor from the very start. The term 'identity' is often used nowadays to cover much that 'telos' refers to, but this can lead to the misunderstanding that what you do as a doctor is primarily to be understood in terms of your personal biography, rather than in the aims, meanings and values associated with what you are doing.

This is not to say that people are always consistent in these attempts; as Schwarz and Sharpe point out (2010: 7), it takes practical wisdom 'to translate the very general aims of a practice into concrete action'.

> People who are practically wise understand the telos of being a friend or a parent or a doctor and are motivated to pursue this aim (Schwarz and Sharpe, 2010: 7).

For Aristotle, the telos of a lifecourse is 'flourishing as a human being'; not flourishing at a particular activity, such as medicine or music, but as a person. This will probably involve intertwining several sorts of practice, as Schwarz and Sharpe imply.

Answering the question 'What should I do?' almost always depends on the particulars of the situation. Friends, doctors, parents, and teachers all need to perceive what others are thinking and feeling. They need to imagine the consequences of what they do. They need to figure out what's possible and not just what's ideal. Practical wisdom is akin to the kind of skill that a craftsman needs to build a boat or a house, or that a jazz musician needs to improvise. Except that practical wisdom is not a technical or an artistic skill. It is a moral skill – a skill that enables us to discern how to treat people in our everyday social activities (Schwarz and Sharpe, 2010: 8).

They too point out that 'character and practical wisdom must be cultivated by the major institutions in which we practice': we need to ask 'whether our institutions are discouraging the wisdom of practitioners' and if so, what can be done about it (Schwarz and Sharpe, 2010: 8–9).

The rules and incentives that modern institutions rely on in pursuit of efficiency, accountability, profit and good performance can't substitute for practical wisdom. Nor will they encourage it or nurture it. In fact, they often corrode it (2010: 9).

Debate about such problems underlines the confluence not only between ethics and politics (regarded as conjoined in the ancient world and up to at least the 18th century) but also between reason and communication, which are aspects of intelligible behaviour rather than spheres separate from it.

The term 'logos', loosely rendered as reasoned discourse or argument and central to the notion of wisdom in the ancient world, is translated by Cicero in the 1st century BC sometimes as 'oratio' (speech), sometimes as 'ratio' (reason). Like Aristotle's contemporary, Isocrates, Cicero held that it is impossible to separate these. For them, too, wise deliberation is part of the communicative life of a society. Cicero excoriated the 'absurd, harmful and deplorable' split 'between the tongue and the mind' (*De Oratore* 3.61), the view that one group of people should concern themselves with communication and a distinct group with thought. Yet, historically, separation between these activities did grow more entrenched. In 1450, Nicholas of Cusa could still take for granted in *Idiota de Sapientia* that the search for wisdom needed to take account of orators as well as philosophers; but by the 17th century this view had become more difficult to defend. During the 19th and 20th centuries, it came to be a prominent Western view that cogitation should distance itself from committed debate in the everyday world of human decision making. (Exceptions to this rule included 19th-century philosophers such as F.H. Bradley [1876] and Bernard Bosanquet [1899], not to mention Karl Marx.) Insight into human life and discussion about how to live it, in other words, became detached from the world of academic debate, both in subject matter and in terms of linguistic conventions. 'Positive psychology' now represents an attempt to return to some of these debates, which can only be an advantage as far as the study of later life is concerned.

They are debates that require careful dissection, responding to the nuances of disparate versions. Thus the lists of variants set out by Birren and Svensson (2005), or Birren and Fisher (1990), should not be regarded as definitive, but as attempts to offer clues to deeply complicated bodies of thought. The 'Christian' approach to wisdom, for instance, is described in one such list as embodying 'a life lived in pursuit of divine, absolute truth' (Birren and Fisher, 1990: 325); this refers extremely tersely to only one of a rich complex of ideas about wisdom in the Christian tradition, and is itself susceptible to a range of interpretations. It omits, too, the sense in which Christianity turned upside down the influential image of the Stoic sage, who was imagined as so much in command of the faculty of reason as to be invulnerable to the blows of fate. Christ is often referred to as wise, but his death as a crucified criminal rendered him a failure in conventional terms. 'Christian' views of wisdom itself may see it as properly associated only with the divine, or on the contrary may envisage Christian wisdom as peculiarly understanding of human imperfections. Some accounts see Christianity as offering communal, interpersonal accounts of wisdom, treating meaning as something that is developed in interaction with others; while others see Christian wisdom as something to be aspired to by individuals in imitation of Christ, a pursuit giving a more solitary version of meaning to their lives.

Since wisdom is regarded as combining profound types of understanding with the most desirable forms of behaviour, disentangling what it means to audiences in different times and contexts depends on reconstructing their taken-for-granted assumptions about the needs and abilities of human beings and the types of excellence or insight they can, singly or jointly, achieve. Virtues commonly associated with wisdom, such as patience or tolerance, have different meanings in different cultural and discursive settings; they cannot be listed as if they had univocal meanings. Hence the need for hermeneutically sensitive ethnographic approaches to the narratives and practices associated with wisdom in different traditions and circumstances, and for a philosophically informed appreciation of what these differences may mean.

Within the history of debates on wisdom, implicit distinctions recur in patterns that cast some light on the ways in which these basic human needs and abilities are envisaged. The question whether knowledge of human affairs can ever encompass certainty is a case in point; 21st-century social theory increasingly often denies this possibility (see for example Gilleard and Higgs, 2013). For Bauman (2000) or Bauman and Donskis (2013), uncertainty is a feature of the age. Classical wisdom can offer a less pessimistic response to this reflection than 21st-century authors may do. Bauman and Donskis call for a return to ethical discourse based on people's capacity to listen to each other (an appeal Ptah-Hotep would have recognised); classical rhetoric explores means by which this can be achieved. Key distinctions in the history of wisdom recur between more and less perfectionist standards – wisdom for the few with esoteric knowledge, or wisdom as a much commoner understanding of the provisional nature of everyday life. They also contrast wisdom as pure insight reached through the striving of a single individual, and wisdom as related more strongly to social and political interaction. These are summarised in Figure 3.

Bearing in mind these distinctions between wisdom envisaged as an extraordinary perfection and in more attainable versions, or between wisdom as reached in isolation and wisdom reached in some form of connection with others, we can see that, for example, the 'philosophical' account of wisdom offered by Sharon Ryan (2013) falls into quadrant III. She defines a wise person as an individual with wide factual and theoretical knowledge, someone who knows how to live well, is successful at doing so and who has very few unjustified beliefs (Woerner and Edmondson, 2008). This is a relatively perfectionist,

Figure 3: Discriminating among theories of wisdom
(adapted from Edmondson, 2013: 199)

I A (tolerance of lack of perfection) high; B (interpersonal as opposed to exclusively individual wisdom) high	II A high, B low
IV A low, B high – that is, expects perfection, but allows for interpersonal wisdom	III A (tolerance of lack of perfection) low, that is, expects perfection; B (interpersonal as opposed to individual) low, that is, stresses individual wisdom

and relatively individualist, version of what wisdom might be. Its link to 'living well' also has the potential to connect it to the 'art of living' literature mentioned in the previous chapter (Curnow, 2008). Curnow (1999: 13) points out that wisdom traditions are not 'simply' collections of 'wise sayings', but bring together those that have been found fit to develop 'into a pattern for living'. His discussion of the history of wisdom highlights the superior status often attributed to the wise, and, in the end, he embraces 'the wisdom of the sages' as an unapologetically 'elitist' notion (1999: 310). In this view, we can hope to learn from wise people, but it is not advisable to hope to acquire much wisdom ourselves. Equally, Ryan's insistence that wise people be 'successful' at living well seems extremely demanding. If people are imprisoned in concentration camps, like Viktor Frankl, they cannot live well; does this prohibit them from being wise? Connecting wisdom with *success* may seem to place it at an excessive distance from struggle with the human condition, as well as from the humble identification with the human predicament often associated with wise people. Individuals regarded as wise, such as Christ or Gandhi, might surely be reluctant to describe themselves as 'successful' at living well. Rural conceptions of wisdom discussed later in this chapter take the opposite tack, treating wisdom as a phenomenon that arises in and through social interaction, in ways that are social rather than stringent; the notion of 'success' does not function well in this cultural setting.

Psychologists working since the mid-1970s tend to distinguish between using 'explicit' methods of studying wisdom, based on definitions they have stipulated themselves, and 'implicit' ones, based on views of wisdom elicited by administering questions to empirical individuals. Often, these are populations of American undergraduate students (Jordan, 2005). The latter approach generally needs to assume that present-day speakers have verbal competencies sufficient to allow them to communicate effectively in respect of complex positions; it cannot fully engage with the fact that debates on ethics or wisdom, not to mention debates on ageing (Cole, 1992), are severely depleted in contemporary times. Gabriel Marcel, for example, points in *The Decline of Wisdom* (1954) to major obstacles to the contemporary practice and understanding of wisdom, associating these hindrances largely with what he considers the overwhelming technical rationality and materialism of the modern world.

Marcel's is a widely shared characterisation that makes it seem dubious to assume that respondents will, by and large, have access to a clear discourse concerning or describing wisdom and be able to access it in a sophisticated and active manner. Not least, such an assumption ignores the impacts of ideology and false consciousness adverted to by Woodward (2003), among others. When we ask members of the public to communicate views connected with wisdom, we are investigating a cultural construct at a particular time and place, with all the advantages and limitations that involves – as, for example, von Hülsen-Esch indicates (see below). She argues that – depictions of Lady Sapientia notwithstanding – wisdom during the Middle Ages became construed as a largely male phenomenon. Had surveys among the public been conducted at that time, they might have warned us not to expect wisdom from females; but that would scarcely justify us in taking such a feature as definitive to research.

It is therefore necessary to contextualise the approach taken by Clayton and Birren (1980) in asking sets of young, middle-aged and older people to judge similarities among a selection of proffered adjectives putatively describing wise people. We can, though, treat this pioneering exercise at least as outlining what a group of late 20th-century respondents in the US might have envisaged wisdom to be. The authors point to a feature of their results that corresponds to historical debates at least in refraining from isolating strict rationality from other features of judgement: their respondents accepted affective, reflective and cognitive elements as aspects of wisdom, a triad later developed in the work of Ardelt (2004, 2011) and attributed by her to other cultures too. Whether or not Clayton's and Birren's respondents knew or could say a great deal in detail about what wisdom might entail or what was meant by the specific terms they associated with it, they agreed in connecting it with understanding and empathy, also with introspection and intuition. Older adults also distinguished between time-dependent cognitive components such as knowledge and experience, and they also saw wisdom as more related to understanding and empathy than to age. That is, older people did not show any tendency to see themselves as wiser – whether or not illustrating the tradition that one does not ascribe wisdom to oneself (Meacham, 1983). For Ardelt, wise people can be identified through particular personal characteristics, not least the capacity to feel deep compassion for others, and we might expect these to guide the meaningful ways they experience their lives.

The point of developing 'implicit' views on wisdom is eventually to make them explicit (Jordan 2005: 167), the direction taken in Robert Sternberg's 'balance' account of wisdom. Sternberg sees wise decision making as bringing into equilibrium intrapersonal, interpersonal and extra-personal interests in any given predicament (1990a). This type of capacity involves both a special variety of practical intelligence and the capacity for moral reasoning. Wisdom, Sternberg argues, is based on 'procedural knowledge', used in 'unusually difficult and complex circumstances'. It is

> the application of tacit knowledge as mediated by values toward the goal of achieving a common good through a balance among multiple intra-personal, inter-personal, and extra-personal interests and in order to achieve a balance among responses to environmental contexts: adaptation to existing environmental contexts, shaping of existing environmental contexts, and selection of new environmental contexts (1998: 353).

He goes on to describe wise people, suggesting that there are specific types of psycho-social disposition conducive to wisdom – though it remains a question how these are acquired. (For Aristotle or Adam Smith, such dispositions can hardly be achieved without participation in the practices characteristic of conducive forms of society.) According to Robert Sternberg,

> The wise person is characterized by a metacognitive stance. Wise people know what they know and what they do not know as well as the limits of what can be known and what cannot be. They apply the processes of intellect in a way that eschews automatization … [T]he wise person seeks truth to the extent it is knowable and evaluates information so as to understand how it relates to truth. Wise people welcome ambiguity, knowing it is an ongoing part of life, and try to understand the obstacles that confront themselves and others in life. They are motivated toward in-depth understanding of phenomena, at the same time that they recognize the limitations of their own understanding. They seek understanding of what will 'work' not only for them but for society as well (Sternberg, 1990b: 157).

For Sternberg, it is characteristic of the actions of such wise people to establish 'balance' with their contexts – where attention to the common good explicitly extends society-wide. This attention to the effects of decisions on their circumstances makes it no accident that his 1998 article ends specifically with a plea to educationalists, placing it within a pedagogic tradition reaching from Isocrates, Aristotle and Cicero onwards. Wisdom, in this view, is not a mere personal predilection but is intended to act effectively on the world. For this reason too, the philosopher Nicholas Maxwell (2007) makes the educational system the focus of his impassioned plea for renewed attention to wisdom.

At the same time, a series of major European studies of wisdom known as the Berlin Wisdom Paradigm evolved under the auspices of Paul Baltes and his colleagues. These studies aim to test empirically the reliability of implicit or explicit cultural-historical (philosophical or religious) theories or beliefs concerning wisdom and wise persons, and explore relevant traits or abilities identifiable in particular individuals. (On the issue of assessing and measuring responses for wisdom, see Ferrari et al, 2013; Glück et al, 2013.) Baltes and Staudinger (2000) see people approaching wisdom as those whose life experience has led them to be 'open-minded and flexible', interested in 'the establishment of social contact and associated empathy', with 'greater tolerance of ambiguity', and 'a greater tendency to refrain from pursuing closure on problems'. It is not so much that each of these capacities is unique, but the way they are 'orchestrated' is crucial. This is held to produce 'an integrative and holistic approach towards life's challenges and problems' (Kunzmann and Baltes, 2005: 111). The notion of orchestration is significant and demands further exploration. Like Sternberg's reference to 'balance' or Aristotle's conception of recognising the right thing to do at the right time, this may refer to titrating the type and degree of empathy (versus, say, realism) appropriate in a situation, estimating the extent to which an interlocutor is capable of change, or predicting reactions to specific forms of behaviour that are likely in a particular social environment. It is no wonder that Cicero underlined the virtually unending nature of the knowledge necessary to wisdom. On the other hand, even though few people may succeed in being consistently wise, the frequency with which the term is used in everyday life suggests that many people approach it at least sometimes.

The capacities identified by the Berlin group are both ethical and interpersonal, and appear also to involve a type of interpersonal imagination, the ability to envisage and understand another person's point of view. In the view of this group, wisdom-related behaviour 'addresses difficult problems regarding the meaning and conduct of life', 'represents truly outstanding knowledge, judgment, and advice', 'is a perfect integration of knowledge and character, mind and virtue', 'coordinates and promotes individual and societal growth', 'involves balance and moderation', 'includes an awareness of the limits of knowledge and uncertainties of the world' and 'is difficult to achieve but easily recognized'. For these researchers, 'lay' conceptions of wisdom entail what they see as cognitive features, such as 'outstanding knowledge about the self and the world', social ones, such as 'the ability to give good advice', emotional ones, such as 'the ability to regulate one's own feelings', and 'motivational' ones, such as 'orientation toward personal growth' (Kunzmann and Baltes, 2005: 113). While the last-named feature seems heavily culturally dependent, the authors contend that these everyday conceptions share with cultural-historical theories at least three assumptions concerning the 'integrative and holistic' nature of wisdom. Not only does it refer to 'outstanding performance', but 'when dealing with fundamental, existential problems related to the meaning and conduct of life, it guides a person's behaviour in ways that simultaneously optimise this person's own potential and that of fellow mortals' (Kunzmann and Baltes, 2005: 116).

Ardelt (2004: 260) has demurred about the term 'expertise' in connection with such an account, its implications that superior forms of *knowledge* are at stake. For her, by contrast, 'wisdom is understood at the experiential level' and 'even the most profound "wisdom literature" remains intellectual or theoretical knowledge until its inherent wisdom is realized by a person'. It is true that some interpretations of the term 'expertise' err in the direction of what we have termed 'perfectionism'; of exaggerating the individual features of the wise person and placing him or her on a level above that of merer mortals. In contemporary culture, the word 'expertise' seems out of harmony with the modesty, even the humility, associated with wise people in many traditions. Like 'skill', the term has been appropriated into the vocabulary of managerialism, colouring it with implications of hierarchy and control, until it no longer connotes simply the results of long, attentive application and effort: the type of skill in communicating with and about people that Homer, say, could recognise in Nestor. It may be this latter sense that the Berlin paradigm is intended to suggest.

Similarly, Ardelt is uncomfortable with the Berlin characterisation of wisdom as knowledge that exists independently of its users (Baltes and Staudinger, 2000), rebutting any attempt to envisage wise individuals as 'carriers' of social 'software'. As we have seen above, in recent discussion of the theory of practices it has also been suggested that the notion of 'carriers' is too crude. It makes sense, however, to read the Berlin writers, who underline familiarity with the ways things are done in the world as well as socially available sources of insight, as referring to social construction and the need to draw on publicly meaningful traditions, discourses and practices in order to be wise in specific social contexts. On the one hand, these practices subsist independently of particular individuals; on the other, they take form only when real people enact them, affected by them and affecting them as they do so.

For the Berlin group, wisdom is something that can be developed, for example through repeated practice in responding to other people's problems. Baltes et al (1995) compare clinical psychologists, other professionals and people nominated by respondents as wise, asking their test subjects how they would respond to a phone call from a friend contemplating suicide. Their aim is to discern whether clinical psychologists score relatively well in wisdom tests because they have genuine knowledge of fundamental life matters, rather than simply sharing a professional background with those developing the scores. The wisdom nominees and clinical psychologists do extremely well in comparison with controls, but show no effect of age; that is, professionals' knowledge seems not to go on evolving continuously during their lifetimes – or at any rate cannot be detected to do so by this method.

The Baltes group, though, do envisage wisdom-related capacities as possessing a temporal aspect. They see them as dealing with the fundamental pragmatics of life in relation to how people manage their lives meaningfully at present, how they plan their lives for the future, and how they review their pasts appropriately. They do not see these as capacities that people possess at birth; their acquisition can be enhanced by appropriate intellectual or emotional dispositions, such as openness to new experience, interest in understanding and helping others or personality traits such as possessing emotional attitudes supportive to others, but also by facilitative contexts fostered by particular social or cultural environments. Ageing as such, they contend, is no guarantee of progress.

For them, the primary foundation for wisdom-related knowledge is laid down in late adolescence and early adulthood, but long, intensive learning and practice is also involved. They suggest that role-models and mentors in the immediate social context, and further societal or cultural conditions such as good educational systems or supportive families, can enhance wisdom (Staudinger et al, 1998). Discussing life-course problems with other persons of choice (spouses, relatives or partners), either in real or in imagined dialogue, may be helpful (Staudinger and Baltes, 1996). Like Dittman-Kohli (1984) or Ardelt et al (2013), therefore, they note the importance of social *influences* on wise people and decisions. This approach can be taken further if we see at least some cases of wisdom as social processes in themselves (Edmondson, 2012, 2013). People in meetings, in therapy sessions, in the complexities of long-term relationships or even in casual encounters can spark off each other to reach insights more profound or more constructive than those the individuals involved could have reached alone. In these cases, wisdom develops in the course of social interaction and need not be the exclusive property of any particular person or persons.

The Berlin researchers connect five criteria in particular with the 'orchestration' of faculties of intellect and character that identify people who come close to wisdom. These are 'rich factual knowledge about human nature and the life course', 'rich procedural knowledge about ways of dealing with life problems', 'awareness and understanding of the many contexts of life, how they relate to each other and change over the lifespan' (life-span contextualism), 'acknowledgement of individual social and cultural differences in values and priorities' (the perhaps misleadingly named 'value relativism' and tolerance) and, lastly, 'knowledge about handling uncertainty, including knowledge about emotions connected with it; and knowledge of the limits of one's own knowledge' (see Baltes and Staudinger, 2000). On this basis, members of the Berlin group have attempted to test for closeness to wisdom by encouraging people to 'think aloud' about hypothetical cases involving existential problems for which there may not be conclusively right or wrong answers. Their replies are evaluated in terms of these five criteria on a one-to-seven scale (for details of how these evaluations are carried out, see Staudinger et al, 1994). One vignette put to participants suggested that 'A 15-year-old girl wants to get married right away. What could one consider and do?' A response might be,

> 'Well, on the surface, this seems like an easy problem. On average, marriage for a 15-year-old girl is not a good thing. On the other hand, thinking about getting married is not the same as actually doing it. I guess many girls think about it without getting married in the end ... There are situations where the average case doesn't fit. Perhaps special life circumstances are involved. The girl may have a terminal illness. She may not be from this country or perhaps she lives in another culture' (Kunzmann and Baltes, 2005: 121).

This participant's response, according to the authors, shows some knowledge about the lifecourse and of teenagers' characteristic contexts, including their emotions, ways of dealing with life-problems, and possible circumstances. It involves an implicit acknowledgement of individual, social and cultural differences in values and priorities, as well as acknowledging the limits of the speaker's own knowledge by refraining from offering a clear Yes or No answer. While 'pure' wisdom itself may be rare, they say, for them this type of answer demonstrates what they term 'wisdom-related knowledge or expertise' (Kunzmann and Baltes, 2005: 121).

Yet it may seem implausible to claim that it is possible to train interview-raters to assess wisdom: Jordan admits that people who are not themselves wise may find it impossible to understand wisdom (2005: 183–4). The Berlin group counter such an objection by pitching their efforts at detecting wisdom-*related* capacities, distinguishing, for instance, between broadly tolerant responses that take into account the possibility of different ways of dealing with a problem, and approaches that do not. The question remains whether this is enough to detect particularly impressive or particularly subtle or surprising forms of insight. Ardelt (2004: 261–3), though she herself rates levels of wisdom using her own (2003) scale, raises the question whether it is excessively detached to elicit responses to abstract problems in laboratories. For her, truly wise people might refrain from judging such vignettes at all, but would insist on involvement in actual, concrete cases.

Ardelt herself examines three who individuals she feels demonstrate what she means by approaching an 'ideal type' of closeness to wisdom (2005: 10). These relatively wise individuals, whom she calls James, Claire and Edna, use 'coping strategies' such as 'reframing' disagreeable events to see them as challenges, making the best of things ('If life gives you lemons, make lemonade': 2005: 11–12) and trying to take control of events rather than waiting for good fortune to befall them. Ardelt remarks, 'No event can make one unhappy unless one allows the unpleasant feelings to fester within' (2005: 12). On the basis of passages in her own work (Ardelt et al, 2013), it seems that Ardelt is drawing on Buddhist conceptions here, but the debate about how vulnerable to unhappiness wise people may be dates from Stoic times. Ardelt describes how she sees the 'reflective' aspect of wisdom as operating:

> By looking at phenomena from many different perspectives and by engaging in self-examination, self-awareness, and self-insight, one can gradually overcome one's subjectivity and perceptions, perceive and accept the reality of the present moment, and gain a more thorough and sympathetic understanding of oneself and others (2005: 8).

This, she continues, can in turn enhance the 'affective' aspect of wisdom, 'a reduction in self-centredness and an increase in sympathetic and compassionate love for others' (2005: 8). The result, a personality 'exceptionally mature, integrated, satisfied with life, able to make decisions in difficult and uncertain life matters, and capable of dealing with any crisis and obstacle they encounter' (Ardelt, 2005: 7), has much in common with the perfectionist ideal the Stoics would have commended too.

For Wink and Dillon, as for most of the writers on wisdom we have examined, wisdom, in whatever forms they discuss it, must include the capacity to transcend self-interest, to respond to uncertainty and to show tolerance. But they cast doubt on the expectation that the three features, cognition, reflection and affect, standardly hold together, seeing them as drawing on different aspects of the personality (Wink and Dillon, 2013: 171). Thus Wink and Helson (1997) examined longitudinal data to argue that there are different types of personal wisdom. They contended that people leaning towards 'transcendent' wisdom tended to be more creative, flexible and intuitive, whereas those closer to 'practical' wisdom had more social poise, enjoyment of mentorship and empathy. (It might also be asked if they populate different quadrants in Figure 4.1 above; the former tend to be more 'perfectionist' in their expectations of wisdom than the latter.) Wink and Dillon (2013) thus ask themselves how specific conceptions of wisdom map with other ideas about insight and meaning. Referring to the Californian longitudinal data to which they have access (see Chapter One above), they argue that if we define personal wisdom in terms that stress *cognition*, wise people will be found to score highly on personal growth, openness to experience, reflection, divergent thinking and perhaps spiritual seeking; whereas seeing wisdom more in terms of *compassion and sympathy* will tend to be more associated with church-based views of religion, conventionality, positive relations with other people and high life satisfaction.

In debates on wisdom it is often asked how likely it is that people are wise in all aspects of their lives. Someone who can advise other people wisely about problems in life is not automatically in a position to advise him- or herself. In fact it may be more difficult to gain insight into one's own prejudices, emotional responses and character traits than into those of others. Ursula Staudinger (2013), extrapolating from the original Berlin Wisdom Paradigm criteria to form a model associated with Bremen, has suggested that 'self-wise' persons should possess rich knowledge of their own cognitive capabilities, emotional responses and motivational and volitional characteristics. People with high degrees of self-related wisdom master heuristics (such as humour) that help them to maintain meaningful social relations and regulate their emotions appropriately in difficult circumstances. They are, she states, capable of reflecting on and having insight into the possible causes of their own ways of behaving and feeling, and have an awareness of their dependency on others. Moreover they should be capable of 'self-relativism' in possessing the ability to evaluate themselves and others critically, showing a tolerant respect for others and only an intermediate degree of self-esteem. They should, too, be able to tolerate ambiguity in managing uncertainties in their own lives and personal developments. This involves a basic trustfulness wherever it is appropriate, and a willingness to develop flexible responses to problematic situations.

Investigating self-related wisdom among adolescents and adults, Staudinger et al (1998) had claimed that openness to new experiences is its most important predictor – surely a highly significant suggestion. It suggests the question what types of 'openness' are involved, and how they operate, in different social circumstances and with what results; modes of and reasons for 'openness' will vary. To give one example, Staudinger et al consider that 'self-wise' people show interest in understanding others' psychological functioning as well as in their own personal growth. They can, too, step outside the realm of common assumptions and rules when confronting problems. On this view they are creative rather than conservative, disinclined to behave in domineering, submissive or conflict-avoidant ways (cf Hahn, 1991). For the most part, as Sternberg's view might also anticipate, they try to understand why something is the case or why it has been done, rather than simply judging whether it is good or bad. A rejection of dogmatism is common to all the explorations of wisdom highlighted in this book, including the work of Erikson or Frankl. This is not to say that wise people are imagined as refraining from taking stands at all; the Berlin group assign a normative social role to wisdom and the wise person. They contend that wisdom, as dealing with 'the fundamental pragmatics of life', 'can define the most general range of what goals and what means are socially acceptable and desirable in human development' (Kunzmann and Baltes, 2005: 127). Like Sternberg or Maxwell, therefore, they are prepared to make the radical claim that wisdom is a meaningful guide for personal and societal development, relevant not only for individuals' lifecourses, but also for the organisation and development of groups, societies and cultures at large.

To comprehend more about what can be understood by 'wisdom' and the ways and extents to which it can be attributed to older people, it is necessary to develop an account of deliberation and reasoning which, like the Aristotelian model, is complex enough to take into account not only what people say directly but also what they do and how they do it; and how modes of reasoning can be both embedded in daily and political practices and amenable to rational criticism. Moreover, if it is the *mode* of wise persons' behaviour that provides key insights into their ethical motivation and hence their wisdom (Rorty 1980), and if meaning is communicated through a wide-ranging variety of languages, symbols, practices and other behaviour (see Figure I.1 above), then as broad a range of vantage-points as possible are required from which to investigate it. Indirect features of communication such as the arrangement of items in a text or conversation, the emphasis given them, and especially the implicit topoi on which arguments are founded, are powerful elements in conveying meaning (Edmondson, 1984). Indeed, practices themselves communicate, often about the lifecourse itself, as in the case of birthday celebrations or funeral customs. This has at least two major implications.

First, there is no alternative to pluralistic, interdisciplinary cooperation in reconstructing what is counted as wise, or as partly wise or approaching wisdom, in different cultures and circumstances, and why it is experienced in this way. For example, indirect and reconstructive ethnographic methods can interrogate and extend significant suggestions from psychology, not least those relating to the transactions by which tolerance or openness to experience may be built up. Sociological methods are required to understand the ways in which constructions of wisdom vary among cultural contexts, as well as their potentially transactional nature; they can scarcely be taken in comprehensively without philosophical analysis. Second, these methods themselves presuppose theoretical views about what people are and how they behave: methods imply philosophical anthropologies. The congeries of methods supported here does not limit attention to any particular field of action or to select people, but is appropriate for discovering interactions that are interpreted as wise in an extremely wide range of social settings. This encourages us to seek relevant behaviour in many or even most places. That is, it is assumed that the brief but illuminating insights of every day will be instructive in showing what is happening, with what effects; the same applies to low-key aspects of daily behaviour – as in the case of the man who visited his depressed neighbour every day for a couple of years, performing farming tasks together in companionable silence. At the same time, we can anticipate the strength and wit attributed to wise conduct by Denning-Bolle or Kunow, permitting us to explore how people who are thought of as wise can resist domination in the cause of justice. These are types of challenge dealt with, not least, in the humanities and arts.

Late-life insight and the human condition: the humanities and artistic production

Especially when we take into account the potency of *styles* of behaviour in communicating meaning, many of the older people reflected in gerontological literature do appear to consider the 'fundamental pragmatics of life', or the human condition. The ways they behave convey the importance they attribute to values such as kindness, tolerance or vitality, and the reasons for which they do so, as well as their expectations about what life has to offer and what should be done about it. Nonetheless, we have seen that they may struggle to access any broadly intelligible set of discourses in whose terms to make these considerations explicit. Jan Baars (2012) is among those gerontologists who stress the relevance of exploring the human condition to understanding life-course meaning, and who underline the role played by the concept of wisdom in this context. This is a conjunction broached very strikingly in artistic works: they and their interpreters are specifically attuned to communicating indirectly rather than directly, and to chronicling the decisive effects such indirect communications can have on social beliefs.

Thus Andrea von Hülsen-Esch (2013) analyses how images, and hence understandings, of ageing and wisdom can be shaped by the iconographic repertoire available at particular times and in particular cultures, either briefly or over very long periods. At the same time, she attempts to disinter major influences on the elements of such repertoires themselves, in particular exploring how images of wise and authoritative women declined in number through the Middle Ages, culminating in 16th-century conventions that represented only older men as wise.

This development took a complex path, leading away from the depictions of abbesses or women expert in medicine and healing that were common at the beginning of the period. Especially in response to the iconography of Church fathers and hermits, 'wisdom' came to be associated with a particular type of venerability, crowding out alternative ways of imagining it, in particular those attaching to authoritative women. An emaciated older male's body came to 'mean' something different – asceticism and insight – from an emaciated older female's. This tendency was accentuated by Church theories of the corruption of the female body, together with medical uses of the female form to illustrate the pains and vulnerability of ageing. Eventually it ceased to seem reasonable to suggest that older female bodies can be read in terms of wisdom. Von Hülsen-Esch shows that by the end of this process, even the Sibyls, who were known to be old, could not be *shown* as old, female and wise. This no longer seemed to make sense; they were represented as sparkling young women instead. This explication is highly significant, not just for its potential in casting light on the way women and female authority are regarded until the present day, but also for its methodological implications. In showing how deeply historical ideologies can affect ideas about insight and wisdom, this account engenders caution about the adequacy of asking people their ideas about wisdom as direct paths to discovering what it 'is'.

Aleida Assmann (1991: 28), reviewing the history of literary treatments of wisdom, draws a distinction between four literary types or figures – all, as it happens, male. She offers 'portraits' of an array of stances that she differentiates by attaching them to particular human figures, some of them fictitious. Her first figure is that of Solomon, who represents kingly wisdom, standing not only for the combination of privilege and power, but also for wise rulers' capacity for a remarkable achievement: blending good counsel with justice (1991: 29–30). Assmann then points to the esoteric, magical wisdom of Prospero, from Shakespeare's *The Tempest*, associated with danger and secrecy, for Jordan (2005) someone with archetypical insights into the workings of the world. Prospero is the opposite of the fatherly wisdom of Polonius in *Hamlet*, the loquacious user of maxims and clichés (Assmann, 1991: 33). Assmann connects Polonius with the stresses and demands of family socialisation and generational relations, with what she sees as the more limited wisdom of every day. Lastly, there is the 'sceptical wisdom' of Jacques in Shakespeare's *As You Like It*: famous for his 'melancholy' and the speech 'All the world's a stage.' For Assmann, this wisdom does not lead to action but away from it; she ascribes it also to Montaigne, of whom she speculates that Shakespeare knew (1991: 40–2). For her, Montaigne's wisdom approaches passivity and quietism, but is nonetheless the type of wisdom that most nearly approaches common intuitions in the present day. It relinquishes a trusting attitude to the world, instead recognising its endless complexity, but for her this stance still retains a commitment to the well-being of other human beings.

Assmann's creative and suggestive account adds to the wisdom literature not least by connecting versions of wisdom with mood and social position. It may be that 'moods', if we interpret them as relatively consistent types of tendency to react and respond to people and predicaments, might be developed to classify person-oriented accounts of wisdom such as Ardelt's, or philosophical-sociological ones such as that offered by Edmondson et al (2009), which argue for accepting emotional and social features as intrinsic to reasoning processes. If so, we might in principle be able to distinguish reasoning like Solomon from reasoning like Polonius. Thus, developing Assmann's work further might involve investigating what, say, everyday wisdom involves: what activities, relationships and forms of judgement characterise it. In the case of Polonius, we might expect a tendency to give special weight to protective types of argument rather than adventurous ones, perhaps. It would need to be asked how essential the link is between Polonius and everyday wisdom: does the latter intrinsically involve busybodying paternalism? Is the use of maxims always tantamount to banality? Edmondson (2012) suggests not: there may be several styles of wise everyday reasoning.

In the case of Montaigne, we might complement trying to sum up what sort of person he was – whether sad or happy, passive or accepting – with exploring the ways in which his deliberations themselves might be termed wise. His celebrated essay 'On the Cannibals' (1580), for example, shows wisdom particularly in its capacity to see the world from the position of the cannibals, achieving the reconstruction of a quite unfamiliar conceptual world so as to make sense of novel emotional and political responses. Montaigne reconstructs abductively what the Brazilians must feel when they express incredulity that Frenchmen can walk the streets undisturbed by the sight of their 'halves' begging at the side of the road. From this one expression, Montaigne infers in imagination to the sense in which the Brazilians embrace a form of radical egalitarianism in which we are all literally bound up in each other. He then goes on to turn the implied criticism of France against his own culture. Montaigne takes the Brazilians so seriously that he is able to produce a critical comparison between the lives and mores of these 'cannibals' and the contemporary Frenchmen of his own time. This is a superb attempt to explore divergent fundamental criteria for a reasonable life: a conceptually adventurous demonstration of some further meanings for 'openness to experience'. Examining cases like this shows the importance of analysing not only the overall personal stance of a person associated with wisdom – informative and suggestive as this is – but also of explicating in detail the implications of that person's reasoning or advice in specific cases.

In addition to someone's personality and reasoning processes, his or her sociopolitical position can be argued to influence that person's capacity for wisdom of a specific type. This may apply to considerations of gender; Glück et al (2009) suggest there may be differences between the ways women and men are expected to enact wise interventions in everyday life. Joseph Falaky Nagy's *The Wisdom of the Outlaw* (1985) analyses early medieval connections between poetic insight and wisdom, the insight of the hunter who lives outside the tribe, in the Irish tradition of Finn Mac Cumhaill. Finn Mac Cumhaill belonged to one of the foremost of the tribes making up the ancient Fianna, the warrior band formed to protect the high king of Ireland, but, owing to quarrels that had taken place before he was born, he was forced to grow up an outcast, hiding in the forest. This is an extreme case of 'openness to experience': Finn learned much animal lore and became so fleet of foot that he could run down any quarry; the adventures he experienced on his way to becoming a poet and seer, qualifications for claiming headship of his tribe, included burning his thumb while roasting the salmon of knowledge over a fire (an image which recurs in Icelandic, Welsh and other stories). When he sucked his thumb against the pain, he achieved access to knowledge that would make whoever possessed it the wisest in all Ireland. Nagy's work examines the special significance of Finn's outsidership, canvassing the possibility that (at least certain sorts of) wisdom may require standing aside from the central, successful, dominant parts of society in order to gain insight into the demands of the human condition. It may be significant that Finn was not his first name, which was Deimne, meaning 'sureness'; he left this name behind when he became prematurely white haired while very young, for 'Finn' means 'fair'. Thus he abandoned certainty at the time when he became wise: symbolically in tune with theories of wisdom from Aristotle's to those of the 21st century.

Gerontological work by Biggs (2004) draws attention to the symbolic and dialogical nature of human experience and the way it is interpreted, as well as older individuals' creative adaptations of social meanings. This can have striking political and ethical implications. Rüdiger Kunow (2009) points to the 'transformative power' of ageing in literary works dealing with special forms of resistance, in which older people may reach heights of courage they were prohibited at earlier stages of their lives, when they depended on powerful individuals and organisations not only for their own quotidian survival but also for that of their families. Kunow deals with a story featuring older black men who specifically give voice to the political bravery that may stem from being over 70. Individuals may gain greater courage to take moral and political actions or stances when they are freed from the fear of losing their jobs or losing conventional respect, or even (at least to some extent) from the fear of death. Kunow's work also draws attention to that of Bly (2004), which explores 'the wisdom of eccentric old men' in the 19th-century novels of Benito Péres Galdós in Spain. Bly refers explicitly to the tradition of the 'wise fool' and the ambiguous status of Don Quixote (2004: 10); for Galdós himself, Pickwick was a superb instance of the wise fool (Bly, 2004: 13). Galdós' 'eccentric' male characters, all old or appearing old, are outsiders in different senses from Finn Mac Cumhaill; they often appear ridiculous or have habits that are regarded as ridiculous by others; some are genuinely mad, at least temporarily. Yet Galdós gradually reveals that these characters possess 'intelligence, moral purpose and subtlety': the reader is forced to regard such people not as fools but as equals (Bly, 2004: 50–1).

For Bly, these characters are entrusted by their author with a 'visionary mission': a 'sudden illumination or vision of what is afoot' that is 'somehow intense and moving' (2004: 170–1). But this is not a magical vision. These eccentrics' capacity for insight derives, for Bly, from their affectionate, devoted and accepting stances towards other people. He compares them with Mr Dick in *David Copperfield*, of whom Dickens makes David Copperfield say that it is his genuine attachment for other beings that gives him a subtlety of perception that outstrips mere cleverness. For Bly, the eccentric old men in Galdós may be 'Laughed at and dismissed as useless for any conventional, productive activity', but they are 'worth more than conventional normal people because of this warmth of human feeling' (2004: 171), which in the final analysis makes their reasoning superior to that of the orthodox world. Here too, we find an assumption that emotional commitment is capable of enhancing reasoning, rendering it not only more meaningful but also wiser.

Examples like these are complemented by Blaikie's (2002) argument to the effect that, rather than embracing cultures of 'consolation' or 'incorporation', older individuals may be able to adopt 'cultures of resistance' to social processes that threaten to homogenise their experience. As we might expect from observations made by Kunow or Erikson about the way in which older people can takes risks for, and identify with, wider groups, love and concern for other human beings have implications for the political arena too. This theme applies too to Leonora Carrington's *The Hearing Trumpet* (1974/2004). Here, when a 92-year-old woman is given a hearing trumpet, she discovers that her family is about to consign her to an old people's home. But she transforms this new environment into an arena of sparkling and astonishing freedom and political rebellion – although, admittedly, the novel is ambiguous about how her project turns out.

Adventurousness and growth are themes that appear in popular work too. Jenny Joseph's 'When I am an old woman I shall wear purple / With a red hat that doesn't go' appeals to many people (Warren and Clarke, 2009), but is not detailed about what the protagonist wants to do and why. A vast range of related questions are explored through the medium of film, often with wide popular impact. German television (ARD and ZDF) routinely shows feature films made for evening viewing, typically at 20:15; many of these deal directly or indirectly with concerns relevant to age and ageing. They are significant for their popular appeal and the fact that they bring profound questions to bear, even if they do not do so in an artistically elaborate manner. Several deal with family quarrels about property ownership, marriage alliances and clashes of world-view; others confront more existential questions about changing capacities and relationships as people age. They deal – often implicitly, but nonetheless centrally – with advances in the wisdom with which protagonists are able to approach daily life, and the meanings they attribute to it.

Four of these can serve as examples here. *Das Glück Klopft an die Tür* (*Happiness Knocks at the Door*) (2006: written by Monika Simon and directed by Christine Kabisch; shown again in 2009 and 2012) explores what happens when unexpected events turn expectations of tranquil later life upside down. When the main protagonist's husband dies suddenly in an accident, it transpires that he has left the family home half to his conventional, unadventurous wife, Gila, and half to a grown-up daughter of whom she has never heard, who has a little son. As the film progresses, Gila is forced to discover unexpected strengths and energies, forging new family alliances and blossoming as an independent character. This is the first of a set of questions explored repeatedly in films of this type: how much can be learned in later life, what sorts of insights can be acquired?

A second theme seems to deal (as to some extent does *Das Glück Klopft an die Tür*) with the consequences of relationships and mistakes made at an earlier stage of life, and individuals' attempts to atone for them or set them right. *Alles Glück der Erde* (*All the Luck in the World*) (2003; written by Maximilian Krückl and Hannes Meier, directed by Otto W. Retzer; shown again in 2009) turns on the fact that one of the characters has had a daughter whom he has refused to acknowledge, but whom he now tries to assist in her career and private life. The action takes place in highly bourgeois circumstances – its characters run expensive hotels, art exhibitions and stud farms – and the fairy-tale nature of the story is accentuated by the fact that the daughter recognises her father by a charm he wears round his neck, which fits a missing place in one she wears herself. Her recognition breaks a spell, in the sense that she becomes able to see the world differently: the world takes on different shape for her. New significances can be attached to people and circumstances, such that previously enigmatic conduct on the parts of other individuals now makes sense.

Für Immer und Einen Tag (*Forever and A Day*) (2008; written by Verena Kurth, directed by Holger Barthel; shown again in 2009 and 2013) deals with a third theme that is prominent in these popular films, the question of how one should spend or give meaning to one's lifecourse. The protagonists have different attitudes to their careers and ideals, and to succeeding generations; an underlying question of the film is whether it is worthwhile for the central female character to give her entire life to building up a celebrated legal practice, even though this makes complex personal relationships impossible. The film appears to argue for the choice made by another character, who is developing an ecologically aware biofuel business that still allows time for a relationship with an orphaned nephew. At the same time, the question of learning in later life appears in this film too. The lawyer's father has recognised the importance of nothing but the law firm and his daughter's career; her mother has been used to interfering in others' affairs for their own good, irrespective of their wishes. Both the parents eventually see the error of their ways and adopt more generous, tolerant approaches to the lives of others.

Lastly, a fourth theme appears in *Der Mann auf der Brücke* (*The Man on the Bridge*) (2009; written and directed by Rolf Silber). This film reprises many of the questions that appear in *Forever and a Day*. One of its central characters is a small boy whose father, the mayor of the city, is so preoccupied with politics that he has no time for the child, who spends much of his time at boarding school; the question of life priorities is significant here too. The second main character is the elderly, misanthropic owner of a newspaper kiosk. Attempting to commit suicide, he fails to do so but, without altogether intending it, succeeds in saving the life of the small boy. While he initially fails to find the child appealing, eventually an alliance builds up between the two. They become embroiled in combating the hypocrisies of power politics in Frankfurt, making explicit the usually discreet counter-cultural tendencies of many of these films. (A similar topic, an alliance between the old and the young that throws into relief the perils of a workaholic culture, can be found in *Charlie and Me* (2008: written by Karen Struck, directed by David Weaver).) This theme, the capacities of the old and the young to ally with each other against the conventional views of those in the years in between, raises the question of what it is that enables them to perceive values and priorities that others cannot. Is it simply that they are free from the pressures of needing to develop careers and can thus assert themselves against the predations of rivals?

Little Miss Sunshine (2006; written by Michael Arndt, directed by Jonathan Dayton and Valerie Faris), which subsequently won an

'Independent Spirit Award', also exhibits a counter-cultural alliance between a grandparent and a child, but its treatment is more complex. In this case, the child, Olive, appears plain and conventional, but she has won the opportunity to enter a Californian beauty pageant for children several hundred miles away from her parents' home. She wishes passionately to do so, and her mother is anxious that she should be able to pursue her goal. Other members of her family sum up a variety of key features of contemporary society. The father is obsessed by the idea of professional success; in his case he hopes it will be based on motivational tapes adjuring viewers to become 'winners – not losers'. His stepson refuses to speak to anyone, sulking systematically and obsessed by his fervour for joining the Air Force as a pilot (which it subsequently transpires he is unable to do, since Olive discovers he is colour-blind). The grandfather has been expelled from an old people's home for taking heroin. Olive's uncle, a Proust scholar also living with the family, has lost his job at Harvard in connection with a gay liaison with a male student, who has rejected him for another man; but it is only when a 'genius award' is bestowed on his rival that he finally (unsuccessfully) attempts suicide. Each working-age male member of the family is preoccupied with the idea of professional success: becoming a winner – not a loser. The role of the work life and its distorting effects on values and behaviour is a recurrent sub-theme in connection with the lifecourse and meaning.

In order for Olive to enter the talent contest, and since they lack the funds for any more reliable form of transport, the family set off in a rickety microbus, with a series of absurd adventures, on the way to California. The father's promotional plan fails, his stepson learns he can never be a pilot, the grandfather actually dies; the pageant proves to be populated by grotesquely sexualised children with whom it seems clear that Olive can never compete. She insists on carrying on with her dance, since it was her grandfather who taught it to her. This turns out to be a bizarrely exaggerated version of a strip-show routine in which Olive divests herself of many of her clothes and growls on all fours at her audience. The pageant organisers are horrified, though the film's audience is clearly meant to find Olive's performance less disturbing than those of her competitors, with their sparkling swimsuits, thick make-up, bouffant hair and fake tans. The family must flee California but the experience has brought them together and freed them from over-investment in phoney ideals.

The political implications of this film have not escaped the attention of the World Socialist Website,[1] which reports that Arndt was moved to write the script in response to hearing Arnold Schwarzenegger state,

'If there's one thing in this world I despise, it's losers.' Arndt wished 'to attack that idea that in life you're going up or you're going down', choosing to concentrate on a children's beauty pageant because it is 'the epitome of the ultimate stupid meaningless competition people put themselves through'.[2] From our point of view, the film's most significant feature is that it is the alliance between the grandparent and the grandchild that allows the ideological spell of competition to be broken. This is not because, as in the German films, the two have simply escaped involvement in the world of work and can thus preserve their moral senses intact. *Little Miss Sunshine* is a more complex production in which both grandparent and grandchild are as deluded as others by the culture they live in. They are simply *unable* to comply with its demands. It is their attempts to do so that highlight these demands' absurdity. Yet the film is predicated on her family's care for Olive, even though it may take misguided form; her innocence in her disastrous attempts unites her family around her, and frees them from the spell. As in both *All the Luck in the World* and *The Man on the Bridge*, the spell in question is a systematic view of the world, in which people, opinions and values are interpreted according to a particular pattern; *Little Miss Sunshine* asserts that such ideological enchantments can be broken, and that intergenerational alliances can be key to this process.

Other recent films also deal with similar questions of value and the human condition. The question of what choices one can make in order to live well in older age is to the forefront of *The Best Exotic Marigold Hotel* (2011; written by Ol Parker and Deborah Moggach, directed by John Madden), and also of *Quartet* (2012; written by Ronald Harwood, directed by Dustin Hoffman). Aagje Swinnen (2010) comments on agency and ageing in her comments on Miyazaki's animé film (2004) of the novel *Howl's Moving Castle* (1986, by Diana Wynne Jones). For the protagonist, Sophie, Swinnen says, changing from a young girl into an old woman frees her to make choices that make personal growth possible. She preserves a sort of sliding scale of age, going from old to young and back again: genuinely able to *forget* her age.

Subsequently, Miyizaki wrote and directed *Ponjo* (2008), an environmentalist morality tale that develops Hans Christian Andersen's 'Little Mermaid'. In this film, relations between the generations play complex roles. The mother of the 6-year-old protagonist, Sošuke, works in an old people's home; when a tsunami arrives she leaves her son alone – 'You're big now' – in order to brave the waters and protect her charges. In her absence, Sošuke forms an attachment to a goldfish or fish-maiden, whom he renames Ponjo. He and Ponjo are forced to defy her father, the king of the sea, trying to overcome the hatred he has for humans because of all they have inflicted on nature. While Sošuke eventually wins over the king through his love for Ponjo, the old people have a special role in the king's magical world. This seems to be both because they are old enough to remember a distant past in which the world was not yet despoiled, and also because they inhabit a liminal world in which they are at least partly freed from the worldly commitments of the middle-aged. In a way they anchor the film as repositories of value. These are older people to whom significance is attached in the fifth of the senses of 'meaning' in Chapter Three above: older people as they are symbolically located in the world by and for others.

Clearly these are not the only recent films to explore the themes of ageing, meaning and intergenerationality from the point of view of the human condition. *Gran Torino* (2008; written by Nick Schenk and Dave Johannson, directed by Clint Eastwood – one of a number of films made by older directors) has as its theme the capacity of older people to achieve heightened moral insight and progress through making unconventional connections with people from other generations, even when initially handicapped by negativity and cynicism. The animated film *Up!* (2009; written by Pete Docter, Bob Peterson and others, directed by Pete Docter and Bob Peterson) deals with the subject of loss in older age, as well as with an alliance between an initially ill-tempered older man and a young child that proves liberating to both of them. In contrast, *Amour* (2012, written and directed by Michael Haneke), concentrates on loss alone. It deals with a couple in their eighties, both musicians; it may be no accident that they are presented so keenly as people living together in time, since time and tempo are so key to music. The film charts in agonising detail what time does to them and how helpless they may be, in the face of great illness, to respond. In this film, the couple's relationship with other generations, in the persons of their own daughter and her husband, seems frozen and stilted. *La Grande Bellezza* (*The Great Beauty*) (2013, written by Paulo Sorrentino and Umberto Contarello, directed by Paulo Sorrentino) also deals directly with the subject of age and how it is experienced. Its main character, an ageing bon vivant in his sixties, is preoccupied with approaching older age and whether he can recapture the literary promise of his youth. Like *Amour*, this film refrains from an upbeat ending, perhaps partly because it is intended as a political allegory of modern Italy, allegedly trapped in the futility of a hollow, superficial, hedonistic life-style. Age, in the case of this character, cannot overcome the influence of the culture around him.

These films, therefore, deal centrally with dilemmas relating to the human condition as it is confronted within particular social and political circumstances. They identify significant questions, many of which are also underlined by writers in gerontology such as Cole, Moody, Baars or Tornstam: in the society I inhabit, how much can I still learn in later life, what can I achieve, what should I aim for, whom should I trust, how much can I change? The perennial nature of these questions is underlined by William Thomas, for whom myths and folktales too offer significant insights into the 'complex and contradictory phenomenon' of ageing (Thomas, 2004: 333). His account of the story of Ulysses quite naturally and intelligibly uses the term 'wisdom'. An enchantress who has fallen in love with Ulysses offers him a potion that will give him eternal youth, which he can spend with her on her island. However, he chooses to return to grow old with his wife, Penelope, embracing 'the bitter fruit of mortality, his and hers'. For Thomas, 'The story suggests that his decision was wise in that it was human' (2004: 332). This is not an unmixed happy ending, even though it offers stature and acknowledgement to Penelope's life-long commitment to her joint course in life with Ulysses (Mueller, 2007; cf Basting on 'Finding Penelope', 2011). Here Thomas conveys something about the struggle involved in ageing by reference to a specific, in this case, fictional, example: Ulysses' fictionality makes the lessons he teaches more general.

Mapping meaning in gerontology with work on wisdom

Like the older people whose comments are reported in gerontological texts, scholars in this field insist that older people can achieve or retain wisdom, not that they automatically will. This maintains what might be termed the sceptical optimism of the ancient world. Even Jordan, though she sees wisdom as a rare attribute that is far from specific to older people, underlines the view held by Baltes and Staudinger (2000) that 'under ideal cognitive and physical health conditions, older adults will demonstrate an advantage due to greater life experience (ie, practice)' (Jordan, 2005: 167). For the same reason, researchers including Smith and Baltes (1990), or Smith et al (1994), suggest that there may be some advantage in wisdom for individuals trained in psychology, theology, family medicine or education policy; this advantage is not invariable and does not seem to increase systematically with age. It has not, as we have seen, classically been maintained that it does; only that, given sufficient effort and a certain amount of good fortune, it *can*. Jordan speculates too that in so far as the capacity for wisdom can be enhanced by circumstances, it might even increase over time down through cohorts; for instance, wider availability of education or enhanced access to life experience through the media might permit recent generations to become relatively wiser than previous ones (2005: 183–5).

While many people noted for being wise have been older, to understand why they are assessed in this way it is important to distinguish between what sort of person someone is in general, and what they do or say on particular occasions, or when faced with particular challenges. Wise interchanges may be glancing or transient, highly significant for participants even if they cannot easily be linked directly to lasting predispositions on the parts of those who contribute to them. Many people contribute wise insights or wise reactions to the situations in which they find themselves without necessarily being regarded as wise, or even nearly wise, in general – perhaps like some of those mentioned in the work by Thompson et al. In their cases, it is the insights they have to offer that strike the reader, and the authors do not necessarily link these to attempts to summarise what sorts of people the speakers are. We saw that Dillon's 'spiritual seekers' often achieved insights, though sometimes without appearing to be wise. If we take the view that wisdom can be reached as part of a social process, where interaction between people who individually might not be wise can still have wise outcomes, we need not expect all (or any of) the people involved to 'be wise' in the sense of possessing permanent dispositions, independent of each other. Sometimes, it is only when looking back to one's childhood that one recognises the constructive influence of particular people on what happens in their surroundings, however flawed those people might have been; or else two individuals who are impatient and intolerant might rub off each other to reach a point where they can both behave more constructively (Edmondson, 2009). Paying attention to 'imperfect' forms of wisdom like this both tells us more about what wise transactions can involve and renders discourses featuring wisdom more serviceable in application to real-life older people. It can bring a new focus to the ways people engage with their own and others' lifetimes, adding to debate on how to conceptualise ageing and lifetime as such.

Everyday wisdom can be noticed in practices, some of which are narrative practices, as in two examples here. They are symptomatic of each of the speakers' distinctive attitudes to life, and to living their own lives; in each case, these attitudes are critical rather than culturally acquiescent. They also cast light on the way people can attribute meaningfulness to their own approaches to living. Each is a *repeated* narrative, told in various ways by each of the speakers on a number of occasions. The first instance is taken from an interview carried out in the US with someone who has been a friend of the author since the 1970s, a man who has spent considerable periods in Europe. Speaking when he was in his late eighties, Howard Bowman related an incident that had occurred in 1945; he made clear the strength of its impact on the view of life he subsequently took. He had also described this incident in print (in *Harper's Weekly*, 29 November 1974, p 5). He had written then,

> I recently returned to Munich after an absence of over a quarter of a century. I saw the city last in late April 1945, when it was in flames and its population mostly fled or huddled in the cellars of the roofless, gutted buildings. I am now a resident of Munich myself, and I perceive no connection between the burning city of 1945 and the affluent, glittering, overbuilt, traffic-choked metropolis of today. When I look at snapshots of the young lieutenant of the U.S. 20th Armored Division and then stare at the lined, bearded face in the mirror, I realize also that not only Munich has changed.
>
> My attitude towards the Germans changed much earlier, however. On 30th April, 1945, we liberated Dachau concentration camp and on that day my resentment of the Germans who had plunged the world into war and had killed my commanding officer and other good men flamed into a gut-searing hatred. It was one thing to read about concentration camps, but to see one and to see and smell and feel its victims was more than I could bear. I could not enter the gates of the camp, but passed on, consumed with anger.

In the interview in 2011, Bowman continues,

> 'About this time, I was driving up the road - the war had just ended, the German troops were to stay where they were, go into fields, park there and rest, and wait for us to collect them. And there was this convoy coming down the road from the Alps, battered trucks and a couple of ambulances, and I stopped them.'

His account in 2011 followed his written version:

I pulled my jeep across the road, blocking the progress of the Germans, and called on the enemy commander to step down. (I speak German.)

I was surprised when the commander turned out to be a German army nurse. She was small and scrawny, there were dark shadows under her eyes, she looked half starved, and she was bristling with indignation. 'Get out of my way!' she snapped.

'You, you,' I blustered. 'You will follow me to the nearest PW *Lager*!'

The nurse was unimpressed and her eyes blazed. 'I will follow you nowhere! You can check my men. They are all wounded and tired and they want to go home. And I am taking them home!'

Bowman engaged in a few more exchanges with the nurse; he reports in 2011 that he said to her, 'You can't do that, it's against the rules.' In the written version, he was thinking 'I hate these people,' when the absurdity of his thought struck him.

And then I realized that it was impossible to hate people in general. These were just people, sick and hurt. The nurse before me was tottering with weariness and her defiance appeared to be rapidly draining away.

'I don't think it will do you much good', I mumbled, 'but I'll write you a pass.'

I scribbled something ... I noticed my case of C rations and I pulled it out and carried it over to the ambulance and dropped it on the floor beside her ... The nurse didn't look grateful or puzzled, but just very tired and sick.

Bowman concludes,

I don't know how much further the convoy managed to travel or whether the nurse got her men home. I shall be eternally grateful to that woman, however, because she and her pathetic convoy drained the hatred from my system. I was satisfied later that the Nazi war criminals were punished and I continued to hate what they stood for, but I no longer hated the German people. Hatred, after all, is bad for the health, for the soul. A good nurse would know that.

Bowman said in 2011, "I was very impressed by this woman, I'll never forget her." He added, too, "I was sure they wouldn't get much further, but I didn't want to be the one to stop them."

This and other aspects of the conversation in April 2011 suggest a certain pessimism on the speaker's part about the possibilities of converting people on a large scale to his own circumspect and humane position. He is telling this story, which may at first appear to be a narrative specifically about his own life, with an eye to what he thinks is the right attitude to other human beings and to the plight of humanity generally. It is true that he experienced this incident as life-changing, even as meaningful in terms of the 'tasks of life' discussed in Chapter Two, in addition to conveying ethical meaning. It also epitomises his reluctance to adhere to the letter of the law when more important values are at stake, and it shows his awareness of the complexity of human endeavours, which cannot be assessed simply in black and white. To this extent it fits with a number of expectations in the wisdom literature. But though Bowman's remarks show his views and something about his character – this narrative can be seen as symptomatic of a quiet scepticism towards official versions of events that has permeated his life – they are not made primarily in order to do this. He is contributing to an on-going debate about national guilt and how we should treat members of populations where crimes have been committed. The views he is expounding are important to him as much because he wants them to be shared as because they are his in particular. The wisdom in what he says resides in the effects of his words on others, as part of an 'activity of understanding' 'something out there in the world'; he is speaking not in capitulation to 'the allure of subjectivism' (Fine, 2015: 218) but as an attempt to shift readers' or hearers' perceptions, and convincing to the extent that the *judgement* expressed in his narrative is found convincing.

Stories that individuals tell more than once may, therefore, be those that have particular significance for them in terms of the attitudes to life that they hold. A similar repeat interview, also expressing something of the speaker's basic attitude to life, was carried out with the matron of a nursing home in the West of Ireland. Though scathing about the rationality of bureaucracies, she had some experience of making immediate, positive impacts on other people, her patients. On the earlier occasion she had said,

> 'A nursing home should be moving away from a hospital situation and making it more of a home. But the rules and regulations won't allow it! Bureaucracy, red tape … The

fire officers came in about fire doors. They insisted on measuring 'running distance' for these people who can't run! ... I think at eighty years of age people should be allowed to do what they want to do ... I had a man who used to drink his whiskey and stay in bed and I think he was very happy. The Health Board attitude was, You should get him up and make him unhappy!' (Edmondson, 2003: 1730).

She had complained about anxiety over litigation:

'Litigation comes in as well nowadays. Everybody's worried about people coming down on their back' (20 April 2001).

While she did not object to regulations per se, she objected to a preoccupation with rules that she saw as undermining the entire aim of the nursing home itself.

Speaking in 2009, she continues to complain about bureaucracy, and also about standardised, task-oriented approaches to care for older people. The inspection authorities "praise when the jobs are done, the baths done ..."; nurses too "feel they have to be doing something. If they've done ten showers they feel they've done a good day's work, but they didn't spend their time talking to the patients." Similarly, psychological and social-scientific approaches to ageing are in danger of becoming too standard:

'The depression scale test – Do you feel happy, do you feel depressed, do you feel other people are better off than you? I think if I asked them these three questions I'd depress them! An awful lot of time is wasted in negativity and stress. There are things I can do something about, and things I can do nothing about.'

She feels that too many recipes are prescribed for the lives of older people, rather than encouraging populations in general to see point in their lives:

'There are a lot of young people whose lives are meaningless and we expect their lives to change suddenly in older age.... It's hardly likely that in your eighties you're going to take up squash or painting if you haven't done them before. We only have one life and we should live it; I think we should experience as much as possible. You should look at it more individually … People who sit by the fire and watch TV, they're not going to do much that's mind-boggling. Rather than looking at older people, we should be getting young people to think about their lives.'

Equally, it is important to realise how differently people can experience the same phenomenon. This speaker often relates how local older people fail to enjoy the spectacular sea views around the nursing home:

'Like I said to you before about how people sit with their backs to the sea, he said the sea meant hard work to him and in most families there had been a drowning, a cousin or a brother. To me, I thought the sea was something you sat by; to him, it was anything but.'

All these experiences of her patients teach her "Tolerance. I think if people were more tolerant of other people, I think there's good in most people, but we tend to look for the bad in others." Lastly, she has been in a position, through her work, to learn vicariously from her patients' experiences, and from practising dealing with them creatively. But she stresses that learning of this type is always filtered through the individual's temperament and outlook.

'It's probably a lot to do with your own ageing, your outlook and your own life experiences…. I wouldn't be a great shopper, I don't believe in material things. I see people go out of here, their possessions could fit in a plastic bag, no matter how rich they were. Your health is your wealth, you hear that as a child but it means more to you as you get older' (21 October 2009).

These are themes to which this speaker characteristically takes recourse; for her, they are a central point of deliberation in explaining the world-view she is commending. Like Howard Bowman's, her reasoning conveys much of the way in which she understands the human condition. On the approach suggested here, we can judge the wisdom of these two narratives in relation to their capacity to illuminate, move and convince hearers or readers. We do not need to try to determine the permanent capacity for wisdom of the speakers in toto.

These two examples can easily be reproduced in textual form because they take largely verbal form; many other instances are more strongly behavioural. In the West of Ireland, for example, extremely low-key verbal interventions, often proverbs, can be used to provoke or inspire heightened wisdom. The communicative import of apparently banal remarks or gestures can indicate much more about how wise interaction works than might be apparent from their surface appearance. First, proverbs are very clearly elements in a cultural storehouse that is locally shared; this makes them especially appropriate for use by people regarded as wise in this particular social setting, which is one in which value is set on social equality. People here do not wish to receive suggestions 'de haut en bas', and nor do they wish to seem to be giving them in this way. Proverbs, too, allow speakers to make conversational interjections without over-personalising them. We have seen that Tim O'Flaherty in South Connemara was described as wise by his son-in-law, Charlie Lennon, because his use of proverbs was based on a swift and apt diagnosis of someone else's difficulty – why it was a difficulty *for them* – and because he could select from a vast store of proverbs precisely the one that could cause *that person* to see the problem afresh. 'The proverb would lay things out for you in a way that made you think about them, think what you would do in the future' (cf Edmondson, 2009). For this to be a transaction that does not misfire, it has to be received as constructive by the other person. The speaker might be skilled in offering this type of intervention, but it is dependent on a suitable reception for it to take effect.

This type of interchange might superficially seem simple and swift, characteristic of the reticent interactive style of the region. But it rests on a remarkable skill in choosing the right time for intervening and a succinct mode of doing so, based on knowledge of and concern for the interlocutor, as well as considerable experience with people in general. Paralleling the point made by Baltes and Staudinger (2000), this is interaction in which age is involved not least because it takes time to acquire this sort of knowledge, and to observe and practise the effects of different types of impact on specific human circumstances. Drawing on the traditions of Aristotle and Smith, it can be added that practitioners will have schooled themselves over time in the type of reactive practice required: the discernment, knowledge, care, concern and – not least – the humour and wit involved.

In these situations, interventions are considered wise when they draw actively on a shared cultural context in a way that is moulded by responding directly and appropriately to the interlocutor's capacities and needs. In the example of Seamus Murphy, whose neighbour was so furious because his own son had lied to him, Seamus responded quizzically: 'Did you make your son tell you a lie?' The neighbour later said it took him more than a year until he realised what had been meant. The time-scale in question is set, in effect, by the hearer. Thus, someone who is behaving inflexibly in a dispute might be brought up by a wry remark – 'Ní thuigeann an sách an seang' or 'The well-fed can't understand the thin' (Edmondson, 2012a). The brevity of such an interjection would respond to a *hearer's* communicative need for surprise. If delivered by a suitable interlocutor, it might well be more effective than hectoring interference. Speaking appropriately like this might enable a sudden transition from one deliberative perspective to another: what we have referred to above as breaking a spell. This type of spell breaking does not only go on between equals in age; perhaps it is even more likely to occur between the generations. The point is that it is a *social* process: the topoi underlying world-views, arguments and gestalts are socially produced, and often it needs a social transaction for insight into using them to be garnered. The interventions in question are wise, less in virtue of some intrinsic quality of what is said than in their impact on others.

Ursula Staudinger (2013: 4) argues that psychological accounts of personal development do in fact deal with the growth of 'personal' wisdom, even though they may not say so. Developmental accounts deal with the end-goals of trajectories in personal growth during the lifecourse, and measure it in terms of features such as tolerance of ambiguity and self-relativism; this, for her, is to talk about wisdom (see also Mickler and Staudinger, 2008). If, as we have argued, discursive treatments of wisdom are fragmented in the contemporary world, we may not expect them to be expounded in detail in gerontology yet: but they do occur there too, as part of a different, though complementary, discourse dealing with what can be done or perceived, what happens between people. To become tolerant of ambiguity or generous to others is something a person can try to develop over a lifetime, but such insights can arise in social situations too. We might perhaps see Gubrium's interlocutor, Rinehart, in this light; his background as a travelling salesman seems to have helped him to take each day as it comes, with an 'equanimity' that does not demand certain progress from the future (Gubrium and Holstein, 2009: 77–9). Gallagher (2008) describes people who give each other highly non-judgemental forms of help in everyday tasks, contributing to making each other's lives qualitatively better. The Eriksons mention the impacts their focal people have on others when they plant apples trees in their gardens or are concerned about the environment. In all these cases, older people are understood in relation to their social contexts and the forms of interpretation to which they give rise.

A transactional approach to wisdom does not ignore the fact that the protagonists are people, one of Ardelt's main stipulations. Perhaps it accentuates the fact more effectively than treating them as cut off from their settings would do, for it shows the effects they have on others. Manheimer (1999), for example, devotes much of the first chapter of a book to describing interactions with his former professor: how he moved, how he spoke, how he smoked his pipe: these details both help us to envisage the effect this professor made on Manheimer, and to understand his reasoning. We are able to envisage something of why he feels moved to say what he does. This is to recur to the importance of *how* people do things that is stressed by Rorty (1980). The Austrian Wastl Schwaiger, in his eighties, makes a habit of greeting strangers in the street, has a 'PAX' number-plate on his car to encourage the idea of peace, sings in the local choir and has galvanised his community to renovate a local mountain chapel (Edmondson, 2005). But it is the manner in which he does these things, humorous and open minded, that lends conviction to the impact he makes on those around him. This style of behaviour makes the difference to how his actions are received. We could describe him as someone from whom wise interventions have come to be expected; this is less demanding than expecting him to be 'a wise person'. This manner of talking about wisdom may seem less stringent than expecting people to be sages, but it does open up a way of appreciating key aspects of the later stages of the lifecourse that is relatively widely attained.

It also gives us an interest in what older people say, a reason for listening to them (de Medeiros, 2014). Gabriel Weston (2009) echoes the classical Greeks in stressing the advantages of avoiding the impetuosity of youth in circumstances where complex judgements are required. Her account of becoming a surgeon is replete with admissions of the self-obsession or narrow-mindedness she showed as a trainee and the experience in moral dilemmas that she needed to overcome them. She writes,

> But the length of training serves another important function. It ensures that, by the time you have any real responsibility, you aren't young any more. This getting old makes you more aware and therefore safer (Weston, 2009: 65).

She repeats this point at the end of the chapter, which is entitled 'Hierarchy':

> Maybe one of the most important reasons we all train for so long is to ensure the self-doubt that is part of getting older. This awareness of one's own limits may prove more life-saving than any knife (Weston, 2009: 80).

Weston's account of her medical training shows that, while medicine cannot be practised constructively without a proper sense of its telos or underlying aim, this is an understanding that accumulates with age. Older doctors can possess significant forms of wisdom that younger ones may not. This is not the only text by a doctor with a similar point in mind; for example, Lown (1996) emphasises the key role in diagnosis of developing the skill of listening to patients. If gerontologists are to succeed in wanting to listen to older people, they need to be alert to all possible reasons for finding their interlocutors interesting; receptiveness to wise contributions offers one such approach.

Notes

[1] http://www.wsws.org/en/articles/2006/08/sun-a26.html.

[2] http://en.wikipedia.org/wiki/Little_Miss_Sunshine.

FIVE

Conclusion: ethics, insight and wisdom in intergenerational life-course construction

Developing meaning in life, carried out in styles of everyday activity as often as in conscious deliberation, is part and parcel of operating within social institutions, groups and practices; but it is core to the human condition. Major contemporary gerontologists, from Cole and Moody to Phillipson, point, like Frankl, Erikson and Elder before them, to a crisis in meaning, one that affects the way in which lifecourses in general can be understood. The fact that people's understandings of themselves and their lives are intertwined with their social contexts does not make them determined by those contexts, but it does make them vulnerable to them. Not least, for writers like Cole and Moody, economistic understandings of the human lifetime have drained the profundity from ageing. The excessive individualism these positions and policies entail is a symptom of a 'war on old age'; without a fundamental reorientation of attitudes to what it is to age, efforts to defend older people or make their life-courses intelligible cannot succeed (Cole, 1992: 181). Thus Moulaert and Biggs (2013) raise the alarm when they note that even in official documents of world organisations supporting older people, references to wisdom and experience are giving way to the assumption that self-sufficiency and independence – not least, financial independence – should be core to defining life-course aims.

Accentuating what gerontological work counterposes to these developments, this book began to explore different aspects of meaning attributed to the world by older people in its texts. Michele Dillon offers evidence of various types of purposefulness with which older people struggle, with absorption and often with pleasure, to determine what is important in their lives. This follows on from work like that of the Eriksons, who see all stages of individuals' lives as marked by the ways they cope with moral and personal challenges, and who show a lively appreciation of the vivacity with which older people embark on their activities; or from Frankl's, whose experiences of life in a concentration camp taught him that retaining hold of meaning can be literally a matter of life or death. For Glen Elder, individuals' development as people, the way they respond to challenges and crises, is key to his work. Though he is conscious of the extent to which responses are constrained by the social and economic circumstances in which people find themselves, how they respond to these challenges affects 'the framework of meanings in which the self is anchored' (1974/99: 145). Thompson et al (1990) build their entire book, *I Don't Feel Old*, on the 'search for meaning' and the 'vital resilience' needed to find it (1990: 245). For them, later life 'is a time of constant reconstruction' (1990: 250). It is a period in principle open to fluid and positive forms of embracing innovation, as Cicero emphasised in *On Old Age*. Correspondingly, Tornstam's work on 'gerotranscendence' focuses on seeing older age in terms of the potential for expanded moral sensibility, the development of broad-mindedness, tolerance and humility.

These discussions of positive features of ageing, however, remain exceptional. Major forms of social exclusion need not be obvious, and they need not involve hostility as such to older people. All that is necessary to prevent any group of people from actively contributing to what goes on is the *absence* of a discourse, of any pervasive set of languages and expectations that anticipate that they will do and say things of importance. 'Within an individualized society, the best way to avoid confronting uncomfortable collective realities is to make them disappear' (Gilleard, 2005: 159). Even those trying to defend older people often find it hard to formulate why they should do so without either exaggerating the advantages of age, mentioned by O'Neill (2011), or falling into denigratory stereotypes. A distinctly and reasonably constructive language is not to hand; this has the rhetorical effect of fading the significance of older people's concerns from public attention – making them vulnerable to negative interpretation instead.

Topics and tactics of debate from health to investment have in common that they deprive older age of *meaning*. 'Expert' discussion of 'demographic time-bombs', or the diagnosis of ageing as a set of biomedical problems to be solved, reinforces the destructive dichotomy between 'success' and 'decline' underlined by Bytheway (2011). 'Successful ageing' is ageing that causes no trouble, whereas the 'chronologisation of everything' in modern bureaucratic states is experienced as implying a steady correlation between age and feebleness. Powerful languages and practices simply rule out assuming that older people and their lives possess notable forms of meaning. Thomas Cole (1992) accentuates modern repugnance at the idea that any vulnerable condition could also be meaningful.

Peter Coleman reports that even the churches, whose business is meaning, tend to behave as if older people had nothing to offer.

While problems connected with meaning are confronted throughout life, often they are evaded except in connection with death – arguably rather late for considering the extent to which older age can involve growth, and how it can do so. While gerontologists interested in these areas, Achenbaum and Orwoll, MacKinlay or Wink and Dillon, take such issues seriously, real problems remain for older people in daily life. Jolanki reports that the discourses readily available for coping with ageing construct it almost exclusively as a health project for the active body; Nichol describes creative and intelligent people searching vainly, in 'vulnerability and confusion', for appropriate language with which to navigate their own ageing (2009: 258). Simone de Beauvoir describes comparable predicaments as cases of real social hegemony: 'the whole meaning of our life is in question in the future that is waiting for us' (1996: 5), and it is striking how effectively this future can be virtually erased.

Philosophers such as Martha Nussbaum or Amélie Rorty accentuate how ethical meanings are in reality woven throughout the large and small practices of daily life, investing it with on-going significance, but Alasdair MacIntyre (1981) dissects the public crisis that affected how ethics was regarded from the 20th century onwards. If ageing can no longer be seen as a moral project, as Cole (1992) urges, this is partly owing to contemporary problems in seeing anything at all as a moral project.

MacIntyre attributes this to the practice of assuming that ethical claims express only feelings and personal preferences, making it impossible to take ethics seriously. Attempts to speak ethically began to be construed, at best, in terms of fear of offending. These developments too fade the meaning from the conduct of the lifecourse, as does neglect of the formerly prominent term, 'wisdom' – in the past, a formidable aim for individuals and societies alike. Chapter Two therefore ended with a return to classical theories of ethics and wisdom, sources of a language able to take seriously how people and practices are involved in deliberation and the development of meaning, one that can embrace their emotional and sociopolitical aspects without disparaging them. Victor et al (2009: 224) complain that few writers have examined in enough detail 'how people make sense of old age through the rhythm, patterns and activities of daily life'. These classical languages precisely expect such daily details to be pregnant with ethical meaning and to form part of the construction of wise conduct.

Chapter Three went on to identify some major responses by gerontologists to the 'problem of meaning' underlined by H.R. Moody and Thomas Cole (1996) or Phillipson (1998), then discussed methods by which they can be explored. The chapter charted three main groups of meaningfulness referred to by gerontologists, excluding the prescriptive ones dealt with by scholars such as Derkx. This is not an exhaustive or a mutually exclusive list, but it outlines significant preoccupations to be found in the field, and in particular it underlines the need to perceive their social dimensions, or what Baars (2012) refers to as the 'inter-human' quality of action. The first group is concerned with connectedness between individuals and wider phenomena; the second with the development of the lifecourse through time; the third with wisdom and understanding the human condition. In each division we can find three further groups, all conveyed through a multiplicity of languages, symbols, practices and even institutions, and sometimes found in combination. Tornstam, for instance, brings together feelings of connectedness with the cosmos with feeling that one is part of the flow of generations; for him, personal 'tasks of life' are also involved, as are questions of spirituality and ethics.

The first group includes pointfulness or purposefulness, including absorption in an activity that consumes the person concerned, that links the individual to some wider state of affairs. Thus, Thompson et al or Dillon portray the purposefulness of their subjects' lives, pointful within networks that are meaningful to other people too, and supported directly or indirectly by their social surroundings. Then there is, second, religious or spiritual connectedness, or a feeling of connectedness with the cosmos; as Derkx (2013a) points out, this is not necessarily an esoteric position but can be very ordinary. It might or might not be religious, perhaps simply accentuating wider values, modulations that are explored in the work of Tornstam or Coleman. Then, third, there are forms of life-course meaning that stress taking human values and relationships particularly seriously. Mehta's subjects in Singapore gain satisfaction from setting a good example to the young; older people in the former East Germany may see their lives as needing to make public, political contributions in order to be truly meaningful. These cases remind us that meaning should not be treated as confined to the individual; whether or not obviously, it makes sense as social behaviour in some immediate or distant social setting.

The next group of meanings of 'meaning' concentrates more directly on the lifecourse itself, beginning with the idea of 'tasks of life' or developments through time. Social and political backgrounds are important here too, whether or not this is apparent to the individuals concerned. Some versions of this approach to meaning emphasise self-development and psychological or spiritual progress, as do the Eriksons, but others do not. They may stress, like Kohli or Mayer, the (positive or negative) structural constraints that educational systems and bureaucracies impose as parts of the meaning of modern lifecourses. The second group of meanings in this set – the fifth overall – concerns the question of pride in one's lifecourse; or, in the case of the 'spoiled' lives sometimes explored in novels dealing with tragedy or disappointment in the lifecourse, the lack of it. Sixth, there is generational meaning; this is not necessarily meant in the sense of family commitments, but in the sense of wanting to contribute to generations of the future. Some societies or institutions may conduce more to generativity than others, and the forms it may take are multiple, ranging from efforts to protect the environment (Moody, 2014), to multi-generational business projects, or occasions when older people instruct younger ones in classrooms or museums (Edmondson and Fairhurst, 2014). And as the writers of ancient texts were aware, the question of transmitting experience is not simply one way: it happens up the generations too.

Within the last group of approaches to meaningfulness, in the seventh sense we have noted, older people are seen as carrying or embodying messages for others – perhaps about how to achieve behaving morally or how to deal with life's vicissitudes; or the process of ageing itself may be seen as pointful or otherwise. Simply the presence of older people in a landscape or cityscape may be understood as reassuring, or not. The eighth sense has to do with the expectation that growing older assists people in understanding the human condition – what can be expected of oneself, of others or of society. Hannah Arendt (1958) points out that this capacity for understanding too is shaped to some extent by social circumstances. Last, there is a number of ways in which ageing can be associated with the enhancement of wisdom, which is explored in more detail in the subsequent chapter.

These approaches to meaning all have implicit or explicit social and political dimensions, which affects the methods by which they can be investigated. Much gerontology depends on individualised data that downplays the 'inter-human' connections that are key, in different ways, to life-course meaning. The rest of Chapter Three discussed how the delicate balance can be maintained between appreciating individuals and acknowledging their embeddedness in larger settings. This must take into account that many of people's deepest experiences and values are not, or not often, spoken, and that they are influenced by the tacit assumptions in shared languages and daily practices. Learning to interpret these involves acknowledging that words and sentences mean different things in different contexts; this poses challenges not only for interpretation but also for how interpretation can be conveyed in texts.

It also needs to take into account time and change, and the chapter examined efforts to perceive time and narrativity with due recognition for their social aspects: in particular in connection with the notion of 'practice' and the question of how to trace practices with different involvements of and impacts upon older people: wise or otherwise.

To discuss and defend meaning in the lives of (older) people, we need to reclaim discourses for doing it. This cannot be politically transformative simply in itself, but it is a necessary, if not a sufficient, condition for change. For this reason, the fourth chapter explored ancient and contemporary approaches to the tradition of wisdom, searching for an account of wisdom that is attentive to the conduct of everyday life and the minutiae that make it important to those who live it. The idea of wisdom has for most of human history been key in making sense of ageing and the lifecourse, and in daily and public usage it still often is. It also retains some presence in work relevant to gerontology and the lifecourse, used by Frankl, Erikson, Moody, Baars and others. While there are many interpretations of the term – some of which are deeply distorted, like uses of 'wisdom' to adjure resignation to the political status quo – major traditions connect it with tolerance, justice and the common good, and debate about what these entail. The chapter tried to weld these into a transactional version that takes into account the ways in which meaning is socially constructed, and that is suitable for use in gerontology.

To do this it drew on classical ideas, as well as developments in positive psychology, the humanities and the arts, and observations of older people and their creative contributions to other people's lives. Not all these ideas attend to the details of deliberation in wisdom, so they need to be augmented with an account of reasoning that keeps it conjoined with feeling and ethics. The approach explored here goes back to a reading of Aristotle that is hospitable to social and political aspects of deliberation: it recognises that constructive discursive habits must be built up in appropriate social and political contexts, since political forms influence the ways people argue within them. This produces a dynamic account that takes account of how people respond to fluid circumstances, where vital decisions must often be taken with insufficient information, and where they assist each other in deliberating on matters of import to the community. This is an account of wise deliberation that sees it as profoundly human: subject to time and the frequent need to see things anew; creative, partly social and emotional, but as reasonable as possible in the circumstances and sensitive to the overall project of living together in a community. While this tradition explores how virtue and wisdom connect in principle, it need not expect individuals to achieve perfection in virtuous behaviour; it can therefore be used to contribute to a quotidian account of what wisdom might be.

This by no means exhausts the ways in which the idea of wisdom has been used to augment the meaningfulness of a lifecourse. Subsequent interpretations of wisdom include complex blends in the major world religions, each of which embraces a number of versions of what wisdom might be like, some of which are compatible with a 'deliberative' account of wisdom and develop it further, and others which contrast with it. To deepen an understanding of what different approaches to wisdom mean in various traditions and social contexts, the practices in question must be studied as they are enacted in circumstances to which they must respond. 'Patience' or 'tolerance', for example, may be taken to indicate contrasting actions and attitudes as they figure in different forms of life. Some ideas of wisdom concentrate on perfection, like that of the invulnerable Stoic sage, whereas others are more hospitable to the idea of cooperation between imperfect individuals, who can nonetheless help each other to reach insights or forms of behaviour that are wiser than the ones they might have achieved alone.

Psychologists writing in recent decades have interrogated the notion of wisdom with special attentiveness, for example exploring associations between 'wisdom' and moral/emotional capacities such as empathy or compassion. Sternberg emphasises achieving balance between different ranges and aspects of the solution to a problem; Baltes and Staudinger see wisdom as 'orchestrating' capacities such as open-mindedness, tolerance, empathy, acceptance of ambiguity and, particularly, openness to experience. They acknowledge that traditions and habits in a social setting may be supportive of wisdom or otherwise, Staudinger taking a special interest in people who approach wisdom in regulating their own lives. Ardelt stresses personal efforts such as the attempt to suppress egotism and bias, whereas Wink and Dillon suggest that there may be different kinds of wisdom, relating to knowledge and compassion, say, in different ways, and offering different perspectives on the human condition.

While many ancient traditions connect wisdom with wit and creativity, or the struggle for justice, not all older traditions commend themselves today: the reluctance to regard older women as wise, for instance, or the association of wisdom with solemnity and magic that Assmann traces as part of its history. But we can expand the idea of 'openness to experience' by examining the work of Montaigne, or 'the wisdom of the outlaw' in ancient societies; or Kunow's reflections on 'the wisdom of eccentric old men'. These discussions reflect preoccupations that are far from recondite and obscure, but continue in popular culture and films, and in daily practices that are part and parcel of local cultures. Small interactions can be part of wise practices or can activate wisdom in others; the ways people do things can be key to what they mean for others, as in Manheimer's (1999) account of his professor's gentle conversational interventions. People who are called 'wise' in the West of Ireland are often those who can activate wisdom in others: 'wisdom' here can be transactional, actively social, and does not entail an impossible degree of perfection. Gabriel Weston's (2009) account of her medical experience also stresses how wisdom can be learned with age, through encounters with other people and the ethical dilemmas these encounters provoke. The variety and vivacity of these ideas about wisdom cast light on everyday interactions: they show how the idea can help us attach significance to the minutiae that make up lived experience.

A discourse of wisdom for gerontology, in other words, would not so much seek out 'wise people' as appreciate perspectives on wise action that can be found in the transactions of everyday life. Confining gerontology to individual-scale evidence helps us to miss cases where wisdom is experienced, as well as diminishing the seriousness with which everyday life should be taken. A transactional account of wisdom, by contrast, augments the centrality to people's lifecourses of talk and behaviour that they experience as meaningful.

If we treat older people in a way that ignores these issues and focuses on technical questions, however much they may be intended to be progressive, by default we support the view that older people's lives lack intrinsic meaning. Attacking this position, Holstein and Minkler explicitly accentuate the work of Gubrium and others in making later life 'visible from the inside' (2003: 788). They acknowledge the role of 'cultural images, representations, symbols and metaphors' in this process (2003: 791); all these go to make up the ways in which *other people* help us to evolve the values and projects according to which we live our lives. However important continuity may be, 'old age is also importantly about transformation as we learn to accept what we cannot change, rage when we must, and adopt new ways of life as needed'. They suggest that we 'return to the ancient question: What is the good life – for the whole of life – and what does it take to live a good old age? What virtues do we strive for and how do we honor difference?' (2003: 795). To do this involves developing a language that recognises (older) people as makers of meaning in an 'interhuman' context. Policy discourse relating to older people should acknowledge this, ceasing to occlude older people's contributions to the meaningfulness of human lifetimes. For Derkx (2013a), it is crucial to living a human lifecourse that one is able to feel one's own life is morally defensible and meaningful; this is a basic expectation that everyone is entitled to have. According to HelpAge International, there are four key domains in which older people's well-being needs to be ensured: income security, health, personal capability and 'enabling environments'. 'Enabling environments' must be thought of as environments in which the meanings of ageing, and older people's meanings, are taken seriously, and in which there are living, effective discourses for doing so.

References

Achenbaum, A. (1995) *Crossing Frontiers: Gerontology Emerges as a Science*, Cambridge: Cambridge University Press.

Achenbaum, A. and Orwoll, L. (1991) 'Becoming wise: A psycho-gerontological study of the Book of Job', *International Journal of Aging and Human Development* 32, pp. 21–39.

Adams, Tim (2014) 'Every single minute: Review – Hugo Hamilton's tribute to Nuala O'Faolain', *Observer*, www.theguardian.com/books/2014/mar/02/every-single-minute-review-hugo-hamilton-nuala (2 March)

Adler, Alfred (1935) 'The fundamental views of individual psychology', *International Journal of Individual Psychology* 1(1), pp. 5–8.

Ahmadi, L.F. (2001) 'Gerotranscendence and different cultural settings', *Ageing and Society* 21, pp. 395–415.

Alasuutari, Pertti (2009) 'The rise and relevance of qualitative research', *International Journal of Social Research Methodology* 13(2), pp. 139–155.

Alasuutari, Pertti (1995) *Researching Culture: Qualitative Method and Cultural Studies*, London: Sage.

Andrews, Molly (1999) 'The seduction of agelessness', *Ageing and Society* 19(3), pp. 301–331.

Andrews, Molly (2014) *Narrative Imagination and Everyday Life*, New York: Oxford University Press.

Arber, S. and Timonen, V. (2012) *Contemporary Grandparenting: Changing Family Relationships in Global Contexts*, Bristol: Policy Press.

Ardelt, Monika (2011) 'The measurement of wisdom: A commentary on Taylor, Bates, and Webster's comparison of the SAWS and 3D-WS', *Experimental Aging Research* 37(2), pp. 214–255.

Ardelt, Monika (2005) 'How wise people cope with crises and obstacles in life', *Revision: A Journal of Consciousness and Transformation* 28(1), pp. 7–19.

Ardelt, Monika (2004) 'Wisdom as expert knowledge system: A critical review of a contemporary operationalization of an ancient concept', *Human Development* 47, pp. 257–285.

Ardelt, Monika (2003) 'Empirical assessment of a three-dimensional wisdom scale', *Research on Aging* 25(3), pp. 275–324.

Ardelt, Monika (2002) 'Effects of religion and purpose in life on elders' subjective well-being and attitudes toward death', *Journal of Religious Gerontology* 12(4), pp. 55–77.

Ardelt, Monika (1997) 'Wisdom and life satisfaction in old age', *Journal of Gerontology* 52B, pp. 15–27.

Ardelt, Monika, Achenbaum, W. Andrew and Oh, Hunhui (2013) 'The paradoxical nature of personal wisdom and its relation to human development in the reflective, cognitive and affective domains', in Michel Ferrari and Nic Weststrate (eds) *The Scientific Study of Personal Wisdom: From Contemplative Traditions to Neuroscience*, New York: Springer, pp. 265–295.

Arendt, Hannah (1958) *The Human Condition*, Chicago: Chicago University Press.

Arensberg, Conrad and Kimball, Solon (1940/2001) *Family and Community in Ireland*, Ennis: CLASP Press.

Asad, T. (1986/2010) 'The concept of cultural translation in British social anthropology', in J. Clifford and G. Marcus (eds) *Writing Culture: The Poetics and Politics of Ethnography*, 2nd edn, Berkeley: University of California Press, pp. 141–165.

Assman, Aleida (1991) 'Was ist Weisheit?', in Aleida Assman (ed) *Weisheit*, Munich: Wilhelm Fink, pp. 15–44.

Atchley, R.C. (2011) 'How spiritual experience and development interact with aging', *Journal of Transpersonal Psychology* 43(2), pp. 156–165.

Atchley, R. (1999) *Continuity and Adaptation in Ageing: Creating Positive Experiences*, Baltimore, MD: Johns Hopkins University Press.

Atkinson, Paul (2005) 'Qualitative research: Unity and diversity', *Forum* 6(3), article 26.

Baars, Jan (2012) *Aging and the Art of Living*, Baltimore, MD: Johns Hopkins University Press.

Baars, Jan (2012a) 'Critical turns of aging, narrative and time', *International Journal of Ageing and Later Life* 7(2), pp. 143–165.

Baars, J. (2007) 'Introduction: Chronological time and chronological age: Problems of temporal diversity', in J. Baars and H. Visser (eds) *Aging and Time*, Amityville, NY: Baywood, pp. 15–42.

Baars, Jan, Dohmen, Joseph, Grenier, Amanda and Phillipson, Chris (eds) (2013) *Ageing, Meaning and Social Structure: Connecting Critical and Humanistic Gerontology*, Bristol: Policy Press.

Baltes, P.B. and Staudinger, U.M. (2000) 'Wisdom: A metaheuristic (pragmatic) to orchestrate mind and virtue toward excellence', *American Psychologist*, 55, pp. 122–136.

Baltes, P.B., Staudinger, U.M., Maerckler, A. and Smith, J. (1995) 'People nominated as wise: A comparative study of wisdom-related knowledge', *Psychology and Aging*, 10(2), pp.155-166.

Baltes, Paul and Baltes, Margaret (1993) 'Psychological perspectives on successful aging: The model of selective optimization with compensation', in Paul Baltes and Margaret Baltes (eds) *Successful Aging: Perspectives from the Behavioral Sciences*, Cambridge: Cambridge University Press, pp. 1–34.

Basting, Anne (2011) Keynote speech at conference 'Theorizing Age: Challenging the Disciplines', 7th International Symposium on Cultural Gerontology/ENAS, Maastricht.

Bauman, Zygmunt (2000) *Liquid Modernity*, Cambridge: Polity.

Bauman, Zygmunt and Donskis, Leonidas (2013) *Moral Blindness: The Loss of Sensitivity in Liquid Modernity*, Cambridge: Polity.

Baumeister, Roy (1991) *Meanings of Life*, New York: Guilford Press.

Beauvoir, Simone de [1970] (1996) *The Coming of Age*, trans. Patrick O'Brien, New York: Norton.

Becker, H. (1963) 'Labelling theory', ch. 9 in *Outsiders: Studies in the Sociology of Deviance*, Glencoe: Free Press, pp. 177–205.

Bellah, R., Madsen, R., Sullivan, W., Swidler, A. and Tipton, S. (1991) *The Good Society*, New York: Knopf.

Benjamin, Walter (1936/1969) 'The storyteller: Reflections on the work of Nikolai Leskov', in *Illuminations*, ed. Hannah Arendt, transl. Harry Zohn, New York: Schocken Books, pp. 83–107.

Berger, Peter, Berger, Brigitte and Kellner, Hansfried (1974) *The Homeless Mind: Modernization and Consciousness*, New York: Random House.

Biggs, S. (2007) 'Thinking about generations: Conceptual positions and policy implications', *Journal of Social Issues* 63(4), p.16.

Biggs, Simon (2004) 'Age, gender, narratives, and masquerades', *Journal of Aging Studies* 18(1), 45–58.

Biggs, Simon and Lowenstein, Ariela (2011) *Generational Intelligence: A Critical Approach to Age Relations*, London: Routledge.

Biggs, Simon and Powell, Jason L. (2001) 'A Foucauldian analysis of old age and the power of social welfare', *Journal of Aging and Social Policy* 12, pp. 93–111.

Birren, James and Deuchman, Donna (1991) *Guiding Autobiography Groups for Older Adults: Exploring the Fabric of Life*, Baltimore, MD: Johns Hopkins University Press.

Birren, J.E. and Fisher, L. (1990) 'The elements of wisdom: Overview and integration', in R.J. Sternberg (ed) *Wisdom: Its Nature, Origins and Development*, Cambridge: Cambridge University Press, pp. 40–55.

Birren, J.E. and Schroots, J.J.F. (2006) 'Autobiographical memory and the narrative self over the lifespan: The recall of happy, sad, traumatic and involuntary memories', in J.E. Birren and K.W. Schaie (eds) *Handbook of the Psychology of Aging*, 6th edn, San Diego: Academic Press, pp. 477–498.

Birren, James E. and Svensson, Cheryl M. (2005) 'Wisdom in history', in Robert Sternberg and Jennifer Jordan (eds) *A Handbook of Wisdom: Psychological Perspectives*, New York: Cambridge University Press, pp. 3–31.

Blackburn, Simon (2001) *Being Good: A Short Introduction to Ethics*, Oxford: Oxford University Press.

Blaikie, Andrew (2002) 'The secret world of sub-cultural ageing: What unites and what divides?', in Lars Andersson (ed) *Cultural Gerontology*, Westport, CT: Auburn House, pp. 95–100.

Blau, Peter (1956) *Bureaucracy in Modern Society*, New York: Random House.

Bly, Peter Anthony (2004) *The Wisdom of Eccentric Old Men: A Study of Type and Secondary Character in Galdós's Social Novels, 1870–1897*, Quebec: McGill-Queen's University Press.

Booth, Wayne (1988) *The Company We Keep: The Ethics of Fiction*, Berkeley: University of California Press.

Bosanquet, Bernard (1899/ 2001) *The Philosophical Theory of the State*, 2001 edn, Kitchener, Ont: Batoche Books.

Botelho, Lynn (2000) 'The 17th CENTURY', in Pat Thane (ed) *Old Age in English History: Past Experiences, Present Issues*, Oxford: Oxford University Press, pp. 113–174.

Bourdieu, P. (1993) *Sociology in Question*, London: Sage.

Bourdieu, P. (1980/1990) *The Logic of Practice*, trans. Richard Nice, Cambridge: Polity Press.

Braam, Arjan, Bramsen, Inge, van Tilburg, Theo G., van der Ploeg, Henk H. and Deeg, Dorly J.H. (2006) 'Cosmic transcendence and framework of meaning in life: Patterns among older adults in the Netherlands' *Journal of Gerontology B*, 61, pp. 121–128.

Bradley, F.H. (1876) 'My station and its duties', ch. 5 in *Ethical Studies*, London: Oxford University Press.

Breen, Keith (2012) 'Reason, production, and rival visions of working life', in Ricca Edmondson and Karlheinz Hülser (eds) *Politics of Practical Reasoning: Integrating Action, Discourse and Argument*, Lanham, MD: Lexington, pp. 147–170.

Brown, Richard Harvey (1987) *Society as Text: Essays on Rhetoric, Reason and Reality*, Chicago: Chicago University Press.

Brückner, Hannah and Mayer, Karl-Ulrich (2005) 'De-standardizatio of the life course: What it might mean? And if it means anything, whether it actually took place?', in Ross Macmillan (ed) *The Structure of the Life Course: Standardized? Individualized? Differentiated?* Amsterdam: Elsevier, pp. 27–53.

Burbank, P.M. (1992) 'Exploratory study: Assessing the meaning in life among older adult clients', *Journal of Gerontological Nursing* 18(9), pp. 19–28.

Burkitt, Ian (2002) 'Technologies of the self: Habitus and capacities', *Journal for the Theory of Social Behaviour* 32(2), pp. 219–237.

Butler, Robert (1975) *Why survive? Being old in America*, San Francisco: Harper and Row.

Butler, Robert (1963) 'The life review: An interpretation of reminiscence in the aged', *Psychiatry* 26: 65–76.

Byrne, Anne, Edmondson, Ricca and Varley, Tony (eds) (2001) 'Introduction to the Third Edition', in Conrad Arensberg and Solon Kimball, *Family and Community in Ireland*, Ennis: CLASP Press.

Bytheway, Bill (2011) *Unmasking Age: The Significance of Age for Social Research*, Bristol: Policy Press.

Bytheway, Bill (1995) *Ageism*, Buckingham: Open University Press.

Carrington, Leonora (1974/2004) *The Hearing Trumpet*, London: Exact Change.

Christie, Agatha (1977) *An Autobiography*, London: Dodd, Mead and Co.

Cicero, *De Senectute* ('On Old Age') in *Selected Works*, ed. and trans. Michael Grant, rev. edn 1971, London: Penguin, pp. 211–249.

Cicero, *Laelius De Amicitia* ('On Friendship'), ed. H.E. Gould and J.L. Whitely, 2013, London: Bloomsbury.

Cicero, *De Oratore* ('The Ideal Orator'), trans. H. Rackham, 1977, London: Heinemann and Harvard University Press: Loeb Classical Library.

Clarke, Ernest (1973) *The Wisdom of Solomon*, Cambridge: Cambridge University Press.

Clayton, V.P. and Birren, J.E. (1980) 'The development of wisdom across the life-span: A re-examination of an ancient topic', in P.E. Baltes and O.G. Brim (eds) *Life-span Development and Behavior*, vol. 3, New York: Academic Press, pp. 103–135.

Clifford, J. and Marcus, G. (eds) (2010) *Writing Culture: The Poetics and Politics of Ethnography*, 2nd edn, Berkeley: University of California Press.

Cole, Thomas (2014) 'Nonviolent resistance and dementia: The story of Walter Wink', paper presented at 8th Symposium on Cultural Gerontology/2nd Conference of European Network of Aging Studies, Galway, April.

Cole, Thomas (1994) 'Generational equity in America: A cultural historian's perspective' in Chris Hackler (ed) *Health Care for an Aging Population*, Albany: State University of New York Press, pp. 19–32.

Cole, Thomas (1992) *The Journey of Life: A Cultural History of Aging in America*, Cambridge: Cambridge University Press.

Cole, Thomas and Gadow, Sally (eds) (1986) *What Does It Mean To Grow Old?* Durham, NC: Duke University Press.

Cole, Thomas, Ray, Ruth and Kastenbaum, Robert (2010) 'Introduction: The humanistic study of aging past and present, or why gerontology still needs interpretive enquiry', in Thomas Cole, Ruth Ray and Robert Kastenbaum (eds) *A Guide to Humanistic Studies in Aging: What Does it Mean to Grow Old?* Baltimore, MD: Johns Hopkins University Press, pp. 1–29.

Coleman, P. (2011) *Belief and Ageing: Spiritual Pathways in Later Life*, Bristol: Policy Press.

Coleman, P. (2009) 'Religious belonging and spiritual questioning: A Western European perspective on ageing and religion', in Ricca Edmondson and Hans-Joachim von Kondratowitz (eds) *Valuing Older People: A Humanist Approach to Ageing*, Bristol: Policy Press, pp. 23–36.

Coleman, Peter, Mills, Marie and Speck, Peter (2006) 'Ageing and belief – between tradition and change', in J. Vincent, C. Phillipson and M. Downes (eds) *The Futures of Old Age*, London: Sage, pp. 125–134.

Cowgill, Donald (1974) 'The aging of populations and societies', *Annals of the American Academy of Political and Social Science* 415(1), pp. 1–18.

Curnow, Trevor (2015) *Wisdom: A History*, Chicago: Redaktion Books.

Curnow, Trevor (2010) *Wisdom in the Ancient World*, London: Duckworth.

Curnow, Trevor (2008) 'Introduction: Sophia's world: Episodes from the history of wisdom', in M. Ferrari and G. Potworowski (eds) *Teaching for Wisdom: Cross-cultural Perspectives on Fostering Wisdom*, Dordrecht: Springer, pp. 1–19.

Curnow, Trevor (1999) *Wisdom, Intuition, and Ethics*, Aldershot: Ashgate.

Dalby, P. (2006) 'Is there a process of spiritual change or development associated with ageing? A critical review of research', *Aging and Mental Health*, 10(1), pp. 4–12.

Dannefer, Dale (2003) 'Cumulative advantage/disadvantage and the life course: Crossfertilizing age and social science theory', *Journal of Gerontology: Social Sciences* 58, pp. 327–337.

Dannefer, Dale (1987) 'Aging as intracohort differentiation: Accentuation, the Matthew effect and the life course', *Sociological Forum* 2(2), pp. 211–236.

Dannefer, Dale and Kelly-Moore, J.A. (2009) 'Theorizing the life course: New twists in the paths', in V. Bengtson, D. Gans, N.M. Putney and M. Silverstein (eds) *Handbook of Theories of Aging*, New York: Springer, pp. 389–411.

Dannefer, Dale and Settersten, Richard (2010) 'The study of the life course: Implications for social gerontology', in Chris Phillipson and Dale Dannefer (eds) *The Sage Handbook of Social Gerontology*, London: Sage, pp. 3–19.

Deleuze, Gilles and Guattari, Félix (1976) *Rhizome – Introduction*, Paris: Éditions de Minuit.

De Medeiros, Kate (2014) *Narrative Gerontology in Research and Practice*, New York: Springer.

Denning-Bolle, Sara (1992) *Wisdom in Akkadian Literature*, Leipzig: Ex Oriente Lux.

Denzin, Norman K. (2001) 'The reflexive interview and a performative social science', *Qualitative Research* 1 (1), pp. 23–46.

Derkx, Peter (2013a) 'Humanism as a meaning frame', in A.B. Pinn (ed) *What Is Humanism and Why Does It Matter?* (Studies in Humanist Thought and Praxis), Durham, UK: Acumen, pp. 42–57.

Derkx, Peter (2013b) 'Ageing and transcendence: A humanist investigation', paper presented at the 5th International Conference on Ageing and Spirituality, Edinburgh, July.

Dillon, Michele (2009) 'Integrating the sacred in creative ageing', in Ricca Edmondson and Hans-Joachim von Kondratowitz (eds) *Valuing Older People: A Humanist Approach to Ageing*, Bristol: Policy Press, pp. 51–72.

Dillon, Michele and Wink, Paul (2007) *In the Course of a Lifetime: Tracing Religious Belief, Practice, and Change*, Berkeley: University of California Press.

Dittman-Kohli, F. (1984) 'Weisheit als mögliches Ergebnis der Intelligenzentwicklung im Erwachsenenalter', *Sprache und Kognition* 2, pp. 112–132

Dixon, Thomas (2003) *From Passions to Emotions: The Creation of a Secular Psychological Category*, Cambridge: Cambridge University Press.

Dohmen, Joseph (2013) 'My own life: Ethics, ageing and lifestyle', in J. Baars, J. Dohmen, A. Grenier and C. Phillipson (eds) *Ageing, Meaning and Social Structure: Connecting Critical and Humanistic Gerontology*, Bristol: Policy Press, pp. 31–54.

Dohmen, Joseph (2002) *Over levenskunst. De grote filosofen over het goede leven*, Amsterdam: Ambo.

Domínguez-Rué, Emma (2013) 'What goes around comes back around: Life narratives and the significance of the past in Donna Leon's *Death at La Fenice*', paper presented at British Society of Gerontology Conference, Oxford, 2013.

Donkin, A., Goldblatt, P. and Lynch, K. (2002) 'Inequalities in life expectancy by social class 1972–1999', *Health Statistics Quarterly* 15, pp. 5–15.

Donovan, Vincent (1978) *Christianity Rediscovered*, West Madison, WI: Fides/Claretian Press.

Duncan, Simon (2011) 'Personal life, pragmatism and bricolage', Sociological Research Online, 16(4) 13, www.socresonline.org.uk/16/4/13.html> 10.5153/sro.2537

Eagleton, Terry (2003) *After Theory*, New York: Basic Books.

Ebrahim, Shah (2002) 'The medicalization of old age: Should be encouraged', *British Medical Journal* 324(7342), pp. 861–863, www.ncbi.nlm.nih.gov/pmc/articles/PMC1122816/ (accessed 4 November 2012).

Edmondson, Ricca (2013) 'A social interpretation of personal wisdom', in Michel Ferrari and Nic Weststrate (eds) *The Scientific Study of Personal Wisdom: From Contemplative Traditions to Neuroscience*, New York: Springer, pp. 191–209.

Edmondson, Ricca (2013a), 'The sociology of ageing', in Tom Dening and Alan Thomas (eds) *The Oxford Textbook of Old Age Psychiatry* (5th edn), Oxford: Oxford University Press.

Edmondson, Ricca (2013b) 'Cultural gerontology: Valuing older people', in Katrin Komp and Marja Aartsen (eds) *Old Age in Europe: A Textbook of Gerontology*, Dordrecht: Springer, pp. 113–130.

Edmondson, Ricca (2012a) 'Practical reasoning in place: Tracing "wise" inferences in everyday life', in Ricca Edmondson and Karlheinz Hülser (eds) *Politics of Practical Reasoning: Integrating Action, Discourse, and Argument*, Lanham, MD: Lexington, pp. 111–130.

Edmondson, Ricca (2012b), 'Intergenerational relations in the West of Ireland: Socio-cultural approaches to wisdom and resilience', *Journal of Family Issues* 33(1), pp. 76–98.

Edmondson, Ricca (2009) 'Wisdom: A humanist approach to valuing older people', in Ricca Edmondson and Hans-Joachim von Kondratowitz (eds) *Valuing Older People: A Humanist Approach to Ageing*, Bristol: Policy Press, pp. 201–216.

Edmondson, Ricca (2007) 'Rhetorics of social science (reflexive sociology, disciplinary boundaries and the paradigmatic role of methodologies)', in William Outhwaite and Stephen Turner (eds) *The Handbook of Social Science Methodology*, London: Sage, pp. 479–498.

Edmondson, Ricca (2005) 'Wisdom in later life: Ethnographic approaches', *Ageing in Society* 25(6), pp. 339–356.

Edmondson, Ricca (2003) 'Social capital: A strategy for advancing health?', *Social Science and Medicine* 57(9), pp. 1723–1733.

Edmondson, R. (2000a) 'Rural temporal practices: Future time in Connemara', *Time and Society* 9 (2/3), pp. 269–288.

Edmondson, Ricca (2000b) 'Health promotion and the study of cultural practices', in Ricca Edmondson and Cecily Kelleher (eds) *Health Promotion: New Discipline or Multidiscipline?* Dublin: Irish Academic Press, pp. 71–94.

Edmondson, Ricca (1998) *Ireland: Society and Culture*, Distance University of Hagen, (Germany) course text.

Edmondson, R. (1984) *Rhetoric in Sociology*, London: Macmillan.

Edmondson, Ricca and Fairhurst, Eileen (2014) 'Counter-cultural constructions of health and wisdom', in Ulla Kriebernegg, Roberta Maierhofer and Barbara Ratzenböck (eds) *Alive and Kicking at All Ages*, Bielefeld: Transcript, pp. 169–186.

Edmondson, Ricca and Hülser, Karlheinz (2012) 'Introduction: Integrated practical reasoning', in Ricca Edmondson and Karlheinz Hülser (eds) *Politics of Practical Reasoning: Integrating Action, Discourse and Argument,* Lanham, MD: Lexington, pp. 1–14.

Edmondson, Ricca and Pearce, Jane (2007) 'The practice of health care: Wisdom as a model', *Medicine, Health Care and Philosophy* 10(3), pp. 233–244.

Edmondson, Ricca and Scharf, Tom (2015) 'Rural and urban ageing: Contributions of cultural gerontology', in Julia Twigg and Wendy Martin (eds) *Routledge Handbook of Cultural Gerontology*, London: Routledge, pp. 412–419.

Edmondson, Ricca, Pearce, Jane and Woerner, Markus H. (2009) 'When wisdom is called for in clinical reasoning', in William Stempsey (ed) *Theoretical Medicine and Bioethics* 30, pp. 231–247.

Edmunds, June and Turner, Bryan S. (2002) *Generations, Culture and Society*, Ballmoor, Bucks: Open University Press.

Elder, Glen (2005) 'Overview of Dr Elder's research: The life course and human development', www.cpc.unc.edu/projects/lifecourse/elder_research (first accessed 30 March 2012).

Elder, Glen (1999) 'The life course and aging: Some reflections', address to American Sociological Association, www.unc.edu/~elder/pdf/asa-99talk.pdf.

Elder, Glen (1974) *Children of the Great Depression: Social Change in Life Experience* (25th anniversary edition, 1999) Boulder, CO: Westview Press.

Elder, Glen H., Jr. and Johnson, Monika Kirkpatrick (2003) 'The life course and aging: Challenges, lessons and new directions', in R.A. Settersten, Jr (ed) *Invitation to the Life Course: Toward New Understandings of Later Life*, Amityville, NY: Baywood, pp. 49–81.

Erikson, Eric H. (1997) *The Life Cycle Completed: Extended Version with new chapters on the ninth stage of development by Joan M. Erikson*, New York: Norton.

Erikson, Eric, Erikson, Joan and Kivnick, Helen (1986) *Vital Involvement in Old Age*, New York: Norton.

Erikson, Erik (1963) *Childhood and Society*, New York: Norton

Estes, C. and Binney, E. (1989) 'The biomedicalization of aging: Dangers and dilemmas', *The Gerontologist 29*(5), pp. 587–96.

Fairhurst, Eileen (1990) 'Doing ethnography in a geriatric unit', in Shiela Peace (ed) *Researching Social Gerontology: Concepts, Methods and Issues*, London: Sage, pp. 101–114.

Fealy, Gerard, McNamara, Martin, Treacy, Margaret Pearl, and Lyons, Imogen (2012) 'Constructing ageing and age identities: a case study of newspaper discourses', *Ageing and Society* 31(1), pp. 85–102.

Featherstone, M. (2010) 'Body, image and affect in consumer culture', *Body and Society* 16(1), pp. 193–221.

Ferrari, Michel, Westrate, Nic and Petro, Anda (2013) 'Stories of wisdom to live by: Developing wisdom in a narrative mode', in Michel Ferrari and Nic Weststrate (eds) *The Scientific Study of Personal Wisdom: From Contemplative Traditions to Neuroscience*, New York: Springer, pp. 137–164.

Fine, Robert (2015) 'The evolution of the modern revolutionary tradition: A phenomenological reading of Hannah Arendt's *On Revolution*', *European Journal of Cultural and Political Sociology* 1(3), pp. 216–233.

Frankl, Viktor (1972) 'Man's Search for Meaning', address in Toronto, www.youtube.com/watch?v=fD1512_XJEw.

Frankl, Viktor (1964) *Man's Search for Meaning: An Introduction to Logotherapy* (rev. edn; original German version published 1946; previous English editions 1959, 1962 by Beacon Press), London: Hodder and Stoughton.

Freeden, Michael (2003) *Ideology: A Very Short Introduction*, Oxford: Oxford University Press.

Friedman, Milton (1970) 'The social responsibility of business is to increase its profit', *New York Times Magazine*, 13 September.

Gallagher, Carmel (2008) *The Community Life of Older People in Ireland*, Oxford: Peter Lang.

Garavan, Mark (2008) 'Problems in achieving dialogue: Cultural misunderstandings in the Corrib gas dispute', in Ricca Edmondson and Henrike Rau (eds) *Environmental Argument and Cultural Difference: Locations, Fractures and Deliberations*, Oxford: Peter Lang, pp. 65–92.

Gaut, Berys (1999) 'Identification and emotion in narrative film', in Carl Plantinga and G.M. Smith (eds) *Passionate Views: Thinking about Film and Emotion*, Baltimore, MD: Johns Hopkins University Press, pp. 200–216.

Geertz, Clifford (1973) 'Thick description: Toward an interpretive theory of culture', in Clifford Geertz, *The Interpretation of Cultures*, New York: Basic Books, pp. 3–30.

Gei␣ler, K., Kümmerer, K. and Sabelis, I. (eds) (2006) *Zeitvielfalt: Wider das Diktat der Uhr*, Stuttgart: Hirzel.

Giddens, A. (1991) *Modernity and Self-Identity: Self and Society in the Late Modern Age*, Palo Alto, CA: Stanford University Press.

Gilleard, C. (2005) 'Cultural approaches to the ageing body', in Malcolm Johnson (ed) *The Cambridge Handbook of Age and Ageing*, Cambridge: Cambridge University Press, pp. 156–164.

Gilleard, C. and Higgs, P. (2013) *Ageing, Corporeality, and Embodiment*, London: Anthem Press.

Gilleard, C. and Higgs, P. (2000) *Cultures of Ageing: Self, Citizen and the Body*, London: Routledge.

Glück, Judith, Strasser, Irene and Bluck, Susan (2009) 'Gender differences in implicit theories of wisdom', *Research in Human Development* 6(1), pp. 27–44.

Glück, Judith, König, Susanne, Naschenweng, Katja, Redzanowski, Uwe, Dorner, Lara, Straßer, Irene and Wiedermann, Wolfgang (2013) 'How to measure wisdom: Content, reliability and validity of five measures', *Frontiers in Psychology* 4, p. 405, doi: 10.3389/fpsyg.2013.00405.

Goodin, R.E., Mahmud Rice, J., Parpo, A. and Eriksson, L. (eds) (2008) *Discretionary Time: A New Measure of Freedom*, Cambridge: Cambridge University Press.

Grenier, Amanda (2012) *Transitions and the Lifecourse: Challenging the Constructions of 'Growing Old'*, Bristol: Policy.

Green, Sheree Louise (2013) '"An unnoticing environment": Deficiencies and remedies – services for adults with learning disabilities', *Journal of Adult Protection* 15(4), pp. 192–202.

Grey, Aubrey de (with Michael Rae) (2007) *Ending Aging: The Rejuvenation Breakthroughs that Could Reverse Human Aging in Our Lifetime*, New York: St. Martin's Griffin.

Gubrium, Jaber F. (2011) 'Narrative events and biographical construction in old age', in Gary Kenyon, Ernst Bohlmeijer, and William Randall (eds) *Storying Later Life: Issues, Investigations, and Interventions in Narrative Gerontology*, New York: Oxford University Press, pp. 39–50.

Gubrium, Jaber F. (1975/1997) *Living and Dying at Murray Manor*, Charlottesville: University Press of Virginia.

Gubrium, Jaber F. and Holstein, James A. (1999) 'At the border of narrative and ethnography', *Journal of Contemporary Ethnography* 28(5), pp. 561–573.

Gubrium, Jaber F. and Holstein, James A. (2009) *Analyzing Narrative Reality*, Thousand Oaks, CA: Sage.

Gullette, Margaret M. (2004) *Aged by Culture*, Chicago: University of Chicago Press.

Gunnarson, Evy (2011) 'Older people's meaning of everyday life and the lived body', in Brian Worsfold (ed) *Acculturating Age: Approaches to Cultural Gerontology*, Lleida: University of Leida Press, pp. 89–104.

Hahn, A. (1991) 'Zur Soziologie der Weisheit', in A. Assman (ed) *Weisheit: Archaeologie der literarischen Kommunikation*, Munich: Wilhelm Fink Verlag, pp. 47–58.

Hamers, Josiane and Blanc, Michel (2000) *Bilinguality and Bilingualism*, 2nd edn, Cambridge: Cambridge University Press.

Hamilton, Hugo (2014) *Every Single Minute*, London: Harper Collins.

Hareven, Tamara (1982) 'The life course and ageing in historical perspective', in Tamara Hareven and Kate Adams (eds) *Ageing and Life Course Transitions: An Interdisciplinary Perspective*, London: Tavistock, pp. 1–26.

Hargreaves, Tom (2011) 'Practice-ing behaviour change: Applying social practice theory to pro-environmental behaviour change', *Journal of Consumer Culture* 11(1), pp. 79–99.

Harvey, David (2005) *A Brief History of Neoliberalism*, Oxford: Oxford University Press.

Hazan, Haim (2009) 'Beyond dialogue: Entering the fourth space in old age', in Ricca Edmondson and Hans-Joachim von Kondratowitz (eds) *Valuing Older People: A Humanist Approach to Ageing*, Bristol: Policy Press, pp. 91–104.

Hepworth, M. (2000) *Stories of Ageing*, Buckingham: Open University Press.

Hepworth, M. and Featherstone, M. (2005) 'Images of ageing: Cultural representations of later life', in Malcolm Johnson (ed) *The Cambridge Handbook of Age and Ageing*, Cambridge: Cambridge University Press, pp. 354–362.

Hertzler, Joyce (1936) *The Social Thought of the Ancient Civilizations*, New York: McGraw-Hill.

Hill, P.C. and Pargament, K.I. (2003) 'Advances in the conceptualization and measurement of religion and spirituality: Implications for physical and mental health research', *American Psychologist* 58(1), pp. 64–74.

Hitchings, Russell (2012) 'People can talk about their practices', *Area* 44(1), pp. 61–67.

Hogan, Michael (2010) *The Culture of our Thinking in Relation to Spirituality*, New York: Nova Science.

Hoffmann, Nora (2013) 'Deficient families in Theodor Fontane's novels: The antithetic roles of mother and father in parent–child relationships', in Tina-Karen Pusse and Katharina Walter (eds) *Precarious Parenthood: Doing Family in Literature and Film*, Vienna: LitVerlag, pp. 23–41.

Holliday, Stephen G. and Chandler, Michael J. (1986) *Wisdom: Explorations in Adult Competence*, Basel: Karger.

Holstein, J.A. and Gubrium, J.F. (2000) *The Self We Live By: A Narrative Identity in a Postmodern World*, New York and Oxford: Oxford University Press.

Holstein, M.B. and Minkler, M. (2003) 'Self, society and the "new gerontology"', *Gerontologist* 43(6), pp. 787–796.

Honneth, Axel (2004) 'Organized self-realization: Some paradoxes of individualization', *European Journal of Social Theory* 7(4), pp. 463–478.

House, J. (2001) 'Understanding social factors and inequalities in health: 20th century progress and 21st century prospects', *Journal of Health and Social Behavior* 43, pp. 125–142.

Hughes, Everett (1971) *The Sociological Eye: Selected Papers*, New Brunswick: Transaction Books.

Hughes, Everett (1945) 'Dilemmas and contradictions of status', *American Journal of Sociology*, March, pp. 353–359.

Hülsen-Esch, Andrea von (2013) 'Men grow wiser, women fall apart', paper to 3rd International Wisdom Workshop, University of Potsdam, June.

Jackson, T. (2009) *Prosperity without Growth?* London: Sustainable Development Commission.

Jacq, Christian (2006/2004) *The Wisdom of Ptah-Hotep: Spiritual Treasures from the Age of the Pyramids*, London: Constable and Robinson.

Jameson, Frederic (1991) *Postmodernism, or, the Cultural Logic of Late Capitalism*, Durham, NC: Duke University Press.

Jeste, D.V., Ardelt, M., Blazer, D., Kraemer, H.C., Vaillant, G. and Meeks, T.W. (2010) 'Expert consensus on characteristics of wisdom: A Delphi method study', *The Gerontologist* 50(5), pp. 668–680.

Joas, Hans (2013) *The Sacredness of the Person: A New Genealogy of Human Rights*, Washington, DC: Georgetown University Press.

John, Eileen (2000) 'Art and knowledge', in Berys Gaut and Dominic McIver Lopes (eds) *The Routledge Companion to Aesthetics*, London: Routledge, pp. 384–393.

Jolanki, Outi (2009) 'Talk about old age, health and morality', in R. Edmondson and H.-J. von Kondratowitz (eds) *Valuing Older People: A Humanist Approach to Ageing*, Bristol: Policy Press, pp. 261–274.

Jordan, Jennifer (2005) 'The quest for wisdom in adulthood: A psychological perspective', in R. Sternberg and J. Jordan (eds) *A Handbook of Wisdom: Psychological Perspectives*, Cambridge: Cambridge University Press, pp. 160–188.

Kattago, Siobhan (2015) 'Introduction: Memory studies and its companions', in Siobhan Kattago (ed) *The Ashgate Research Companion to Memory Studies*, Farnham: Ashgate, pp. 1–19.

Katz, Stephen (2009) *Cultural Aging: Life Course, Lifestyle, and Senior Worlds*, Toronto: University of Toronto Press.

Katz, Stephen (1996) *Disciplining Old Age: The Formation of Gerontological Knowledge*, Charlottesville: University Press of Virginia.

Keeling, Sally (2013) Review of Komp, Kathrin and Carr, Dawn (eds) (2012) *Gerontology in the Era of the Third Age: Implications and Next Steps* (New York: Springer), *Ageing and Society* 33(2), pp. 364–365.

Kekes, John (1997) *Moral Wisdom and Good Lives*, Ithaca, NY: Cornell University Press.

Kelly, Christopher and Committee on Standards in Public Life (2013) *Standards Matter: A Review of Best Practice in Promoting Good Behaviour in Public Life*, www.public-standards.org.uk/Library/Standards_Matter.pdf.

Kimball, Solon (1979) 'Warner, W. Lloyd', *International Encyclopaedia of the Social Sciences*, 18, pp. 791–796.

King, Anna (2014) 'An alternative gathering: Public space and shared agency in the lived experience of multicultural Ireland', unpublished PhD thesis, National University of Ireland, Galway.

Kohli, Martin (2007) 'The institutionalization of the life course: Looking back to look ahead', *Research in Human Development* 4(3–4), pp. 253–271.

Kohli, Martin (1986) 'Social organization and subjective construction of the life course', in A. Sorenson, F.E. Weiner, and L.R. Sherrod (eds) *Human Development and the Life Cycle*, Hillside, NJ: Laurence Erlbaum Associates, pp. 271–292.

Kohli, Martin and Meyer, John W. (1986) 'Social structure and social construction of life stages', *Human Development* 29, pp. 145–149.

Komp, Kathrin and Carr, Dawn (eds) (2012) *Gerontology in the Era of the Third Age: Implications and Next Steps*, New York: Springer.

Kondratowitz, H.-J. von (2009) 'The long road to a moralisation of old age', in R. Edmondson and H.-J. von Kondratowitz (eds) *Valuing Older People: A Humanist Approach to Ageing*, Bristol: Policy Press, pp. 107–122.

Kotre, John (2004) 'Generativity and culture: What meaning can do', in Ed de St Aubin, Dan P. McAdams and Tae-Change Kim (eds) *The Generative Society: Caring for Future Generations*, Washington, DC: American Psychological Association, pp. 35–50.

Kotre, John (1999) *Make It Count: How to Generate a Legacy that Gives Meaning to Your Life*, New York: Free Press.

Kotre, John (1996) *Outliving the Self: How We Live on in Future Generations*, 2nd edn, New York: W.W. Norton & Co.

Krause, Neal (2009) 'Deriving a sense of meaning in late life: An overlooked forum for the development of interdisciplinary theory', in Vern Bengtson, Merril Silverstein, Norella Putney and Daphna Gans (eds) *Handbook of Theories of Aging*, New York: Springer, pp. 101–116.

Krekula, Clary (2011) 'Åldersdiskriminering i svenskt arbetsliv. Om ålderskodningar och myter som skapar ojämlikhet [Age discrimination in Swedish working life. On age codings and myths that create inequality]', *Official report from the Ombudsman for Discrimination*, Stockholm: Karlstad University.

Krekula, Clary (2009) 'Age coding: On age-based practices of distinction', *International Journal of Ageing and Later Life*, 4(2), pp. 7–31, www.ep.liu.se/ej/ijal/.

Krekula, Clary (2007) 'The intersection of age and gender: Reworking gender theory and social gerontology', *Current Sociology* 55(2), pp. 155–171.

Küng, Hans (2006) '22nd Niwano Peace Prize commemorative address', *Buddhist-Christian Studies* 26, pp. 203–208.

Kunow, Rüdiger (2010) 'Old age and globalisation', in Thomas Cole, Ruth Ray and Robert Kastenbaum (eds) *A Guide to Humanistic Studies in Aging: What Does it Mean to Grow Old?*, Baltimore, MA: Johns Hopkins University Press, pp. 293–318.

Kunow, Rüdiger (2009) 'The coming of age: The descriptive organization of later life', in A. Hornung and R. Kunow (eds) *Representation and Decoration in a Postmodern Age,* Heidelberg: Winter, pp. 295–309.

Kunzmann, U. and Baltes, P. (2005) 'The psychology of wisdom: Theoretical and empirical challenges', in R.J. Sternberg and J. Jordan (eds) *A Handbook of Wisdom – Psychological Perspectives*, Cambridge: Cambridge University Press, pp. 110–135.

Laslett, P. (1991) *A Fresh Map of Life: The Emergence of the Third Age*, Cambridge, MA: Harvard University Press.

Laslett, P. (1965) *The World We Have Lost*, London: Methuen (rev. edn 1971).

Le Menestrel, Marc (2002) 'Economic rationality and ethical behavior: Ethical business between venality and sacrifice', *Business Ethics: A European Review* 11(2), pp. 157–166.

Leceulle, Hanne (2013) 'Self-realisation and ageing: A spiritual perspective', in Jan Baars, Joseph Dohmen, Amanda Grenier and Chris Phillipson (eds) *Ageing, Meaning and Social Structure: Connecting Critical and Humanistic Gerontology*, Bristol: Policy Press, pp. 97–118.

Leceulle, Hanne and Baars, Jan (2014) 'Self-realization and cultural narratives about later life', *Journal of Aging Studies* 31, pp. 34–44.

Lerner, Michael (1996) *The Politics of Meaning: Restoring Hope and Possibility in an Age of Cynicism*, New York: Helix/Harper Collins.

Levenson, Michael R. and Aldwin, Carolyn (2013) 'The transpersonal in personal wisdom', in Michel Ferrari and Nic Weststrate (eds) *The Scientific Study of Personal Wisdom: From Contemplative Traditions to Neuroscience*, New York: Springer, pp. 213–228.

Lie, M., Baines, S. and Wheelock, J. (2009) 'Citizenship, volunteering and active ageing', *Social Policy and Administration* 43(7), pp. 702–718.

Lown, Bernard (1996) *The Lost Art of Healing: Practicing Compassion in Medicine*, Boston, MA: Houghton Mifflin.

McAdams, Dan (2006) 'The redemptive self: Generativity and the stories Americans live by', *Research in Human Development* 3(2&3), pp. 81–100.

McDowell, Josh and Hostetler, Bob (1998) *The New Tolerance*, Carol Stream, IL: Tyndale House.

MacIntyre, Alasdair (1981) *After Virtue: A Study in Moral Theory*, London: Duckworth.

McKee, P. and Barber, C. (1999) 'On defining wisdom', *International Journal of Aging and Human Development* 49, pp. 149–164.

McKerlie, T. (1989) 'Equality and time', *Ethics* 99(3), pp. 475–491.

MacKinlay, Elizabeth (2005) 'Understanding the ageing process: A developmental perspective of the psychosocial and spiritual dimensions', in Francis Turner (ed) *Social Work Diagnosis in Contemporary Practice*, Oxford: Oxford University Press, pp. 213–219.

MacKinlay, Elizabeth (2001) *The Spiritual Dimension of Ageing*, London: Jessica Kingsley.

Malešević, Siniša (2002) 'Rehabilitating ideology after poststructuralism', in Siniša Malešević and Iain MacKenzie (eds) *Ideology after Poststructuralism*, London: Pluto Press, pp. 87–100.

Malette, Judith and Oliver, Luis (2006) 'Retirement and existential meaning in the older adult: A qualitative study using life review', *Counselling, Psychotherapy, and Health* 2(1), pp. 30–49.

Manheimer, Ron (2009) 'Gateways to humanistic gerontology', in R. Edmondson and H.-J. von Kondratowitz (eds) *Valuing Older People: A Humanist Approach to Ageing*, Bristol: Policy Press, pp. 283–287.

Manheimer, Ronald (1999) *A Map to the End of Time: Wayfarings with Friends and Philosophers*, New York: W.W. Norton.

Mannheim, Karl (1923/1952) 'The problem of generations', in Karl Mannheim, *Essays on the Sociology of Knowledge*, London: Routledge and Kegan Paul, pp. 276–322.

Marcel, Gabriel (1954) *The Decline of Wisdom*, transl. Manya Harari, London: Harvill Press.

Marrus, Michael (1985) *The Unwanted: European Refugees in the Twentieth Century*, New York: Oxford University Press.

Maxwell, Nicholas (2007), *From Knowledge to Wisdom: A Revolution for Science and the Humanities*, 2nd rev. edn, London: Pentire Press.

Mayer, Karl Ulrich (1986) 'Structural constraints on the life course', *Human Development* 29(3), pp. 163–170.

Meacham, J.A. (1983) 'Wisdom and the context of knowledge: Knowing that one doesn't know' in D. Kuhn and J.A. Meacham (eds) *On the Development of Developmental Psychology*, Basel: Karger, pp. 111–134.

Mehta, Kalyani (2009) 'Spirituality: A means for achieving integration in personality and community spheres in an ageing Singapore', in R. Edmondson and H.-J. von Kondratowitz (eds) *Valuing Older People: A Humanist Approach to Ageing*, Bristol: Policy Press, pp. 37–50.

Mickler, Charlotte and Staudinger, Ursula (2008) 'Personal wisdom: Validation and age-related differences of a performance measure', *Psychology and Aging* 23(4), pp. 787–799.

Miller, P.N., Miller, D.W., McKibbin, E.M. and Pettys, G.L. (1999) 'Stereotypes of the elderly in magazine advertisements, 1956–1996', *International Journal of Aging and Human Development* 49(4), pp. 319–337.

Minkler, M. and Cole, T. (1992) 'The political and moral economy of aging: Not such strange bedfellows', *International Journal of Health Services* 22(1), pp. 113–124.

Montaigne, Michel de (1580/1997) 'On the Cannibals', in *The Complete Essays*, ed. and transl. M.A. Screech, London: Penguin, pp. 228–241.

Moody, H.R. (2014) 'Gray is green: Elders and the care of the earth', talk presented at 8th Symposium on Cultural Gerontology/2nd Conference of European Network of Aging Studies, Galway, April.

Moody, H.R. (2010) *Aging: Concepts and Controversies*, 6th edn, Thousand Oaks, CA: Pine Forge Press.

Moody, H.R. (2003) 'Conscious aging: A strategy for positive change in later life', in J.L. Ronch and J.A. Goldfield (eds) *Mental Wellness in Aging: Strength-based Approaches*, Winnipeg: Health Professions Press, pp. 139–160.

Moody, H.R. (2002) 'The soul of gerontology: Reconciling science and religion', *The Gerontologist* 42(5), pp. 713–716.

Moody, H.R. (1993) 'Overview: What is Critical Gerontology and why is it important?', in Thomas Cole, W. Andrew Achenbaum, Patricia L. Jakobi, Robert Kastenbaum (eds) *Voices and Visions of Aging: Toward a Critical Gerontology*, New York: Springer, pp. xv–xliii.

Moody, H.R. (1992) 'Gerontology and critical theory', *The Gerontologist* 32(3), pp. 294–295.

Moody, H.R. (1988) *Abundance of Life: Human Development Policies for an Aging Society*, New York: Columbia University Press.

Moody, H.R. (1986) 'The meaning of life and the meaning of old age', in Thomas Cole and Sally Gadow (eds) *What Does It Mean To Grow Old? Views from the Humanities*, Durham, NC: Duke University Press, pp. 9–40.

Moody, H.R. and Cole, Thomas (1986) 'Aging and Meaning: A bibliographic essay', in Thomas Cole and Sally Gadow (eds) *What Does It Mean To Grow Old? Views from the Humanities*, Durham, NC: Duke University Press, pp. 247–253.

Moody, H.R. and Sood, Sanjay (2010) 'Age branding', in Amy Drole, Norbert Schwarz and Carolyn Yoon (eds) *The Aging Consumer: Perspectives from Psychology and Economics*, New York: Routledge, pp. 229–245.

Moulaert, Thibauld and Biggs, Simon (2013) 'International and European policy on work and retirement: Reinventing critical perspectives on active ageing and mature subjectivity', *Human Relations* 66(1), pp. 23–43.

Mückenberger, U. (2011) 'Local time policies in Europe', *Time and Society,* 20(2), pp. 241–273.

Mueller, Melissa (2007) 'Penelope and the politics of remembering', *Arethusa* 40, pp. 337–362.

Mulley, Graham (2007) 'Myths of ageing', *Clinical Medicine* 7(1), pp. 68–72.

Mumford, Katharine and Power, Anne (2003) *East Enders: Family and Community in East London*, Bristol: Policy Press.

Nagy, Joseph Falaky (1985) *The Wisdom of the Outlaw: The Boyhood Deeds of Finn in Gaelic Narrative Tradition*, Berkeley, CA: University of California Press.

Nhongo, Tavengwa (2008) 'Death and dying – perceptions and implications for poor older people in Africa', paper presented at 6th International Symposium on Cultural Gerontology, Lleida, Spain, 18 October.

Nichol, James (2009) 'Does eldership mean anything in the contemporary West?', in Ricca Edmondson and Hans-Joachim von Kondratowitz (eds) *Valuing Older People: A Humanist Approach to Ageing*, Bristol: Policy Press, pp. 249–260.

Nussbaum, Martha (2006) *Frontiers of Justice: Disability, Nationality, Species Membership*, Cambridge, MA: Harvard University Press.

Nussbaum, Martha (2004) *Upheavals of Thought: The Intelligence of Emotions*, Cambridge: Cambridge University Press.

Nussbaum, Martha (1990) *Love's Knowledge: Essays on Philosophy and Literature*, Oxford: Oxford University Press.

O'Neill, Desmond (2011) 'The art of the demographic dividend', *The Lancet* 377(9780): pp. 1828-1829, 28 May.

O'Rourke, Fran (2012) 'Aristotle's political anthropology', in Ricca Edmondson and Karlheinz Hülser (eds) *Politics of Practical Reasoning: Integrating Action, Discourse and Argument*, Lanham, MD: Lexington, pp. 17–38.

Orwoll, L. and Perlmutter, M. (1990) 'The study of wise persons: Integrating a personality perspective', in R.J. Sternberg (ed) *Wisdom: Its Nature, Origins and Development*, Cambridge: Cambridge University Press, pp. 160–180.

Ostrom, Elinor (1991) *Governing the Commons: The Evolution of Institutions for Collective Action*, Cambridge: Cambridge University Press.

Pain, R. (2001) 'Gender, race, age and fear in the city', *Urban Studies* 38(5/6), pp. 899–913.

Parekh, Bhikhu (2000) *Rethinking Multiculturalism: Cultural Diversity and Political Theory*, London: Macmillan.

Pearce, Jane (2013) 'Wisdom and some creative processes in art and psychotherapy', paper presented at 3rd International Wisdom Workshop, University of Potsdam, 17 June.

Peirce, C.S. (1958) *Collected Papers*, volumes VII and VIII, ed. Arthur W. Burks, Cambridge, MA: Harvard University Press.

Phillips, Judith, Walford, Nigel and Hockey, Ann (2011) 'How do unfamiliar environments convey meaning to older people? Urban dimensions of placelessness and attachment', *International Journal of Ageing and Later Life* 6(2), pp. 73–102.

Phillipson, C. (1998) *Reconstructing Old Age: New Agendas in Social Theory and Practice*, London: Sage.

Pincharoen, S. and Congdon, J.G. (2003) 'Spirituality and health in older Thai persons in the United States', *Western Journal of Nursing Research* 25, pp. 93–108.

Powell, Jason and Biggs, Simon (2003) 'Foucauldian gerontology: A methodology for understanding aging', *Electronic Journal of Sociology*, http://www.sociology.org/content/vol7.2/03_powell_biggs.html (first accessed 4 November 2011).

Powell, Kathy (2009) 'Neoliberalization: Uneven geographies of class power: An essay on David Harvey's *A Brief History of Neoliberalism*', *Journal of Power* 2(2), pp. 326–337.

Randall, William (2011) 'Memory, metaphor, and meaning: Reading for wisdom in the stories of our lives', in Gary Kenyon, Ernst Bohlmeijer and William L. Randall (eds) *Storying Later Life. Issues, Investigations and Interventions in Narrative Gerontology*, Oxford: Oxford University Press, pp. 20–38.

Rau, Henrike and Edmondson, Ricca (2013) 'Time and sustainability', in Frances Fahy and Henrike Rau (eds) *Methods of Sustainability Research in the Social Sciences*, London: Sage, pp. 173–190.

Ray, Ruth (2000) *Beyond Nostalgia: Aging and Life Story Writing*, Charlottesville: University of Virginia Press.

Reckwitz, A. (2002) 'Toward a theory of social practices', *European Journal of Social Theory* 5(2), pp. 243–263.

Reker, G.T. (2000) 'Theoretical perspectives, dimensions, and measurement of existential meaning', in G.T. Reker and K. Chamberlain (eds) *Exploring Existential Meaning: Optimizing Human Development Across the Life Span*, Thousand Oaks, CA: Sage, pp. 39–55.

Richardson, Laurel (2000) 'Writing as a method of inquiry', in N. Denzin and Y. Lincoln (eds) *Handbook of Qualitative Research*, Thousand Oaks, CA: Sage, pp. 923–948.

Richardson, Laurel (1990) 'Narrative and sociology', *Journal of Contemporary Ethnography* 19(1), pp. 116–135.

Ricoeur, Paul (1980) 'On narrative', *Critical Inquiry* 7(1), pp. 169–190.

Riley, M.W. (1987) 'On the significance of age in sociology', *American Sociological Review* 52 (February), pp. 1–14.

Riley, M.W., Kahn, R. and Foner, A. (1994) *Age and Structural Lag: Society's Failure to Provide Meaningful Opportunities in Work, Family and Leisure*, New York: Wiley Interscience.

Riley, M.W., Kahn, R. and Foner, A. (1972) *Aging and Society, vol. 3: A Sociology of Age Stratification*, New York: Russell Sage.

Rorty, Amélie Ocksenberg (2011) 'Aristotle on the virtues of rhetoric', *Review of Metaphysics* 64(4), pp. 715–733.

Rorty, Amélie Ocksenberg (2004) 'Enough already with "theories of the emotions"', in Robert Solomon (ed) *Thinking about Feeling: Contemporary Philosophers on Emotions*, Oxford: Oxford University Press, pp. 269–278.

Rorty, Amélie Ocksenberg (1980) 'The place of contemplation in Aristotle's *Nicomachean Ethics*', in A.O. Rorty (ed) *Essays on Aristotle's Ethics*, Berkeley, CA: University of California Press, pp. 377–394.

Ross, Jen (2010) 'Was that infinity or affinity? Applying insights from translation studies to qualitative research transcription', *Forum: Qualitative Social Research* 11(2), www.qualitative-research.net/ (first accessed 12 May 2012).

Rothermund, K. and Brandstädter, J. (2003) 'Coping with deficits and losses in later life: From compensatory action to accommodation', *Psychology and Aging* 18, pp. 896–205.

Rowles, Graham and Bernard, Miriam (eds) (2013) 'The meaning and significance of place in old age', in G.D. Rowles and M. Barnard (eds) *Environmental Gerontology: Making Meaningful Places in Old Age*, New York: Springer, pp. 3–24.

Ryan, Anne (2009) *Enough is Plenty: Public and Private Policies for the 21st Century*, Ropley, Hants: O Books.

Ryan, Assumpta, McKenna, Hugh and Slevin, Oliver (2012) 'Family care-giving and decisions about entry to care: A rural perspective', *Ageing and Society* 32(1), pp. 1–18.

Ryan, Sharon (2013) 'Wisdom', *The Stanford Encyclopedia of Philosophy* (Summer 2013 edn), Edward N. Zalta (ed) http://plato.stanford. edu/archives/sum2013/entries/wisdom/, in *Stanford Encyclopedia of Philosophy*, online at http://plato.stanford.edu/entries/wisdom/ (first accessed 19 August 2013; first edition 2007)

Sánchez Rodrigez, Marta, de Jong Gierveld, Jenny and Buz, Jose (2014) 'Loneliness and the exchange of social support among older adults in Spain and the Netherlands', *Ageing and Society* 34(2), pp. 330–354.

Sayer, A. (2000) *Realism and Social Science*, London: Sage.

Schachter-Shalomi, Z. and Miller, R. (1995) *From Age-ing to Sage-ing: A Revolutionary Approach to Growing Older*, New York: Warner.

Scharf, Thomas, Timonen, Virpi, Carney, Gemma and Conlan, Catherine (2013) *Changing Generations: Findings from New Research on Intergenerational Relations in Ireland*, Dublin and Galway: SPARC and ISCG.

Schatzki, T.R. (1996) *Social practices: A Wittgensteinian Approach to Human Activity and the Social*, Cambridge: Cambridge University Press.

Scheff, T.J. (1997) *Emotions, the Social Bond, and Human Reality: Part/ whole Analysis*, Cambridge: Cambridge University Press.

Scheper-Hughes, Nancy (1977) *Saints, Scholars and Schizophrenics: Mental Illness in Rural Ireland*, Berkeley, CA: University of California Press.

Schwartz, Barry and Sharpe, Kenneth (2010) *Practical Wisdom: The Right Way to Do the Right Thing*, New York: Riverhead.

Scott-Maxwell, Florida (1968) *The Measure of My Days*, New York: Penguin.

Settersten, R.A., Jr (2003) 'Propositions and controversies in life-course scholarship', in R.A. Settersten, Jr (ed) *Invitation to the Life Course: Toward New Understandings of Later Life*, Amityville, NY: Baywood, pp. 15–45.

Shahar, Shulamith (2004) *Growing Old in the Middle Ages: 'Winter Clothes Us in Shadow and Pain'*, London: Routledge (new edn; first edn 1995).

Sherman, E. (2010) *Contemplative Aging: A Way of Being in Later Life*, New York, NY: Gordian Knot Books.

Sherman, Nancy (1989) *The Fabric of Character: Aristotle's Theory of Virtue*, Oxford: Clarendon Press.

Shove, E. (2004) 'Changing human behaviour and lifestyle: A challenge for sustainable consumption', in L. Reisch and I. Røpke (eds) *The Ecological Economics of Consumption*, Cheltenham: Edward Elgar, pp. 111–131.

Shove, E. and Pantzar, M. (2005) 'Consumers, producers and practices: Understanding the invention and reinvention of Nordic walking', *Journal of Consumer Culture* 5, pp. 43–64.

Sinclair, David, Swan, Amy and Pearson, Anna (2007) *Social Inclusion and Older People: A Call for Action*, London: Help the Aged.

Smith, Adam (1790) *The Theory of Moral Sentiments*, ed. D.D. Raphael and A.L. MacFie, 1976, Oxford: Oxford University Press.

Smith, J. and Baltes, P.B. (1990) 'Wisdom-related knowledge: Age/cohort differences in response to life-planning problems', *Developmental Psychology* 26(3), pp. 494–505.

Smith, J., Staudinger, U.M. and Baltes, P.B. (1994) 'Occupational settings facilitative of wisdom-related knowledge: The sample case of clinical psychologists', *Journal of Consulting and Clinical Psychology* 64, pp. 989–1000.

Stange, Antje and Kunzmann, Ute (2008) 'Fostering wisdom: A psychological perspective', in Michel Ferrari and Georges Potworowski (eds) *Teaching for Wisdom: Cross-cultural Perspectives on Fostering Wisdom*, Dordrecht: Springer, pp. 23–36.

Staudinger, Ursula (2013) 'The need to distinguish personal from general wisdom: A short history and empirical evidence', in Michel Ferrari and Nic M. Westrate (eds) *The Scientific Study of Personal Wisdom: From Contemplative Traditions to Neuroscience*, Dordrecht: Springer, pp. 3–20.

Staudinger, Ursula and Baltes, Paul (1996) 'Interactive minds: A facilitative setting for wisdom-related performance?', *Journal of Personality and Social Psychology* 71, pp. 746–762.

Staudinger, U., Maciel, A. and Baltes, P.B. (1998) 'What predicts wisdom-related performance? A first look at personality, intelligence, and facilitative experiential contexts', *European Journal of Personality* 17, pp. 1–17.

Staudinger, U.M., Smith, J. and Baltes, P.B. (1994) *Manual for the Assessment of Wisdom-related Knowledge* (Technical Report No.46), Berlin: Max Planck Institute for Human Development.

Steger, M., Frazier, P., Oishi, S. and Kaler, M. (2006) 'The Meaning in Life Questionnaire: Assessing the presence of and search for meaning in life', *Journal of Counseling Psychology* 53, pp. 80–93.

Steger, M.F., Kashdan, T.B., Sullivan, B.A. and Lorentz, D. (2008) 'Understanding the search for meaning in life: Personality, cognitive style, and the dynamic between seeking and experiencing meaning', *Journal of Personality*, 76(2), pp. 199–228.

Sternberg, Robert (1998) 'A balance theory of wisdom', *Review of General Psychology* 2, pp. 347–365.

Sternberg, Robert (1990a) 'Understanding wisdom', in Robert J. Sternberg (ed) *Wisdom: Its Nature, Origins, and Development*, Cambridge: Cambridge University Press, pp. 3–9.

Sternberg, Robert (1990b) 'Wisdom and its relation to intelligence and creativity', in Robert J. Sternberg (ed) *Wisdom: Its Nature, Origins and Development*, Cambridge: Cambridge University Press, pp. 142–159.

Strathern, Marilyn (2000) 'The tyranny of transparency', *British Educational Research Journal* 26(3), pp. 309–321.

Sutton, J. and Windhorst, C. (2009) 'Extended and constructive remembering: Two notes on Martin and Deutscher', *Crossroads* 4(1), pp. 79–91.

Swinnen, Aagje (2010) '"One nice thing about getting old is that nothing frightens you": From page to screen: Rethinking women's old age in Howl's Moving Castle', in Heike Hartung and Roberta Meierhofer (eds) *Narratives of Life: Mediating Age*, Bielefeld: Transcript Verlag, pp. 167–182.

Taylor, Charles (1989) *Sources of the Self: The Making of the Modern Identity*, Cambridge, MA: Harvard University Press.

Taylor, Lawrence (1995) *Occasions of Faith: An Anthropology of Irish Catholics*, Philadelphia, PA: University of Pennsylvania Press.

Temkin, L. (1993) *Inequality*, Oxford: Oxford University Press.

Thane, Pat, ed. (2005) *A History of Old Age*, London: Thames and Hudson.

Thane, Pat (2000) *Old Age in English History: Past Experiences, Present Issues*, Oxford: Oxford University Press.

Thomas, William (2004) *What Are Old People For? How Elders Will Save the World*, Acton, MA: VanderWyk and Burnham.

Thompson, Paul, Itzin, Catherine and Abendstern, Michele (1990) *I Don't Feel Old: Understanding the Experience of Later Life*, Oxford: Oxford University Press.

Tornstam, L. (2011) 'Maturing into gerotranscendence', *Journal of Transpersonal Psychology* 43(2), pp. 166–180.

Tornstam, L. (2005) *Gerotranscendence – A Developmental Theory of Positive Aging*, New York: Springer

Tornstam, L. (1989) 'Gero-transcendence: A reformulation of the disengagement theory', *Aging*, 1, pp. 55–63.

Treanor, Brian (2010) 'Turn around and step forward: Ideology and utopia in the environmental movement', *Environmental Philosophy* 7(1), pp. 27–46.

Turner, B.S. (1998) 'Ageing and generational conflicts: A reply to Sarah Irwin', *British Journal of Sociology* 49(2), pp. 299–304.

Turner, Roy (ed) (1974) *Ethnomethodology: Selected Readings*, Harmondsworth: Penguin.

Turner, Stephen (1994) *The Social Theory of Practices*, Chicago: University of Illinois Press.

Twigg, Julia (2013) *Fashion and Age: Dress, the Body and Later Life*, London: Bloomsbury.

Twigg, Julia (2012) 'Adjusting the cut: Fashion, the body and age in the UK high street', *Ageing and Society* 32(6), pp. 1030–1054.

United Nations (2002) *Report of the Second World Assembly on Ageing*, Madrid, 8–12 April.

Uslaner, Eric (2002) *The Moral Foundations of Trust*, Cambridge: Cambridge University Press.

Victor, Christina (2010) *Ageing, Health and Care*, Bristol: Policy.

Victor, Christina (2005) *The Social Context of Ageing: A Textbook of Gerontology*, London: Routledge.

Victor, Christina, Scambler, Sasha, and Bond, John (2009) *The Social World of Older People: Understanding Loneliness and Social Isolation in Later Life*, Maidenhead: Open University Press.

Vincent, J. (2005) 'Understanding generations: Political economy and culture in an ageing society', *British Journal of Sociology* 56(4), pp. 579–599.

Vincent, John (1995) *Inequality and Old Age*, London: Routledge.

Warde, Alan (2005) 'Consumption and theories of practice', *Journal of Consumer Culture* 5, pp. 131–53.

Warren, Laura and Clarke, Amanda (2009) '"Woo-hoo, what a ride!" Older people, life stories and active ageing', in Ricca Edmondson and Hans-Joachim von Kondratowitz (eds) *Valuing Older People: A Humanist Approach to Ageing*, Bristol: Policy Press, pp. 233–248.

Warren, Marjory (1943) 'Care of the chronic sick: A case for treating chronic sick in blocks in a general hospital', *British Medical Journal* 2, pp. 822–823.

Weber, Max (1922/1968) *Economy and Society: An Outline of Interpretive Sociology*, Günther Roth and Claus Wittich (eds), New York: Bedminster Press.

Weber, S.J. and Mitchell, C. (eds) (2004) *Not Just Any Dress: Narratives of Memory, Body, and Identity*, New York: Peter Lang.

Weston, Gabriel (2009) *Direct Red: A Surgeon's Story*, London: Jonathan Cape.

White, Michael and Epston, David (eds) (1990) *Narrative Means to Therapeutic Ends*, New York: Norton.

Whittle, Andrea, Kenny, Kate and Willmott, Hugh (2011) *Understanding Identity and Organizations*, London: Sage.

Wiggin, Kate Douglas (1902) *Penelope's Irish Experiences,* London: Gay and Bird.

Wilińska, Monika (2012) 'Is there a place for an ageing subject? Stories of ageing at the University of the Third Age in Poland', *Sociology* 46(2), pp. 290–305.

Wilkinson, P. and Coleman, P. (2011) 'Coping without religious faith: Ageing among British Humanists', in P. Coleman (ed) *Belief and Ageing: Spiritual Pathways in Later Life*, Bristol: Policy, pp. 97–111.

Winch, Peter (1958) *The Idea of a Social Science and its Relation to Philosophy*, London: Routledge and Kegan Paul.

Wink, Paul (2003) 'Dwelling and seeking in late adulthood; The psychosocial implications of two types of religious orientation', *Journal of Religious Gerontology* 14 (2/3), pp. 101–117.

Wink, P. and Dillon, M. (2013) 'Religion, spirituality, and personal wisdom: A tale of two types', in Michel Ferrari and Nic M. Westrate (eds) *The Scientific Study of Personal Wisdom: From Contemplative Traditions to Neuroscience*, Dordrecht: Springer, pp. 165–212.

Wink, Paul and Dillon, Michle (2002) 'Spiritual development across the adult life course: Findings from a longitudinal study', *Journal of Adult Development* 9(1), pp. 79–94.

Wink, Paul and Helson, Ravenna (1997) 'Practical and transcendent wisdom: Their nature and some longitudinal findings', *Journal of Adult Development* 4, pp. 1–14.

Woerner, Markus H. (2000) 'Untimely meditations on ageing, the good life and a culture of friendship', in Ricca Edmondson and Cecily Kelleher (eds) *Health Promotion: New Discipline or Multi-Discipline?* Dublin: Irish Academic Press, pp. 205–218.

Woerner, Markus H. (2000a) 'Sokratische Widerlegungen', in Ernest W.B. Hess-Lüttich and H. Walter Schmitz (eds) *Botschaften Verstehen: Kommunikationstheorie und Zeichenpraxis*, Frankfurt am Main: Peter Lang, pp. 285–298.

Woerner, Markus H. (1999) 'Elements of an Aristotelian theory of political discourse', in D.N. Koutras (ed) *Aristotle's Political Philosophy and its Influence*, Athens: Society for Aristotelian Studies 'The Lyceum', pp. 56–73.

Woerner, Markus H. (1998) 'Rhetorik als logic der Rede', in Dieter Krallman and H. Walter Schmitz (eds) *Perspektiven einer Kommunikationswissenschaft* (v. 2), pp. 423–432.

Woerner, Markus H. (1990) *Das Ethische in der Rhetorik des Aristoteles*, Freiburg/Br.: Alber Verlag.

Woerner, Markus H. (1989) 'Eternity', *Irish Philosophical Journal* 6, pp. 3–26.

Woerner, Markus H. and Edmondson, Ricca (2008) 'Towards a taxonomy of types of wisdom', in Fiachra Long (ed) *Yearbook of the Irish Philosophical Society*, pp. 148–156.

Woodward, James (2008) *Valuing Age: Pastoral Ministry with Older People*, London: SPCK.

Woodward, Kathleen (2003) 'Against wisdom: The social politics of anger and aging', *Journal of Aging Studies* 17 (1), pp. 55–67.

Wright, F. (2004) 'Old and cold: Policies failing to address fuel poverty', *Social Policy and Administration* 38, pp. 488–503

Wuthnow, R. (1998) *After Heaven: Spirituality in America in the 1950s*, Berkeley, CA: University of California Press.

Yan Chi Kwok, Jackie and Ku, Ben H.B. (2013) 'Growing old in Hong Kong: A life story research', paper presented at British Society of Gerontology Conference, Oxford, 2013.

Young-Eisendrath, Polly (2000) 'Psychotherapy as ordinary transcendence: The unspeakable and the unspoken' in Polly Young-Eisendrath and Melvin Miller (eds) *The Psychology of Mature Spirituality: Integrity, Wisdom, Transcendence*, Hove: Routledge, pp. 105–114.

Index